D1270290

CULTURE, LITERACY, ~~WITHDRAWN~~ and LEARNING ENGLISH

Voices from the Chinese Classroom

Edited by **KATE PARRY** with Su Xiaojun

Boynton/Cook Publishers
HEINEMANN
Portsmouth, NH

献 给 我 的 启 蒙 老 师
Xiàn gěi wǒ de qǐ mēng lǎo shī

邬 展 云
Wū Zhǎn Yún

To Wu Zhanyun,
who introduced me to Chinese literacy

Boynton/Cook Publishers, Inc.
A subsidiary of Reed Elsevier Inc.
361 Hanover Street
Portsmouth, NH 03801-3912

Offices and agents throughout the world

© 1998 by Kate Parry

All rights reserved. No part of this book may be reproduced in any form or by any electronic or mechanical means, including information storage and retrieval systems, without permission in writing from the publisher, except by a reviewer, who may quote brief passages in a review.

Library of Congress Cataloging-in-Publication Data
Culture, literacy, and learning English : voices from the Chinese classroom / edited by Kate Parry
  with Su Xiaojun.
     p. cm.
   Includes bibliographical references.
   ISBN 0-86709-448-6
     1. English language—Study and teaching—Chinese speakers.   2. English language—
Study and teaching—China.   3. English language—Social aspects—China.   4. Language
and culture—China.   5. Literacy—China.   I. Parry, Kate.   II. Su, Xiaojun.
PE1130.C4C85   1998
428'.007'051—dc21   98-52584
                                                                                                       CIP

Editor: Scott Mahler
Production: Abigail M. Heim
Cover design: Darci Mehall, Aureo Design
Manufacturing: Louise Richardson

Printed in the United States of America on acid-free paper

02 01 00 99 98 DA 1 2 3 4 5

Contents

Introduction   *vii*

Acknowledgments   *xvii*

Part One   The Culture of Chinese Literacy   *1*

1   Literacy at Home   *3*

   1   Four Generations
     Zhu Xiaowen   *8*

   2   My Experience of Childhood
     Sheng Ping   *12*

   3   Literacy in My Home
     Zhu Minghui   *14*

   4   Reading and Writing Within a Family
     Ding Lu   *16*

   5   The Beginnings of Literacy for Rural Children
     Lu Wanying   *18*

   6   From the Womb to the Cradle: The Practice of *Tāi Jiào*
     Xu Ju   *22*

   7   Education at Home
     Li Xiaozhong   *25*

   8   The Importance of Early Education
     Luo Ningxia   *27*

   9   Education Outside School
     Qin Haihua   *29*

  10   Literacy Acquisition: The Difference Between Urban and Rural Areas
     Zhang Weinian   *31*

2   The Social Context of Schooling   *33*

   1   Chinese Examinations in Historical Perspective
     Su Xiaojun   *37*

2 The Influence of Confucianism on China's Education
   Wu Liangzhe   40

3 Good and Bad Schools
   Yang Hongqi   42

4 Problems in Chinese Primary Education
   Zhu Xiaowen   45

5 Literacy at School
   Zhao Guangzhu   49

6 Ideological Teaching Through Early School Literacy
   Lu Wanying   52

7 Chinese Children in Primary School
   Qin Haihua   56

8 The Heavy Burden of Chinese Children
   Gu Tiexia   58

3 Learning the Written Language   *61*

1 Form, Pronunciation, and Meaning in Chinese Characters
   Chang Qian   67

2 Comprehending Word Meanings in Chinese
   Xu Ju   70

3 Step by Step: Reading in Primary School
   Wang Jian   73

4 How Chinese Children Learn Chinese in School
   Zhu Minghui   79

5 Reading Aloud in Learning Chinese
   Wang Kui   85

6 Classical Chinese Reading in Junior-Secondary School
   Wu Lili   89

Part Two   The English Language in China   *99*

4 The Social Meaning of English   *101*

1 Chinese Attitudes Towards English
   Liu Yuanyan   106

2 English in China
   Chen Ting   109

3 Why Chinese People Learn English Now
   Zhu Minghui   *112*

4 The Present Craze for English: Negative Aspects
   Du Qunhua   *117*

5 English Loan Words in Chinese
   Wu Lili   *119*

6 My Experience of Learning English
   He Yue   *122*

7 Why Do We Study a Foreign Language?
   Sun Wenjing   *125*

8 What Is English?
   Qin Haihua   *127*

5 English in the Chinese Classroom   *129*

   1 Approaching English
      Rao Zhiren   *136*

   2 Two Teachers
      Zheng Guolong   *138*

   3 Problems of English Teaching in Secondary School
      Bao Jingying   *140*

   4 English-Language Teaching in China: The Gap Between
      Secondary School and College
      Gu Tiexia   *145*

   5 Traditional and Communicative Approaches in China's
      College English Teaching
      He Yue   *152*

   6 The College Entrance Exam and College English Test Band 4:
      Effects on English Teaching
      Du Qunhua   *157*

6 Strategies for Reading in English   *169*

   1 Learning a New Way of Reading
      Bao Jingying   *176*

   2 Getting to Know a New Genre: Academic Articles
      Du Qunhua   *178*

   3 Reading Two Articles: A Comparison
      Zhu Xiaowen   *182*

4 Extensive Reading in College English: Attitudes, Strategies, and Problems
Wang Kui   187

5 Chinese Students' Reading Strategies: A Study in Contrasts
Wang Jian   195

7 New Directions in Teaching   *207*

1 Improvement in Classroom Teaching of English
Zhang Jianying   212

2 Vocabulary Teaching or Vocabulary Learning?
Li Xiaozhong   216

3 Towards a Reader-Centered Approach in Intensive Reading
Zhang Weinian   223

4 Let Them Speak: A New Approach to Intensive Reading
Xu Ju, Sheng Ping, and Chang Qian   230

Conclusions   *245*

Appendix I Questionnaire for Eliciting Personal Information   *253*

Appendix II Assigned Readings   *257*

Appendix III Research Topics   *259*

Contributors   *261*

References   *263*

Introduction

What is the relationship between cultural background and individual behavior? The question can be simply stated, but the two variables it posits are so complex, so diverse, and so hard to isolate that it is virtually impossible to come up with a satisfactory answer. Yet it is important for educators to consider the question, because in these days of frequent and pervasive international communication, the classroom has become a place not only for passing on to students and thereby perpetuating the traditions of their own culture, but also for introducing to them and thereby propagating the ideas and ways of ones that are alien. How the students respond is crucially dependent not only on their individual personalities, but also on the cultures from which they come.

No one is more aware of this issue than teachers of English to speakers of other languages, especially those who teach culturally diverse groups in English-speaking countries and those who, as native speakers of English, go abroad to teach in foreign environments. Such teachers are constantly faced with the task of interpreting their students' behavior—why does José write so abysmally when he can speak so fluently? Why does Eun Sook insist on looking up every word in the dictionary? How can Musa think that the answer he has given is relevant? Why is Xiao Li so reluctant to speak in class? Even the choice of names for such fictitious individuals brings us up against the problem in question; for the names are associated not only with individuals, but also with particular cultural groups, and so, in the minds of teachers at least, are the kinds of behavior described.

In dealing with such problems of interpretation, it is all too easy to resort to stereotypes, and stereotypes are dangerous because they can blind us to the richness of individual variation and prevent us from recognizing individual potential. Yet it has to be acknowledged that stereotypes come from somewhere: Membership of a culture entails the absorption of cultural norms that are then made manifest, to a greater or lesser degree, in the behavior of individuals. And while we may not be able to know in any depth the norms that inform the behavior of all our students, it would certainly be helpful to understand the processes by which those norms are first absorbed and then displayed in what our students do as they work to learn English.

The question is, however, too large to be dealt with in its entirety—at least, within the confines of one book. This book, therefore, is an attempt to address it with respect to one particular kind of behavior—learning a language through reading—and one set of cultural practices—those having to do with literacy. It further narrows the field by focusing on a specific and unusually well-defined cultural group—educated Han Chinese in the People's Republic of China. In other words, it approaches the broader question through a narrower one: What is the relationship between the literacy practices of this particular—and peculiarly literate—culture and the English reading strategies of individual Chinese students?

The opportunity to approach this narrower question came when I was teaching at Nanjing University in China in a program called the Nanjing University/United Board College English Teacher-Training Program. The program was (and is) funded by the United Board for Christian Higher Education in Asia, and its purpose is to raise the professional standards of those teaching "College English" in Chinese universities and colleges—college English being English taught to undergraduates who are not specializing in foreign languages. There are two million such students, and while English is not their primary interest, they desperately want to learn it, for it is required in many universities for getting a degree[1] and it is an important asset in getting a job. Yet this population has been somewhat neglected, the best teachers and resources being devoted mainly to students who are working for degrees in English. The Nanjing University program is directed towards this problem. The participants are graduates who are already teaching English to students working for other degrees, and a team of two Chinese and two foreign faculty members teach them courses designed to give them some understanding of linguistics, to help them apply this linguistic knowledge to their teaching, and to improve their own proficiency in English.[2]

This book grew out of one of the proficiency courses, that in reading and writing. When I first taught in the program, in the autumn term of 1992, I used this course as an opportunity to learn about China: The program participants wrote essays about various social issues, including the Chinese education system and Chinese attitudes towards English. The success of these essays suggested a more systematic approach for the second time I taught in the program, in the academic year of 1994–95: Instead of having the participants write on a wide range and somewhat random selection of topics, I asked them to focus particularly on the very skills—reading and writing—that they were practicing. Thus, during the first term, they developed their academic reading skills by reading articles from both the ethnographic literature about literacy and the pedagogical literature about strategies used for reading in a second language; they developed their writing skills by producing essays of their own that were linked thematically to what they read. Then, during the second term, they built on this foundation by carrying out and writing research projects of their own, many of which were based on the teaching practice they were doing at the

1. Students may elect to take their foreign-language exam in a language other than English—in Japanese or Russian, for example—but the vast majority choose English.
2. The structure of the program is to be changed in the future with the number of foreign faculty members being reduced to one (David Vikner, personal information, February 13, 1997).

same time. The present book consists of a selection of this group's essays and research papers, together with a few of the essays of the 1992 group of participants, whose writing had first inspired the idea.

In thus reading and writing about reading and writing, the program participants were achieving a number of purposes. First and of most immediate importance, they were improving their own proficiency so they could, by the end, read academic articles in English with relative ease, and they could at least imagine writing articles in English for publication. For some of the participants, the development of their reading skills was quite dramatic, as can be seen from two of the essays in Chapter Six. Second, they became much more aware of the issues involved in learning a foreign language, particularly in learning to read in English—an appropriate focus for them since it is on this skill that the college English curriculum lays most emphasis.[3] Third, in developing their own ideas about literacy and reading, the participants were making a real contribution to our knowledge of the subject, for not only were they presenting information about China—which, to too many Westerners, still constitutes a great unknown—but they also were helping to fill a large and somewhat surprising gap in the general literature about literacy.

The process of acquiring literacy has, of course, been much studied, especially in various English-speaking communities—consider the influential work of Heath (1983) and the edited collections of Cazden, John, and Hymes (1972), Cook-Gumperz (1986), Foorman and Siegel (1986), Hedley and Baratta (1985), Schieffelin and Gilmore (1986), and Street (1993). Variation in reading strategies is also an increasingly popular subject of research, including reading strategies in English as a second or foreign language—see Block (1992), Davis and Bistodeau (1993), Hansen-Strain (1989), Johnson, Shek, and Law (1989), Koda (1988), Oxford (1990), Oxford and Anderson (1995), Pritchard (1990), and Wenden and Rubin (1987). Few attempts have been made, however, to link these two kinds of research, largely, I think, because most classroom ethnographers are not themselves teachers—at least, not teachers of English as a second or foreign language—while many of those who publish research on ESL or EFL are native speakers of English in English-speaking countries who have little opportunity to study closely the cultural backgrounds of their students.

The participants in the Nanjing College English Program were well placed to fill this gap. Of course, they could speak only of China, but given its size, its increasing economic influence, and its enormous numbers of people studying English, it is unnecessary to argue that China is important; nor is it necessary to argue that it is interesting, given its long, independent, and non-alphabetic tradition of literacy. As Chinese themselves, they were and are

---

3. This emphasis may well be a function of the extreme influence on the curriculum of the college-English exam, which is taken at the end of the undergraduates' second year; for it is generally believed that reading skills are easier to test than listening, speaking, or even writing. See Hill and Parry (1992).

participants in this tradition, and could report from their own experience on how it was and is transmitted from one generation to the next. Furthermore, as teachers and learners of English, they could provide interesting insights on how a background of literacy in Chinese affects the way they and their students study written English. Such evidence is, of course, common knowledge in China, but that "common knowledge" is largely unknown in the English-speaking world, and gathering it together in one place is a necessary prerequisite to more systematic data collection. Finally, during their teaching practice, the participants were in an ideal position to collect primary data themselves: not only did they have ready access to students of their own, but also, because they were working in teams, they could observe while one of their colleagues conducted the class, or they could ask their colleagues to record responses while they themselves taught.[4]

The information presented here does, of course, have limitations. In a country as large as China, it is impossible for one group of twenty-five people to be fully representative. Moreover, this particular group was by no means randomly selected: The participants are all university graduates, and this fact alone means that they belong to an intellectual élite. To establish the group's social characteristics, I asked the participants in the 1994–95 program to fill in a questionnaire about their family background and upbringing (see Appendix I). Because two of them were absent on the day the questionnaire was distributed, the following is a summary of the information given by the remaining twenty-three, with added comment on the other two where I know the facts in question.

   First, where do these writers come from? China is an enormous country with a great deal of regional variation, so it is not insignificant that most of them live in the east-central provinces on the lower Yangzi River, thirteen of them in Jiangsu (of whom ten live in Nanjing, the capital), five in Wuhan (which is the capital of Hubei Province), and one in Shanghai. Of the rest, three live in northern provinces (two in Liaoning and one in Ningxia), one lives in Urumqi (the capital of Xinjiang in the far west), and of the two who were absent, one lives in Qinghai (another far western province) and the other in Jiangxi, in the south. The predominance of people from the east-central region can be explained partly by the location of the program: It is particularly attractive to teachers in Nanjing because they do not have to leave their families, and they can continue teaching while attending courses. Another factor, however, is the higher level of education achieved in this part of China; Jiangsu is particularly favored in this respect, having a larger number of students enrolled in university than any other province.[5]

4. For me personally, there was yet another source of information—namely, my own experience of trying to become literate in Chinese. The fact that I was myself working on the language enabled me to appreciate much more fully what the participants were telling me, and we had many fruitful discussions of how the strategies I used to interpret Chinese text were affected by my literacy in English.

5. This information was supplied by the Nanjing University Institute of Education, February 1996; I am grateful to Wang Haixiao for obtaining it for me.

As university teachers, most of the participants—twenty of the twenty-five—live in provincial capitals. Of the remainder, one lives in Shanghai, which is directly under the central government, and one lives in Suzhou, which is the wealthiest city in Jiangsu, though not the capital. The group as a whole, then, can be said, in their present lives, to represent the prosperous, urbanized areas of China.

Not all of the participants, however, had always lived where they are living now, and the changes of residence they reported in the questionnaire are an interesting reflection of China's present pattern of economic development. Sixteen said they had moved; of these, four had moved between the east-central provinces and four had moved from the north and west to the south and east (in two cases, these moves reversed those made by the previous generation, when the participants' parents had "followed the Party's call" to go to the remote areas of China to work). Eight had made moves within their home provinces, and here the pattern was always from village or small town to the provincial capital. Such moves are difficult to make in China because it is hard to get a residence permit (*hùkŏu*) to live in a big city; the possibility of getting such a *hùkŏu* is one of the benefits that a university education offers (Kristof and WuDunn 1994).

Because all the program participants are teachers, and language teachers at that, it is no coincidence that they are predominantly women (twenty-one in the 1994–5 group, as opposed to only four men). In traditional Confucian society, teachers were much respected, but in present-day China, a teaching career is not considered particularly desirable because it is much less lucrative than working in commerce or manufacturing—university teachers, despite their high qualifications, earn less than most factory workers. Men, however, feel the pressure to make a good salary more than women do, and they also find it easier than women to get good jobs. Add to this the fact that women are expected in China to be better at languages (and worse at science subjects) than are men, and it is easy to see that in a group of university language teachers, especially at junior levels, women almost certainly will be in the majority.[6]

Of the twenty-one women in the 1994–95 program, seventeen were married, one was divorced, and three were single. Ten had children; that is, one child each, as allowed in the present-day Chinese family. Their concern for their one child was a major factor stimulating their interest in the processes of language acquisition and literacy development. Of the men, two were already married when they came to the program (one to another participant), one found a wife at Nanjing University, and one was unmarried. None of the men had children.

The composition of the households in which the participants live reflects modern urban lifestyles rather than traditional ones; that is, most of those who are married live alone with their spouse and their child if they have one; only

6. For a fuller discussion of the status of women in China's educational system, see Rosen (1992).

two said they lived with their parents-in-law. Those who are single, however, do not live on their own: Before coming to the program, two of them were living with their parents and two in rooms at the universities where they taught. The households in which the participants grew up reflected older patterns of domestic life rather more. Of those who answered the questionnaire, only eleven had grown up with their parents alone; ten had grown up with one or more grandparents in the house as well, and two said their households had included an uncle or an aunt as well. Thus, their perceptions of literacy were formed under the influence of a variety of adults in the family.

While all the participants were graduates, the institutions they attended varied considerably in prestige, a factor of some importance in China, where the educational system is organized in a rigidly hierarchical way (Henze 1992; Rosen 1984). Of those who answered the questionnaire, seven had attended "key" universities, which are administered by the central government and are considered the best; four had attended "state" universities, which are also administered by the central government, though they are not of such high status; ten had attended "provincial" universities; and two had attended "normal colleges," that is, teacher-training colleges. Which kind of institution they attended was determined by the marks they got in the national College Entrance Exam (CEE), which they took on leaving secondary school; as their teacher, however, I could see no direct correlation between the prestige of the institutions they had attended as undergraduates and their performance as graduate students in the program. It is worth pointing out, too, that entry into Chinese universities is so competitive that any graduate must be strong academically.

Another important factor in determining the kind of education the participants received was their age, and hence the years in which they had attended school and university. Their average age was 27:3 and their median age was 28:11, so most of them had begun school in the early 1970s, early enough to remember the slogans of the Cultural Revolution but late enough to have been encouraged to pay serious attention to school work and to have been taught English in secondary school. Four of them, however, being in their mid-thirties, received most of their schooling during the Cultural Revolution years, and this meant that their experience of literacy acquisition was radically different from that of those born later (see Chapter One). The three who were under twenty-five also had different perceptions in some ways from the others because they had no direct memories of the deliberate denigration of formal learning that had characterized the decade of 1966–1976.

There was variation, too, in the amount of education that the participants' parents had received. Table 1 shows the educational status of the fathers and mothers of those who answered the questionnaire (with the exception of one, whose answer was uninterpretable).

It is striking how many of the participants had fathers who had been to university, and though their mothers, on the whole, were less well educated, the proportion of university graduates among them is still high. Most of the

Table 1

Highest level of education achieved by the participants' parents

	University	Secondary School	Primary School	None
Father	14	3	3	2
Mother	7	8	4	3

essays in this book, therefore, are written by people who are not only intellectuals themselves, but who also come from intellectual families. Two of the participants, however (Lu Wanying and Zhu Minghui), said that neither of their parents had any formal schooling at all, showing that upward mobility through education is at least possible for children of uneducated parents. It is interesting to note that both of these participants grew up in peasant households in the countryside (see their essays in Chapter One).

The questionnaire also asked about the educational status of the other adults with whom the participants grew up, and here there were more indications of educational mobility within families. Of the grandparents about whom information was given, one grandfather and one grandmother had received tertiary education, two grandfathers and two grandmothers secondary, three grandfathers primary, and as many as nine grandmothers were characterized as illiterate. Thus, at least nine of the participants had grown up with at least one illiterate adult. That does not mean that education was any less valued in their households (cf. Ho 1982, who cites many instances where boys were encouraged in their studies by women who could not read themselves), but it does mean that the participants were strongly aware of the educational difference between generations, especially for women, and this awareness shows clearly in their essays.

Finally, a word about the participants' language background. None of the participants belonged to any of China's ethnic minorities, so they all spoke "Chinese" as their first language. But Chinese varies greatly in its spoken forms to the extent that some of its varieties might more properly be considered distinct languages (Ramsey 1987). One of the major functions of the education system, therefore, is to teach a single standard variety that is based on the one spoken in Beijing (DeFrancis 1984). This variety, called *Pǔtōnghuà*, or "common speech," is virtually the same as the official variety, Mandarin, that was used before 1949 in mainland China and is still used in Taiwan. All of the participants speak it, and it was the variety they generally used among themselves, at least when they were in my presence. However, only six claimed to have learned it at home, and of those six, four said that they spoke another variety too. Eight said that they had learned Putonghua in primary school, and Lu Wanying claimed that she had not really learned it until she went to university. Most of them had learned to read, therefore, in a standard language as a second dialect, yet they did not pick up on the suggestions made in what they were reading that the imposition of a standard variety on nonstandard speakers could be educationally damaging (see Chapter Three).

The essays in this book come largely from the writers' own experience, but they also were formed by the process through which they were written; what follows, therefore, is a description of what happened in the reading and writing course. When I met the participants in September 1994, I explained to them what I intended to do and gave them as their first reading an article by myself entitled, "The Social Construction of Reading Strategies" (Parry 1993a). This article spells out the argument that since the uses of literacy in the home affect children's performance as readers in school, and since reading strategies acquired in the first language may be transferred to reading in a second language, we are likely to find interesting relationships between the ways in which people are first exposed to text and the ways in which they deal with foreign texts later in life. The argument is supported by a review of the literature about "the social construction of literacy" (Cook-Gumperz 1986) on the one hand, and about sociocultural variation in reading strategies on the other. Thus, at the outset, the participants were introduced to the basic premise of the course and were given an overview of the research from which it was derived; and since they found the article difficult, they had an opportunity to consider, in light of what it said, the strategies that they used to understand it (see Bao Jingying's and Zhu Xiaowen's contributions in Chapter Six).

For the rest of the autumn term, the participants read one or two articles each week, receiving them on a Tuesday and handing in written responses the following Friday. Often I helped them before they did the reading by explaining the context from which the articles came—for example, before they read Collins (1986) and Philips (1972), we discussed the concern that is felt in the United States about the persistently poor performance in school of African-American and Native American children. In some cases, I guided their reading by describing the genre of which the article was an example (the participants found such guidance particularly helpful when they read reports of experimental research). Then, after they had read the articles, we discussed how the material related to the Chinese situation, and this discussion served as a stimulus to the participants' own writing. I also tried to structure the reading so that by the end of the term, the participants had become familiar with different academic genres—with review articles as well as research reports and with simple narrative accounts as well as discussions of theory—and had read about a variety of research methods. For a list of the readings assigned and the themes to which they related, see Appendix II.

As for the writing, in addition to producing an informal response to every article that they read, the participants wrote in the first term four formal essays of their own. Each essay was written in three drafts, to the first of which I responded in terms of its content and organization, and to the second in terms of its grammar, vocabulary, and style, with additional comments on content if necessary. The third draft was the final version, which I considered for inclusion in this book. The participants were quick to respond to this treatment, so that by the second essay they were anticipating and answering the questions they expected me to ask on the first draft (my comments on content being nearly always couched as questions). Their writing thus became increasingly rich and detailed, and at the same time becoming more accurate in terms of grammar and use of vocabulary. Each of the four essays was based on a broadly defined theme, which was, of course, reflected in the readings too: the first theme was "Literacy at Home"; the second, "Literacy in School"; the third, "Approaching English"; and the fourth, "Making Sense of English Text."[7]

A month before the end of the first term, I asked the participants to consider topics for their own research, bearing in mind the opportunities that would be offered by their teaching practice and the practical limitations within which they would have to work (the main one to be considered was time—the teaching practice lasted only six weeks). Through a series of class and individual discussions, each participant finally came up with a topic that was practicable, though in some cases it was not fully defined until the following term; their final research topics are listed in Appendix III.

During the spring term, our work was structured differently. We all met every week for a research-methods course, in which we used Nunan's *Research Methods in Language Learning* (1992) as a textbook; in addition, I met all the participants individually or in groups of two or three for tutorials. The participants were given a schedule at the beginning of term in which I specified when I expected them to have finished each section of their research paper. I identified four sections—introduction, methodology, findings, and conclusions—for each of which I allowed three weeks; in the event, of course, there was variation in how long each section took, but on the whole, the participants kept to the schedule remarkably well. The participants developed their own bibliographies, but these were limited because in China there is not much material available in English on applied linguistics research. In any case, I was more concerned that the participants, as teachers, should learn how to collect primary data by observing what goes on with actual students in actual classrooms. By the middle of May, most of the participants had finished drafting their papers, which left three weeks for word processing and editing. At the beginning of June, they made oral presentations of their work to their colleagues and faculty from the department.

It is the participants' formal essays and research papers that constitute the material for this book, with the order of the chapters generally reflecting the order in which topics were covered in the course. Chapters Two and Three, however, together represent the work done during the second three-week period in 1994; Chapters Five and Six include both essays written in the autumn term and research papers written in the spring; and Chapter Seven consists mostly

7. My original plan was for the participants to write five essays, but since we lost some time over an extended National Day holiday and everyone was getting very tired, I decided to drop one. The one dropped was on "Literacy in Society," and it was under that head that I originally included the readings by Gee (1986) and Goody and Watt (1968).

of research papers, together with an essay sent to me in 1995 by a previous participant. Each participant in the 1994–95 program is represented by at least one piece, and a few from the 1992–93 group are represented too, where their essays fitted in and I could get their permission.

The essays and papers were selected on the basis of both their intrinsic quality and their capacity to fit in with the others in the chapter to form a coherent and informative whole. I have edited each piece for language and have had to reduce considerably the length of the research papers, but I have tried to maintain the integrity of the argument in each case and to allow the writer's own voice to come through. Su Xiaojun helped me by checking the Chinese characters and Pinyin transcriptions, but the introduction to each chapter is my own, and any interpretations offered are solely my responsibility. They are the product, however, of extensive discussions with the program participants and of intense reading of their work—not only the pieces published here, but also the many other essays and papers they wrote for me—and I hope that they will be seen, by the participants and by my other Chinese friends, as a fair representation of their views on literacy and the English language in China.

Note on Chinese Names

The names in this book are all given in the Pinyin transcription except for those of a few historical figures for which older spellings are already well established in the English-speaking world. Following Chinese custom, the surname is always given first, followed by the given name. Where the given name consists of two characters, it is represented in English as a two-syllable word; in the bibliography, however, each of the two syllables is initialized so as to reduce the number of apparently identical names.

Acknowledgments

I could not have produced this book without the help of a great many people. I owe thanks, first of all, to the United Board for Christian Higher Education in Asia for making the project possible, and especially to its president, David Vikner, and its China secretary, Anne Ofstedal, for their consistent support while I was in China and since my return. I also must thank Nanjing University for its generous hospitality, especially the staff of the Foreign Affairs Office and the faculty of the Department of Applied Foreign Language Studies, in which the College English Teacher Training Program is housed. I would like to make particular mention of Yang Zhizhong, the chair of the department; Wang Haixiao, the vice-chair; Liu Chunbao, the then-director of the program; Wang Xueli, the present director; Xu Xiaomei, the administrative assistant; and Zheng Changke, who photocopied many articles for me and taught me Chinese while doing so. Wang Haixiao and Wang Xueli were especially helpful, and they have, moreover, answered many questions that have arisen as this book was being prepared. Sarah Towle, my American colleague in the program, was a delight to work with and a most helpful and encouraging reader of early versions of each chapter. I thank Don Snow, too, of the Amity Foundation, for his helpful feedback, and Stephen Ting and Wen Qiufang for their friendship and encouragement. In the United States, too, I have many people to be grateful to: Professor Allan Brick of the Department of English at Hunter College helped me obtain leave to go to China, Ann Raimes looked after my major responsibilities while I was away, and my sister, Elizabeth Parry, took charge of my house, my money, and my dog. I am indebted to them all.

On behalf of the contributors, I would like to thank the faculty and students of the various institutions where they did their teaching practice and classroom observations. Particular thanks are due to the Nanjing University students in Wang Jian's class, especially to the two who did think-aloud protocols for her, Liu Wanli and Lin Wanqing; to the students and teachers at Jinling Women's College, where Chang Qian, Sheng Ping, and Xu Ju taught; and to the students in Yang Hongqi's class at Nanjing Institute of Chemical Technology, where Wang Kui collected her data, especially the four students she interviewed; Zhou Xiaobin, Wang Shuan, Chen Qianjin, and Qian Hong.

Above all, I would like to acknowledge the participants in the Nanjing University/United Board College English Teacher-Training Program, both those of 1994–95 and those of 1992–93. They have taught me quite as much as I have taught them, and I deeply appreciate their continued friendship.

Part One

The Culture
of Chinese Literacy

1

Literacy at Home

Much of the literature about literacy has emphasized the importance of the lessons about language that children learn from their caretakers when they are still very young. Scollon and Scollon (1981), for example, argue that their daughter, Rachel, was learning about approaches to language that are characteristic of Western literate culture long before she could actually read. As children grow older and begin to read themselves, they learn how to relate to written text and what part they can expect it to play in their own social lives—not, usually, from explicit instruction, but from observing the role that such text plays in the lives of the adults around them. That role, according to the work of Heath (1983, 1986), Street (1984, 1993), and many others, can vary greatly among cultural groups, and there is every reason to believe that Chinese practices will be particularly distinctive. For their first sequence of assignments, therefore, the participants in the 1994-95 Nanjing program were asked to examine literacy in their own homes, as experienced either by themselves when they were young or by their own children now; or they could, if they wished, compare the experience of two or more generations.

The participants began the sequence by reading Heath's article, "What No Bedtime Story Means: Narrative Skills at Home and School" (1986); with this article as a model, they were asked to write the first draft of an essay of their own on the theme of "Literacy at Home." I suggested that they might write about their own experiences or about those of their children, and that they might consider such questions as the following: Were there books in the home? Did parents or other people read children stories? Were children allowed to play with books? Did they have any "literacy toys" such as cards or blocks with characters on them? Were there many public uses of literacy in the environment? Did people talk about books? What happened if a child messed up a book? I also suggested that their essays might take the form of general descriptions of childhood or detailed descriptions of specific events, and that they might want to give point to their descriptions by comparing different environments or periods. Thus primed, the participants wrote their first essays, the final drafts of which form the bulk of this chapter. Between the first and the second drafts, they also read Hatano's "How Do Japanese Children Learn to Read? Orthographic and Ecocultural Variables" (1986); between the second and third drafts they read Lee, Stigler, and Stevenson's "Beginning Reading in Chinese and English" (1986). These last two articles are more quantitative than qualitative in focus and depend more on experimental than ethnographic research, yet they both stress the importance of home background and early exposure to literacy, and they are of special interest in the Chinese context because they consider children who are learning non-alphabetic orthographic systems.

The point that comes out most dramatically in this first set of essays is the extent of the changes that have taken place in China during the past several decades. Zhu Xiaowen, whose essay is presented first because it serves as a frame for the others, takes a particularly long view: She describes the education of four generations of her family, from her grandfather, who was brought up on classics that date back two millennia, to the child that she may expect to have, who will be exposed to the full effects of China's modernization and opening up to the Western world. The changes have been enormous, and yet, Zhu argues, there is continuity, for even through the traumatic years of the Cultural Revolution, and now facing the onslaught of Western culture, many Chinese cling to their traditional literature and seek to ensure that their children learn both its forms and the moral teaching associated with it.

The Cultural Revolution is the historical context of several of the essays, naturally enough, for many of the participants grew up during that time. For some of them it brought terrifying experiences: Sheng Ping, for instance, describes the effects of the Red Guards' activities against her neighbors and her own family because of their undesirable class background. Even when families were not under attack, their lives were profoundly affected: Teenagers roamed about the country denouncing their elders, and many adults had to spend so much time at political meetings—in order, frequently, to defend themselves against denunciation—that their children had to be left in the care of older siblings or grandparents. In these circumstances, the kind of parent-child interaction that Heath (1986) reports among the "Townspeople" was not possible; however, for these writers, there were compensatory factors, such as in the case of Zhu Minghui, who writes of the influence that her elder brother and sister had on her early experiences of reading. Nor was distancing of children from parents a universal experience. Ding Lu gives a delightful account of the close relationship he had with his parents during this period; for him his parents' banishment to the countryside meant more contact with them rather than less.

The Cultural Revolution affected the processes of literacy acquisition not only indirectly through the patterns of parent-child interaction, but also directly in its treatment of different kinds of written text. On the one hand, the Red Guards invaded the houses of intellectuals and burned books that were not written by officially approved authors. Both foreign (i.e., Western) books and traditional Chinese literature were targets of attack, and it was such an attack that Sheng Ping describes. (There are a number of more detailed accounts in English of these Red Guard activities; see Cheng 1986 and Chang 1991. For a literary historian's interpretation of these events, see Spence 1981 and 1990.) On the other hand, the revolutionary forces used written text a good deal themselves: the "little red book" of Mao Zedong's work became prescribed reading for all; an important form of propaganda was slogans posted prominently in public places; and certain writers, such as Guo Muoruo and Lu Xun, were officially approved. Thus, it was in houses that had only a limited range of books and among streets where writing was to be seen everywhere that most Chinese children grew up in the 1960s and 1970s. Such is the setting for all the accounts of this period, but the environment is described in most detail by Lu Wanying in her essay about rural China.

Traditional Chinese literature may have been condemned and books may have been destroyed, but one theme that comes out strongly in these essays is the ways in which the older traditions of literacy nevertheless endured. In the village that Lu Wanying describes, for example, the public display of government notices and revolutionary slogans seems to have been assimilated to an older custom of promoting good fortune by displaying scrolls on the gateposts of a house whenever the household had some special occasion to celebrate. Moreover, the content of the burned books was by no means forgotten. Some condemned books in fact were preserved, and Ding Lu describes how his family borrowed them illicitly and made sure that he learned about them. Even those who had no access to books (including some who could not read) could tell the stories to their children, as Lu Wanying's account demonstrates. A striking feature of all of these essays is the loyalty that the adults in these writers' lives showed to the old ideals of education and the efforts that they made to ensure that their children acquired the kind of literacy that they themselves had been taught to value.

The changes that China has experienced since the late 1970s have been less painful but no less dramatic than the Cultural Revolution. From the point of view of literacy acquisition, perhaps the most important has been the introduction of the population-control policy in 1979. Since then, each couple has been allowed to have only one child, and though exceptions are made for special groups, the policy has been largely adhered to, at least in urban areas. As a consequence, city-dwellers in their thirties now have a single child on whom they lavish all their attention and to whom they try to give everything of which they were deprived—and the most important thing they seek for this child is success in education.

In such circumstances, it is not surprising that adults spend a good deal of time on their children and that much of this time is spent on teaching them to read or preparing them to do so. The process of preparation begins even before the child is born, as Xu Ju vividly describes in her essay, "From the Womb to the Cradle: The Practice of *Tāi Jiào*." Li Xiaozhong and Luo Ningxia both take the story further by recounting the ways in which they, respectively, have tried to prepare their children for literacy from the time when they were born. Li emphasizes the teaching of Chinese characters and provides for English readers interesting insights into how the enormously complex system can be introduced so that a child can remember some of the basic elements and use them as a foundation for later learning. Luo writes of the materials that she uses in largely oral interactions with her daughter. These materials represent two kinds of education, both of which were decried in the Cultural Revolution: some are from traditional Chinese sources, especially the poems of the Tang Dynasty; others are from foreign sources, such as collections of fairy tales from Europe and stories from Japan. In both essays, and in many of the others that are not published here, it is clear that these teachers are determined to do the best they can for their children and that this, for them, means introducing the children to literacy skills at an early age.

Chinese parents, in urban areas at least, not only have more time to spend with their children than they did in the recent past, but also have more money with which to buy books, toys, tape-recorders, and television sets. Over and above all this, many parents are apparently spending surplus income on extra tuition for their children, even while the children are still very young. Qin Haihua describes this phenomenon. She herself is one of the younger students in the group, which may be why she seems to have enjoyed more access to books as a child than did most of the others. However, the children that she knows now are given much more than she was, a development that she describes as disturbing, both because it puts children under undue pressure and because it exposes them to information that is not valuable while distracting them from information that is.

Another note of warning is sounded by Zhang Weinian, who compares the situation of urban children with that of their rural contemporaries. While urban children may be growing up in a hothouse atmosphere of intense exposure to literacy, their rural counterparts live apparently in much the same way as their parents did in the 1960s and 1970s: Peasant parents still have little time to spend with their children and little money to spare for books. So, although the rural population is largely literate, as is suggested in Lu Wanying's essay, this literacy is limited, and there is an increasingly large gap in educational achievement between rural and urban areas. The gap is made manifest, as Zhang points out, in the results of the annual university entrance exam: Few young people from rural areas are able to pass this exam, which means that they are obliged to stay in their villages and earn their living as peasants like their parents. (For further discussion of the differences between urban and rural education, see Lo 1984.)

The difficulties experienced by rural Chinese in competing with their urban counterparts echo the problems reported by Heath (1983) as experienced by Trackton and Roadville children. It is clear from Lu Wanying's and

Zhang Weinian's essays that rural Chinese, like the "non-mainstream" children that Heath describes, are fully part of a literate culture: Written Chinese plays a regular part in their daily lives, and the stories with which they are entertained are some of the staples of traditional Chinese literature. But the ways in which children of peasant backgrounds are taught to interact with text differ markedly from the ways in which the children of the teachers who have written these essays are learning to do so. Given the intense competition to get into Chinese universities, such children are under-represented in most institutions of higher education, especially in the more prestigious ones such as Nanjing University itself. They do, however, account for an increasingly high proportion of those who attend teachers' colleges, partly because these colleges (in contrast to others) do not require their students to pay fees, and partly because positions as teachers are no longer considered desirable, there being so many opportunities now in other fields (cf. Paine 1992). The implications for future social and educational development are interesting and disturbing: the teachers'-college graduates will be expected to return to their home areas in the countryside to teach in secondary schools, while graduates of the more prestigious universities will have good chances of getting jobs in the rapidly expanding cities. Thus, it looks as if literacy in China—far from being an equalizing factor—will serve rather to widen the gap between urban and rural and between rich and poor.

The diversity of literacy practices described in this chapter has implications, too, for those who teach English to Chinese-speaking students in other parts of the world. Despite their common linguistic heritage, such students may have widely different backgrounds, especially if we include those who do not come from mainland China. While it is valid to say that all such students are likely to value Chinese literacy as an important form of participation in their own culture, the extent to which it will be associated with pleasant childhood experiences and with close family relationships may vary considerably, and so also may the extent to which the students are imbued with classical Chinese literature. Their perceptions of reading may be correspondingly various, and so may their attitudes towards the classical cultures of Europe; these may be important factors governing the strategies that they find helpful in learning to read in English.

1. Four Generations

Zhu Xiaowen

The literacy education of Chinese children differs drastically from one generation to another, yet it is always strongly influenced by Chinese traditional culture.

According to Heath (1986), the style of one's literacy education is closely related to social circumstances, in which moral values, customs, traditions, status relations, and many other factors are subject to change. Thus, it is easy to understand the changes in literacy education that have taken place among generations as China's social structure has been shaken and reconstructed by the three important revolutions of this century,[1] as well as the economic reform that is now taking place. I would like to describe the changes in the literacy education of different generations by focusing on my own family.

My grandfather, who was born in Zhejiang Province in the southeastern part of China in about 1918, belongs to the last generation that had a *sīshú* system. *Sīshú* was a kind of traditional, private, educational institution that existed long before the public school came into being.

From his *Recollections,* which is his own written account of his life, I learn that his literacy education was typical of his community at that time. My grandfather came from a middle-class family, and his father was a local businessman who owned several grocery stores in the town. Like almost all the other children from similar families, he had little chance to learn to read and write before he was sent to *sīshú* at the age of about eight. The written words that children could see were the stone titles on the facades and the names or prices of items on sale. At night, he would see his father or the accountant writing and using an abacus to do calculations. So my grandfather and his younger brother watched and observed the adults' activities, and thus learned to read words by connecting adults' repetition of the names of the items with the written forms that appeared in his surroundings—written forms that were more complicated than the characters we now use.

However, his parents seldom deliberately taught him any words. Only occasionally, when his father was free from his work, would he take one of the books he liked best from his very small book collection and read aloud the lines he enjoyed. At this time, he would explain a bit to his sons. From such

---

1. The first of these revolutions was that of 1911 when the Qing Imperial Dynasty was overthrown; it is known in China as the Bourgeois Revolution or the Xin Hai Revolution. The second is considered by Chinese historians to have begun in 1919 and to have culminated in 1949, with the Communist Party's takeover of power; it is described as the People's Revolution or as the New Democratic Revolution. The third is the Cultural Revolution of 1966–1976.

instruction by their father, my grandfather and great-uncle got to know many historical figures, such as the great thinkers, Confucius and Mencius; the first emperor, Qin Shihuang; the national hero, Yue Fei; and the most famous poets of the Tang Dynasty, Li Bai, Du Fu, and Bai Juyi. My great-grandparents also used the ideology, thought, and life stories of these historical figures to teach their sons moral lessons in order to make them behave themselves and grow up to be promising young men.

From my grandfather's *Recollections,* I also learn that the traditional materials for beginning literacy instruction were the anonymous *Three-Character Primer* and *A Hundred Surname Characters;* two other elementary books were *A Thousand-Character Essays* and *A Thousand Poets' Poems,* which my grandfather's father also taught his sons to read and recite. The *Three-Character Primer* and *A Thousand-Character Essays* are actually text-books of moral lessons. My grandfather and great-uncle could recite many lines from them but were not able to recognize the characters. *A Hundred Surname Characters* is a book on the origins of Chinese family names and the historical evolution of the nation. The two children could at least write one of the names—their own surname.

Both my grandfather and great-uncle learned to use a writing brush at *sīshú* and to read much more of the classics of Confucius and Mencius, all by rote-learning. At home, every morning, their parents (usually their mother) would supervise them reciting their lessons and practicing their brush-writing.

This traditional education was what my grandfather's ancestors had received. But he was born after the Bourgeois Revolution of 1911, which introduced modern Western culture into China and, as a result, two public schools were established in the town in his childhood.[2] After two years of *sīshú* education, both my grandfather and my great-uncle were sent to public schools to learn more than the Chinese classics, which were the only subject they had at *sīshú*. Although at these schools they learned many modern subjects, such as math, physiology, and geography, as well as vernacular Chinese (*Bái Huà Wén*), what they practiced at home was still Chinese handwriting and reciting classical literature.[3] Moral lessons combined with traditional culture were consistently given to them throughout the process of growing up.

Twenty years later, in my father's generation, there were no more *sīshú*. The *sīshú* and their tutors were replaced by public schools and trained teachers. But before my father went to school at the age of seven in 1948, he received at home a moral and cultural education similar to that of my grandfather.

Because his family considered education important, my father was deliberately taught to read *Three-Character Primer* and *A Hundred Surname Characters* at the early age of four. My father often recalled that his grand-

---

2. For an account of the transition from traditional to modern education, see Hayhoe (1992). (Ed.)
3. The establishment of vernacular Chinese as a written form was one of the most important linguistic changes of the Republican period. See DeFrancis (1984, 234–5) and Ramsey (1987, 10). (Ed.)

mother always sat beside him and supervised him copying calligraphy and reciting classics from simple to more complicated pieces, usually poems by Li Bai or some other poets. His grandmother was very strict with him, my father said: No matter how cold it was in winter, he was not allowed to get up late and skip morning reading and writing. Whenever he was being naughty or trying to play some tricks to avoid her assignments, his grandmother would scold him by telling him stories, citing either good or bad examples from history. These moral lessons were the same as my grandfather had received. My father also told me that he learned from his grandmother's teaching many Chinese idioms and the stories on which they are based.[4] However, his grandmother seldom explained the written words my father copied in his daily morning handwriting exercise, for the few characters she knew were not enough for her to explain the beginning literacy material to her grandson.

At primary school, my father learned *zhù yīn fú hào,* a phonetic writing system that is different from the Pinyin that we now learn, but it is the same as the phonetic system used in Taiwan (see Lee, Stigler, and Stevenson 1986), and he studied simple standard modern Chinese *(Bái Huà Wén).* Also, instead of classical works, he read many beautiful essays by modern Chinese writers such as the poet Guo Muoruo, the essayist Zhu Ziqing, and the essayist and novelist Lu Xun.[5] He also learned ancient poems at school, many of which were already included in his calligraphy book, and he continued his calligraphy exercises until he left his hometown and went to high school at the age of thirteen. But as for Confucius' and other ancient authors' works, he only studied a few of them later in high school.

When I look at my own childhood, it seems that the traditional cultural education was abruptly cut off in my generation, for my childhood was during the ten-year Cultural Revolution (1966–1976), which condemned the tradition and culture of the feudalistic past as worthless. Old books and historical heroes, as well as Western Capitalist culture, were "swept into the trash-can of history," as the newspapers and magazines of the time put it. It was a nightmare for all Chinese. Like many other children of my age, I began to learn characters from the political slogans everywhere in my surroundings. There were so many slogans that I could read and write many words before I went to primary school.

In their free time, my parents (usually my mother) would teach me to sing children's rhymes from the books they bought for me. All these verses were written in praise of our great leader, the national heroes whom Chairman Mao had praised (i.e., Lei Feng, Liu Hulan, and Dong Cunrui, who all died for the Chinese revolutionary cause), and our socialist society. But my mother also taught me a few ancient poems because she loved them so much. Like many other Chinese, she never believed deep down in her heart that those literary

---

4. For an example of such Chinese idioms, see Xu Ju's essay in Chapter Three. (Ed.)
5. These writers developed during and after the "New Cultural Movement" of the 1920s, which condemned the political ideology of imperial China as decaying and corrupt, and promoted the twin ideas of "science and democracy" while trying to preserve the essence of Chinese traditional culture.

treasures were historical rubbish. The Chinese simply dared not teach them openly to the next generation.

At night when my parents were fulfilling their daily obligations—reading Chairman Mao's works or going out for political meetings—we children would read picture books, which were similar in content to the children's rhymes mentioned previously. These books were simple and colorless, but we loved them as they were the most interesting materials we could have.

After the "nightmare," I went to secondary school where I had an opportunity to recover from its effects. Many traditional as well as foreign literary and scientific works again were included in the textbooks, and I came to read some classical Chinese collections that somewhat made up for my lack of traditional culture.

Compared to the foregoing generations, the generation born in the 1990s is very lucky. As I have no child yet, I have no idea how I will begin his or her literacy education at home, but as far as I can see, the social environment and family circumstances of the present are highly favorable for learning. Children have more television and radio programs, beautiful attractive pictures and storybooks, various toys that promote literacy, and also the most helpful parents who have such great expectations for them. There are indeed many negative factors, such as the mass media's overemphasis on Western culture, the unrealistic expectations of some parents, and the tendency for children to be passive recipients of information rather than active and creative learners. Nevertheless, the present generation's average literacy ability is much higher than that of previous generations, at least at the time before formal schooling.

Although social developments have brought so many changes in the past few generations, there is still much consistency in the beginning education at home. Our traditional culture and morals are always respected, for they are as precious to us as pure gold, the more so because they have survived so many revolutions and reforms, and they will always be passed on from one generation to the next. Take the Tang poems as an example. Although they were created almost thirteen hundred years ago, their vocabulary is so simple that even our modern children have no difficulty understanding their surface meaning. On the other hand, the verses are so skillfully composed and contain so much beauty and so many profound meanings that any adult, of whatever walk of life, can get spiritual nourishment from them. Another example is traditional Chinese handwriting. We do not now use a writing brush for purposes of daily communication, but there are still numerous parents who require their children to practice calligraphy in order to develop such valued moral qualities as persistence and patience. Others may teach calligraphy to their children as an artistic skill because, through its thousands of years of development, Chinese calligraphy has become a unique art form.

In short, more young parents have realized that literacy education is cultural education. If our traditions and culture are considered as expressing a unique Eastern aesthetic, how can we reject or abandon the treasures left to us by our ancestors?

2. My Experience of Childhood

Sheng Ping

I spent my childhood in an unusual period, the so-called Great Cultural Revolution. It meant a revolution that opposed feudalism and bourgeois culture. Its principal aim was that the working class should dominate everything. The intellectuals had to transform their outlook by doing physical labor and receiving reeducation from the working class.

At that time, I didn't know what the Cultural Revolution was. I only remember I saw many strange things happen around me, which often made me frightened. One day, one of my kind neighbors, Uncle Lei, as I used to call him, committed suicide by hanging himself at home. I didn't understand what had happened, but the neighbors guessed he had done so for some political reason. Another day, a group of Red Guards rushed into my house and searched everywhere for something. They destroyed some furniture and some of my father's books that he had failed to hide well. When they left, one of them cursed me as the whelp of a landlord. Later I asked my grandma why they wanted to search our house, but she didn't say a word. From then on, I had a sense of inferiority and dared not go out to play with other children for fear that they would look down on me and curse me too. I often stayed at home with my grandma since my father was sent to Xi'an to receive reeducation from the working class and my mother was busy with her work. I felt very lonely sometimes. Maybe that is the reason why I am shy and timid now.

During the Cultural Revolution, it seemed that most people didn't work and study; they just held meetings every day to criticize one person after another. They wanted to overthrow some revolutionary cadres who once took part in the War of Liberation and also to undermine the authority of some knowledgeable teachers. There used to be a slogan, "Whoever has knowledge is a reactionary element." They burnt and destroyed many valuable books— everything, in fact, except books of Chairman Mao's quotations. People couldn't buy any good books in bookstores. Generally speaking, most parents wouldn't teach their children to read at home, for they thought it was useless to read and write. And some families were so poor that the children often went hungry, so there was no question of buying books to read. However, most children saw text around them from their earliest days, since Chairman Mao's pictures were everywhere, accompanied by phrases like "Long live Chairman Mao," "Long live the Communist Party; without the Communist Party there would be no New China," "Never forget the class struggle," and "Serve the people with heart and soul." Some slogans were painted on walls, some were painted on the lids of cups, some were on towels and in other places. Everyone could read those few words at that time, I think. The children also were supposed to read and recite Chairman Mao's teachings.

However, I was a bit lucky in some respects, for I had a relatively good family background. My mother had a good job and got a high salary, for she came from a poor worker's family, which suggested she had a "glorious" class origin. At that time, the working class played a leading role, which meant my father had to obey my mother's orders. My mother assured the party organization that she would help my father transform his world outlook and become a member of the working class.

Whenever I heard these words later, I couldn't help laughing, for I thought it funny and ridiculous. My father once studied in the Chinese Department of Hunan University, during which time he specialized in ancient Chinese poetry. After graduation, he became a teacher teaching Chinese in a school. Thus, he belonged to the intellectual class, which is why he had such a hard time during the Cultural Revolution. When he returned from two years in Xi'an, he came back to his original school and continued his teaching career, but many classrooms in the school were now empty; most students refused to attend class under the influence of the fallacy, "Whoever has knowledge is a reactionary element."

Yet, no matter what happened, my father still attached importance to his children's education. Every time he came home from work, he would bring me something such as blocks, cards, a colorful paper organ that could make sounds, picture books, storybooks for children, and pencils. He bought me a little dog to accompany me. With great patience, he taught me to read and write whenever he was free. He taught me to recite the famous poetry written in the Tang Dynasty, and he also taught me simple arithmetic. I still remember some stories told by him: *Journey to the West,* which tells how Xuan Zhang, a monk in the Tang Dynasty, traveled to India with his pupils in search of Buddhist scriptures; *The Tale of the White Serpent,* which describes the love story between a white serpent spirit and a young man; and *The Little Match Girl,* the story by Hans Anderson about a poor little girl who sold matches on Christmas Eve and died of cold and hunger.

I was also interested in revolutionary stories about heroes and heroines who devoted their lives to the Anti-Japanese War and the War of Liberation. My father taught me to love our motherland, for he believed that the abnormal situation in China was temporary. He often said China was a great country with a long history. He was proud of her and he firmly believed China had a good future. Influenced by him, I had deep feelings for new China when I was very young. I still remember I loved to sing the songs for children extolling Chairman Mao and the Communist Party. Whenever I saw a picture of Chairman Mao, I called him "Grandpa Mao" and pointed to it. I tried to keep Grandpa Mao's teaching firmly in mind, "Study hard and make progress every day," and I resolved to serve our motherland with heart and soul in the future.

3. Literacy in My Home

Zhu Minghui

When I was a child, I had no storybooks, cards, or other toys that encouraged literacy. Nobody ever read any bedtime stories to me. I had a mechanical toy tank that was passed on to me from my brothers and sisters. That was my only toy. But I did have certain experiences of literacy before school.

I have two brothers and two sisters. My second sister and second brother are six and four years older than me. At that time, my parents were too busy to look after me, so it was always my second sister and second brother who did so. They were then old enough to go to school. After school, they took me home from the nursery every day. As they were doing their homework, I played by myself beside them. I sometimes listened casually to what they read, perhaps admiring their ability. When they practiced writing Chinese words, I was so interested in writing that I asked them to teach me. Sometimes they taught me to write just to keep me quiet so that they could finish their homework.

I was born in 1968. That was soon after the beginning of the "Great Cultural Revolution." The revolution was initiated by Mao Zedong, who did it originally to propose a kind of new thinking in people's minds. The Chinese people respected him very much, thinking it was he who brought them new lives. So there were pictures of Chairman Mao in almost every family. On each picture, there were always these characters "毛主席万岁," *Máo Zhǔxí wàn suì,* which mean "Long live Chairman Mao!" My literacy at home began from these words.

People saw and heard these words often in their daily life, so my brother and sister naturally chose them to teach me first. They were glad at their successful teaching because I was able to write these words very soon. So they taught me some other simple Chinese characters. I myself was proud that I knew something that my playmates didn't know, and my success encouraged me to learn more words. My sister and brother also taught me how to count and write numbers from one to a hundred. These were all I knew before entering primary school.

Frankly speaking, I didn't get much literacy at home, but I was considered very clever at that time in my hometown, just because I could recognize and write some words and numbers. Because of this, I was given permission by the schoolmaster to go to school at the age of seven, while my playmates of the same age could not because children were usually expected to go to school at eight.

Compared with other children in my hometown, I was lucky, because they couldn't get even the little literacy I had. My brothers and sisters all went to school, were interested in learning, and got high grades, and I had the chance to be influenced by them. All five of us were also lucky to have our parents' support. My family was not wealthy, just like other families, and after I went to school my parents had to pay the fees for all five of us, which was very difficult for them. However, my parents often said to us, "If only you can read on (i.e., have the ability to go on studying), we will pay for you. Even if we don't have money, we will support you by borrowing money."

Many parents would not do this. Sometimes, if they couldn't afford to send their children to school, they would just let them stop studying and expect them to return home to help support the family. In their minds, life for their children would be the same with or without knowledge from school, and so they saw little reason to encourage literacy at home. I often heard this in their homes: "What's the good of going to school?" or "It's only a waste of money!"

Another reason why many children could not get literacy at home was that their parents were too busy. My home was in a rural area, and adults worked from morning till night when I was a child. After they came back from the fields and finished their supper, they were too tired to sit with the children to talk with them.

And there is one more important point. Many of the parents were illiterate. They just could not read to their children.

4. Reading and Writing Within a Family

Ding Lu

Almost everybody is deeply and closely connected with his family, and I am no exception. In particular, my parents helped me greatly in becoming the literate person that I am now.

I was born in Nanjing, which is a big industrial and cultural center in China. But two years later, in 1969, my family was sent to Yangzhou, a much smaller city and my father's hometown, because of the period of persecution that was called the Great Proletarian Cultural Revolution (1966–1976). At that time, in order to strengthen the government, the classical élite type of literacy and Westernized literacy were alike attacked, and the so-called revolutionary literacy, which centered on Mao Zedong's work and quotations and eight model Beijing operas, was promoted. Many intellectuals and political cadres were sent to the countryside to help the peasants and their children. My father, a schoolteacher, was posted to a school for peasants' children in the countryside near Yangzhou. So my life in nursery school, which I attended for just one year, was cut off, and my parents began to act as my tutors. To keep me well informed of and familiar with city life, my parents took me to Yangzhou at regular intervals.

As a small city, Yangzhou had kept its own historical and cultural color. It still had its bird and flower market and classical painting and calligraphy works display. Besides this, some gardens with special architectural characteristics were kept intact. So I got chances to look around and began to cultivate in myself a sense of classical culture. I followed my parents to the movies, ate at the famous restaurants that served regional food, had showers, and visited some of my parents' workmates. The most important thing was that I gradually became really excited at going to the bookstores, where I spent a lot of time searching around the shelves, pointing at the books displayed, inquiring and asking to buy. Many of the books were on revolutionary themes and presented stories of modern Socialist construction, but some were more "neutral," being about ancient Chinese philosophy, or simply being collections of fables. My parents always found it difficult to resist my pleading, so my mother would pick out and pay for some picture books and magazines, and I would go home with my own copy of *The Long March,* for example, or *The Young Pioneer.*

On the way home, I would ask various kinds of questions, and my father never tired of answering them to satisfy my desire for learning. Sometimes, tired by the day's activities, I would almost fall asleep sitting on the front bar of the bicycle. My father would keep talking to me in order to keep me awake and to prevent me from getting ill from the wind blowing against us.

16

The next day, my mother would make me sit on a stool in front of her and would go through the picture books and magazines page by page, reading aloud, explaining patiently, and vividly depicting the settings and the plots. I would ask many questions—"Can I do that when I grow up?," "Why do people die?," "Will we die someday?," and so on. However foolish they were, she always answered them. Some of the stories were made up so poorly that I couldn't believe they were true; the stories about the class struggle, for example, were too badly knitted together. But I really loved the instructive fables and philosophical stories. After we finished a book, my mother would ask me to retell the story immediately, and I could usually remember the same words and expressions my mother had used. If occasionally my memory failed me, she would offer help by showing me the page in question again, and as I told and retold the stories, she always kept me excited and encouraged. Even as a boy of four, I could sense the progress day by day.

In addition, when relatives and guests paid a visit, they would like to hear me telling stories out of *The Journey to the West, Outlaws of the Marsh,* and *The Three Kingdoms.* All these books are classical Chinese novels, and at the time they were forbidden books. It was my father who wanted me to learn from these books and borrowed them through connections in the library. On these occasions, I usually got praised a lot, and so I built up a sense of achievement.

Besides all this, my father was extremely strict with me. In his opinion, the trend of attacking classical culture and knowledge would be reversed, and a strong China would need intellectuals and professionals. So he tried to direct me to use the abacus, making me familiar with the rules of arithmetic, and he was especially rigid in instructing me to write Chinese characters in the standard square exercise books, according to the relationship between radical and space. Only by doing this could I have good and correct handwriting, an important point, because the theory that handwriting matches the person who does it has been accepted for many centuries. Furthermore, according to his requirements, I could only use a pencil or fountain pen. My father regarded the ball pen as the killer of good handwriting, and he was right, for the ball pen made one casual with the structure. Finally, he asked me to practice calligraphy. I practiced for three years, using a brush and following the style of the Tang Dynasty calligrapher, Liu Gongquan.

In the course of learning, I really appreciated the help given me by my parents. Indeed, I owed a lot to the Great Proletarian Cultural Revolution, for without it my family would not have been sent to the country, and my parents would not have been so free or so resolute to instruct me. In that time of turmoil, they believed that the younger generation was the only hope of the country; and, without question, God said to them "You are right."

5. The Beginnings of Literacy for Rural Children

Lu Wanying

Literacy at home differs from one country to another and also from urban to rural areas within the same country. Living in the Chinese countryside as a child, I know quite clearly how the rural children of my age acquired their initial literacy at home.

Generally speaking, rural Chinese parents of that time (the late 1960s) received little education. Most of them knew only a small number of characters besides their own names and the Arabic numerals. Consequently, they were of little help to their children's literacy acquisition. Nonetheless, rural children could and did begin their literacy at home, unconsciously and in a very special way, for it was through an old traditional custom.

For many centuries, Chinese people, especially rural Chinese, have had a tradition of attaching antithetical couplets to their gates on special days, such as the Spring Festival, wedding days, or funerals of old people. An antithetical couplet is a pair of scrolls of long red paper (yellow, green, or white for a funeral) of exactly the same size, hung vertically on either side of the door frame. On the scrolls, strictly rhymed phrases, usually of seven characters, are written to show all sorts of good wishes. A typical couplet is shown in Figure 1-1.

On the left scroll, the characters shown in Figure 1-1 read:

和	顺	一	门	有	百	福
hé	*shùn*	*yī*	*mén*	*yǒu*	*bǎi*	*fú*
harmony	smoothness	one	door	have	a hundred	fortune

It means harmonious and smooth family relationships will bring the family good fortune. On the right scroll, the characters read:

平	安	二	字	值	千	金
píng	*ān*	*èr*	*zì*	*zhí*	*qiān*	*jīn*
peace	safety	two	character	deserve	thousand	gold

It means peace and safety are invaluable assets. The horizontal scroll usually includes four or five characters that summarize the couplet. In this case, they read:

万	事	如	意
wàn	*shì*	*rú*	*yì*
ten thousand	affairs	as	one wishes

Figure 1-1
An antithetical couplet

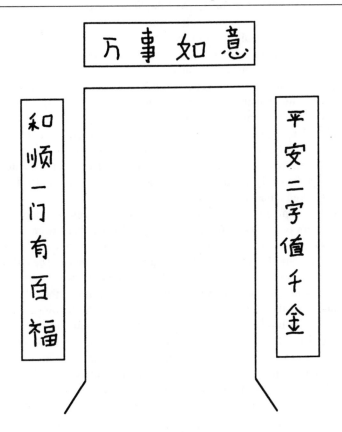

When I was a child, every family would put antithetical couplets up on their gates to celebrate the lunar new year. Because the calligraphy on the couplets was beautiful and varied, and also because the couplets expressed the best wishes of each family, all the villagers were ready and glad to read and comment on them. At these times, young children would look at the couplets and listen to adults talking about them. Sometimes the adults would point at some simple Chinese characters to teach the children. For example, they might point out 天, *tiān* (sky) in 普天同庆, *pǔ tiān tóng qìng* (all the people celebrate together) or 人, *rén* (person) in 人寿年丰, *rén shòu nián fēng* (long live the people, good harvest in the new year). They just read out and repeated such characters as *tiān tiān* or *rén rén,* and the children would follow and say, *"tiān, tiān"* or *"rén, rén."* Time and again, the children might memorize the characters. Wherever they found the already learned words, they would point at them and cry out *"tiān"* or *"rén,"* as described previously.

Attaching couplets to the gates of the houses was a very old tradition. It began thousands of years ago and it continues to the present. Even during the Cultural Revolution, this tradition was not abolished. Antithetical couplets formed part of the traditional Chinese culture, and they played an important role in rural children's literacy acquisition.

Besides antithetical couplets, children were exposed to other written materials. There were always some slogans written on the walls in white lime to publicize government policies or laws such as the anti-illiteracy campaign, the family-planning policy (in the 1970s), the water law, or the public-security law. Thus, rural Chinese were never cut off from the literate environment of their culture in spite of the fact that they had no toys or blocks or cards. They were not deliberately instructed in literacy, but they—or at least some of them—acquired it nonetheless.

Another source of literacy at home for rural Chinese children was their elder brothers or sisters or literate villagers. Usually there were some small picture books passed from house to house. These books played an important part in the cultural life of the children. Popular books such as *The Orphan San Mao's Adventure* (set in Shanghai before Liberation) were very amusing. Whenever some literate children obtained one such book, they would squat down and read the captions, as well as appreciate the pictures, while their young illiterate brothers or sisters or neighbors listened and watched attentively. Occasionally, the young ones who could not read would ask some questions. In doing so, these young children were beginning to acquire literacy. The children also might learn something from their elder siblings' textbooks or when the elder ones did their assignments. My brother sometimes held my hand and taught me to write some simple words such as Arabic numerals or Chinese characters; for example, 口, *kǒu*, mouth, or 手, *shǒu*, hand. In that way, the young children enlarged their stock of characters.

A third way in which rural children were prepared for literacy was by listening to stories during summer nights. When it was too hot to go to sleep at night, all the villagers enjoyed the cool in the open air. Sometimes some people would voluntarily tell some well-known ancient legends like *The Tale of the White Serpent,* about the love between a young doctor and the spirit of a white snake. They also liked to tell famous historical stories such as *The Three Kingdoms,* an historical novel about how three feudal warlords tore the country apart at the end of the Han Dynasty, and *Outlaws of the Marsh,* which describes the uprising of 108 outlaws in Liangshan Marsh against the imperial court at the end of the Northern Song Dynasty. At such times, the children would sit around the adults and listen admiringly. They might not understand what the stories were, but they had some vague ideas about them.

Thus, rural Chinese children of that time (the late 1960s) got little direct instruction from their parents about how to read and write. However, they were in frequent touch with literate sources. They acquired their literacy unconsciously and naturally, even though it was very limited.

Things have changed a great deal in the countryside of today. Now rural parents are of more help to their children's education. However, some customs, such as attaching antithetical couplets to the gates, are still kept and are, indeed, becoming more fashionable. Children may still acquire literacy through that particularly Chinese folk tradition, and it will be handed down for a long time.

6. From the Womb to the Cradle: The Practice of *Tāi Jiào*

Xu Ju

In today's China, many parents or would-be parents are attempting to mold themselves again for their child's sake. Some parents who did not receive a good education go to the open universities and study hard for the purpose of teaching their child; some who used to like reading stories and watching television plays about crime, battle, or romance sacrifice their own preferences in order to be qualified parents and turn to cartoon television and picture books, laughing at themselves as "recovering their childhood."

Besides caring for the only child's physical well-being, parents focus on the child's intellectual development. Fostering the only child's literacy begins even before the child is born. Sometimes when you go out in the dusk, you will meet a pregnant woman leisurely ambling under a canopy of street trees or along a peaceful winding path. She is murmuring to the fetus in her womb. Sometimes it is just aimless talk. Sometimes it is a children's rhyme. Sometimes it is a song. This beautiful picture is the practice known as *tāi jiào*, or educating the fetus.

There are in Chinese many legends, folktales, fables, and children's rhymes dating from ancient times. All of these can become materials for *tāi jiào*. The following are some examples:

> *Xiǎo tùzi guāi guāi,*
> *Bǎ mén kāi kāi.*
> *Wǒde bǎo bǎo yào jìn lǎi.*

It can be translated into English as follows:

> Good little rabbit,
> Please open the door.
> My baby wants to come in.

The last words of the three lines, *guāi, kāi,* and *lǎi,* all rhyme. A little child, even a fetus, may be alert to the sounds when they are repeated several times.

Animals are the most attractive things to little children. Fairy tales such as *Xiǎo māo diào yú,* "A kitten goes fishing," naturally become lively materials for *tāi jiào* because the sounds made by different animals and onomatopoeic words describing the animals' actions can be vividly imitated by the expectant mother. *Xiǎo māo diào yú* tells a story about how a kitten wasn't attentive to her fishing and was distracted successively by a multicolored butterfly, a

22

nimble dragonfly, a flying squirrel, and a flock of swallows, and so got nothing for a whole day. While telling such a story to a fetus, the future mother puts emphasis on the details of sounds and gestures through her exaggerated tones of voice. Normally, no attention is paid to the moral of the story.

Tang poems are among the best teaching materials for the child and the fetus, especially those with four lines and five characters in each line. They are easy to read aloud and understand. Here is a poem written by Li Bai, the greatest romantic Tang poet:

Chuáng qián míng yuè guāng,
Yí shì dì shàng shuāng.
Jǔ tóu wàng míng yuè,
Dī tóu sī gù xiāng.

The English version is:

The bright moon is shining in front of my bed,
I wonder if it is the frost on the ground.
Raising my head, I look at the moon,
Lowering my head, I think of my home.

The last characters of lines 1, 2, and 4, *guāng*, *shuāng*, and *xiāng*, respectively, rhyme, and the rhyme can easily come to a little child's or even a fetus's notice.

Generally speaking, *tāi jiào* remains at the level of attracting the attention of the fetus to the sounds of words. It is not the character forms that a fetus can reach; it is an impression with which parents hope to imbue the child. The impression and reflection of sounds, however, can have a direct effect on the child's subsequent interest and performance in literacy.

Here I will talk about a couple, both of whom are postgraduates and my friends. The wife is pregnant. The husband often nestles up against the wife's belly, listening to the sound made by the fetus or speaking in a tender voice. He tells the little creature how sincere his love is for him and how earnestly he expects the child to come to the human world, and how wonderful the outside world is. The father tries to talk about everything to his unborn child, even things about an American president. Now and then, he slightly pats the wife's belly and asks his child: "Did you hear what I said?," "Do you agree with me?" In the father's opinion, he has been fully heard and understood.

The situation described mainly exists in the urban areas. How about the rural areas then? Because money is often limited there, there are not so many sources of knowledge acquisition. Peasants solve the problem by drawing on local resources—legends, folktales, and children's rhymes that have existed among the local people for generations. In the moonlight of summer nights, the pregnant country woman sits peacefully in the court under the trees with a palm fan in her hand and talks to her unborn child. The fetus thus grows in a leisurely and carefree atmosphere and is nurtured by the old and primitive culture.

In *tāi jiào*, the fetus is exposed not only to sounds, but also to ideas. A pregnant woman may extend her thoughts and emotions to her unborn child through the interaction of their hearts. The information that the fetus receives will be part of the content that the words will bear for him when he studies them in the future. Such transmission of meaning, as well as exposure to sound, is a forerunner to the child's later training in literacy. For example, I know a particular father and son who are extremely similar not only in their figures, countenances, and voices, but also in their styles of thought. The father died several years ago, but I always realize that he is still alive every time I meet his son. The case makes me begin to believe that such a transmission of ideas can really take place.

How great is the effect of *tāi jiào*? Nobody has systematically studied the question and drawn a conclusion. However, many young parents born in the 1960s and 1970s believe it can have an active, far-reaching effect on their only child and that it is an important first step in education. It is done in thousands of only-child families and constitutes a peculiar phenomenon of today's China.

7. Education at Home

Li Xiaozhong

I think the new generation of Chinese children are luckier than their parents, for they have more chance to receive education than their parents had. Take my son, for example. His case is somewhat similar to the "Townspeople" described by Heath (1986). After he was born, I began to buy him books, cards, and toys. At first, he had not much interest in learning Chinese characters, so I read the stories to him and he only looked at the pictures. He wanted me to repeat the stories again and again, and later he himself could "read" the stories by following the pictures.

When he was about two and a half years old, I gradually taught him some simple Chinese characters like 人, *rén;* 大, *dà;* 上, *shàng,* and 下, *xià,* which mean respectively "people," "big," "up," and "down" in English. At first I taught him these characters separately, for he was still young, and too many characters at a time would have confused him. However, I did associate the character with what was familiar to him. For example, when I taught him 太, *tài,* which means "too," I first told him this character is formed by adding a dot to 大, *dà,* "big," and then I explained to him 太 is one of the characters in 太阳, *tài yáng,* which means "the sun" in English. When he was older, I tried to teach him characters in relation to each other. I would teach him 春, *chūn;* 夏, *xià;* 秋, *qiū;* and 冬, *dōng,* which mean "spring, summer, autumn, winter" all together. Sometimes I would give him four cards that have 妈, *mā;* 姐, *jiě;* 妹, *mèi;* and 奶, *nǎi* on them. The English for these characters is "mother," "elder sister," "younger sister," and "grandma." I asked him to find the part that is the same in all these characters, and then I told him that the common element, 女, *nǚ,* is often used to refer to female, though of course there are exceptions, like 娃, *wá,* which means "baby" in English. By making connections of this sort, he could remember the characters more easily.

I think my son's real interest in learning Chinese characters began at about four years old. He learned fast and actively wanted to learn. Maybe his stage for learning characters had come. I began to teach him four Chinese characters a day with cards that have characters on one side and pictures on the other. Of course, reviewing exercises would be done every day too; that is, if I taught him four words after breakfast, we would review them after lunch and supper. As time went on, this seemed to be part of his daily routine and he just took it for granted. I think he had already developed a habit, because when occasionally I was too busy to teach him, he would come over and say, "Mum, it's time for me to learn new characters."

To keep his interest, I used various games for teaching him. For example, if he had learned 吃, chī, "eat," on one card, I would teach him 西瓜, xīguā, "watermelon" on another, and then put the two together to make the phrase 吃西瓜, "eat watermelon." If possible, I let him make sentences, like 飞机快, fēi jī kuài, which means "a plane is fast," and 火车慢, huǒ chē màn, "a train is slow." Sometimes we divided the cards between us, and we two read the characters on the cards in turn. At times, I pretended to mispronounce some characters and he immediately corrected me. In this way, his vocabulary increased, and so did his interest. He would take all the cards down and read the characters on them and make associations between the characters. For example, if he found a card with 听, tīng, "listen," he would try to find the card that had 唱歌, chàng gē, "sing a song." Then he would read these together as "tīng chàng gē," which means "listen to a song." Sometimes when my husband and I read books of our own, he would come and pick out the characters he knew. The same thing happened when we watched television, which now and then shows characters in the names of films and in advertisements, and when we walked in the streets, which are full of signs with characters on them.

In the process of our interaction around characters, I often gave him rewards, which I think stimulated his motivation to learn. Sometimes I praised him to my colleagues in his presence. My compliments to him played an important part in his developing literacy.

Now my son seems to have learned about two hundred Chinese characters. When I come back home in a year (he will be six years old then), I am going to teach him Pinyin, and then he can read by himself.

I should say that my work has kept me very busy, so I have taught my son only at odd times, and not in a planned and systematic way. I think if I had more time, my son's literacy would be much more fully developed than it is. Yet, to my delight, he has learnt to enjoy reading in a way, moreover, that is consistent with what he will experience in school.

8. The Importance of Early Education

Luo Ningxia

There were not many books around me during my childhood. My parents only bought me some little books with pictures before my school education. So I didn't read a great number of books as a student. Sometimes when my classmates talked about somebody or something in some books, I could do nothing but look at them quietly.

So, four years ago when my daughter was born, I had an idea that I would develop her reading habit from the very beginning and that she should be educated in reading. I bought her a lot of books for children, such as *Famous Fairy Tales of the World* and *A Picture Book for Children,* and I began to read stories to her when she was one year old, such as "Little Red Riding Hood," "Snow White," and "Doctor Duck." She liked to listen to my reading even though she could not really understand the stories. Later, when she was two and a half, I sometimes asked her questions about what I was reading. For example, while I was reading her "Little Red Riding Hood," I wanted her to answer such questions as "Why do people call the little girl 'Little Red Riding Hood'?", "Was she brave?", and "Was she afraid of wolves when she went to her grandmother's home for the second time?" At first she couldn't answer them correctly, but I encouraged her and helped her with the comprehension of the story. Later, she was able to answer questions by herself without my instruction.

Since she liked stories, I bought her some tapes for children, such as "Children Telling Stories," which is a set of six tapes altogether. For some time, as soon as she got up in the morning, she would turn on the tape-recorder to listen to her stories. She would sit at the tape-recorder for an hour or more; indeed, she enjoyed them. I also got her a Chinese book called *Three Hundred and Sixty-five Nights* and another Japanese storybook called *Flower Fairy Maiden.* To my delight, every evening after we finished supper, she would ask me to read her these books.

Before I told her a new story, I always required her to tell me the one I had told her the day before. Gradually, she could tell a good story to us all. To develop her narrative skills, I got the idea a few months ago that as soon as I finished reading my stories, she should retell what I had read in her own way, or else she should make up a story of her own. Now she is four and a half years old and is able to tell not only the stories I read her, but also ones from her own experience; she can describe something or somebody very well.

I often get both Chinese and foreign books for her, and she is always happy if I buy her a new book. She can read stories to her little friends and teach her little cousin to recite some famous Tang poems, such as "Missing my hometown quietly at night,"[6] which I taught her at the age of three. Because I am a teacher, I realize the importance of this early education; if I continue to focus on my daughter's reading, I believe that she will certainly be good at reading and also at writing in the future.

My daughter's childhood is different from mine. I often ask myself: If I had been educated well in reading in my early childhood, and if I had been given a large number of books to read then, what would the results have been?

6. This is the poem cited by Xu Ju on p. xxx. (Ed.)

9. Education Outside School

Qin Haihua

In China, children usually go to school at the age of seven, some a bit earlier, some a bit later. But, actually, children receive their first knowledge of reading and writing long before they go to school. Especially nowadays, most couples are allowed to have only one child, which results in children getting more attention in the family. In consequence, education before school has become more common, there being several sources from which children get their preschool knowledge.

Children of my generation used to have picture books as our first access to Chinese characters and what they mean. A lot of us owned our own books. Our parents may not have taught us to read, because they were busy themselves, but when we were curious about what the book was telling us, they would briefly introduce the content. We figured out the rest by ourselves. Now I still remember the charming figures of the twelve beauties and their stories in my picture book *The Dream of the Red Chamber,* which I got as a birthday gift at the age of five. At this age, children cannot read a lot and understand the meaning, but they are curious and interested in books, which will help them do well in their study later on.

Storytelling is another way in which children get "enculturated" if their elders' time is available. Once I firmly believed that there were beautiful fairies living in heaven and the sea and that I could also become one as long as I behaved well. These illusions came from the stories my mother told me before I went to bed, and then, when I could read myself, I found these stories in fairy tales by the Brothers Grimm and other people. Even now I still like little stories and novels with exciting plots and charming characters.

In recent years, a new phenomenon has developed: Children receive their preschool education not only from their parents and elders, but also from the tutors their parents get for them. When my little niece was two years old, my sister taught her to recite ancient poems. Of course, that was mere imitation of sounds without any understanding of the meaning. Now my sister has made an appointment with me that I should teach my niece English next summer, and at that time she will be only four years old! How can I teach such a little child a second language when she hasn't grasped her native language, and, still more important, in an environment where no English is spoken?

Nowadays, it is quite common for college students to take part-time jobs as tutors. There are great demands for tutors of all kinds. For preschoolers, the parents usually seek tutors who teach Chinese, English, or musical instruments. Parents also get tutors of these kinds for their children who are studying at school. A short while ago, I met a father whose nine-year-old daughter is learning to play the piano and studying English at the same time. Besides her schoolwork, she has to practice her handwriting and recite ancient poems. When I asked whether he felt he was putting too heavy a burden on his daughter, he said, "I have no way out. I mean to do her good. All the other children are learning all these things. If she doesn't learn enough, she will be left behind." Now children are pushed forward by their parents' goodwill, but I am wondering whether this really does them good.

As television intrudes more deeply into our lives, children also are greatly affected by the programs they watch. One of my colleagues told me that her three-year-old nephew is never willing to count the numbers beyond ten, but he is always ready to sing the words of an advertisement on television for a computer with the brand name of "Little King," which is especially designed for children's study. This advertisement includes many of the numbers that he usually refuses to count.

This summer, I helped one second cousin of mine with her Chinese and mathematics. She is in Grade Five in an elementary school. She is neither hard-working nor clever in her schoolwork, but when she is talking about television programs, movie stars, or singers from Hong Kong, she knows so much that a great deal of what she says is beyond my knowledge. This suggests that television and movies are not really sources of literacy, but hindrances to it. It is good for children to know something outside their textbooks, but information about what a movie star likes or the exposure of someone's romance is neither valuable nor helpful to children. It only distracts their attention and energy from studying well.

People receive most of their education from school, but literacy at home forms a firm and indispensable foundation for their life. It helps children become open and receptive to knowledge and to develop good attitudes toward learning. It can cultivate their interest in new things. If correctly led in their preschool education, children will be better prepared for more serious studies later. At the same time, however, parents should not put too much pressure on their children, for such pressure can seriously hinder their development.

10. Literacy Acquisition: The Difference Between Urban and Rural Areas

Zhang Weinian

In China, there is a college entrance examination in July every year. Examinees and their parents are all involved in the "struggle." The examination is called a struggle because there is only one sitting in a year, many students take part in it, and, according to the official report by the State Education Commission (SEC), only the most excellent four percent are permitted to pass. In China people call this phenomenon "too many people going over a one-log bridge." Students in China are under great pressure, especially those living in rural areas, because if they fail the examination, they will have to stay in the countryside and become peasants like their parents. In China, being a peasant means working harder and having less money than people in the cities. Although students who fail can take part in the examination again, it puts even greater pressure on them because it costs them a great deal of money and most rural families are poor. Unfortunately, rural students regularly do worse than those living in the cities, and the regulations put them at an even greater disadvantage, because to enter colleges in big cities such as Beijing or Shanghai, they are required to achieve higher scores than those who are already resident there. So most of them cannot break the pattern by which their families have been peasants generation after generation. It is not that they lack the will to do so; it is chiefly that they are constrained by economic conditions. But another important factor is the way in which they initially acquire literacy.

When children begin to learn language, they first learn it from their parents, elder brothers and sisters, and perhaps their neighbors; but as for literacy, the pattern of learning is different in different regions. In cities, people have better economic circumstances, more education, and more time. When their children are almost four years old, parents usually provide them with blocks or cards that have Chinese characters and corresponding pictures on them. In addition, the parents teach their children to recite the alphabet and some simple poems. After that, when the children get a little older, the parents teach them how to write characters. When I was a little child less than five years old, my parents taught me how to write and gave me assignments that they checked every day. Because my grandparents, my unmarried uncle, and my aunt all lived together with my parents and me, they became my teachers too. After work, my uncle often taught me to recite children's songs. My aunt told me many stories and said they were all in books—so it made me very interested in books. My parents often bought me books and asked me to read them, and I,

31

for my part, was eager to learn. Brought up in such a good environment, I was more than ready to go to school at the age of five.

In rural areas, however, parents work in the fields every day, even on Sundays. After work, they have to cook meals and feed the pigs and the sheep and do other chores. When they finish, they have to rest because tomorrow's work is waiting for them. They have no time or energy to look after their children. Moreover, in the countryside there are few kindergartens, so the parents take the children to the fields with them or ask the elder children—that is, those under seven, who are not yet in school—to take care of the little ones. In the rural areas, a child between four and seven years old can do a lot of housework, such as sweeping the yard, feeding chickens, or herding oxen, but he or she knows nothing about characters or Pinyin. Although there are public notices everywhere and everyone puts up antithetical couplets at the Spring Festival, this material is too limited for children to learn more than a few characters.

I have an uncle on my mother's side who lives in the countryside. He has four children. His five-year-old daughter cannot read characters or recite poems at all. She only knows counting from one to ten. My uncle and aunt are busy working every day for their living. They have to work all day long in the fields and have to do all kinds of chores at home. They sleep early at night because they are tired after a day's hard work, and they get up early the next morning to prepare for the new day's work. They have almost no time to teach their children.

The literacy of rural children also is affected by the low educational status of their parents. In my own parents' time, most people in the cities received a secondary education, but in the countryside, most people did not finish primary school. In the time when my own generation became parents, almost everyone in the cities had graduated from secondary school and one-third of them had attended college or university; from my own secondary school, for example, nearly everyone graduated. In rural areas, by contrast, fewer young parents had a secondary education, and still fewer had received any higher education. The present generation of children is directly affected, because if people receive more education, they will be more qualified and have more ideas in teaching their children. The children brought up in a well-educated family are lucky because they will acquire more knowledge.

With China's economic reform and opening to the outside world, the case in a few rural areas has changed a little, especially in economic development zones and the areas along the coast. People there pay more attention to their children's education. But in most rural areas, the situation remains the same, so it is not strange that students from these areas usually get lower marks than those from the cities. There are eight hundred million peasants in our country. It is urgent to change their conditions, because these conditions determine the educational quality of the majority of Chinese. If they do not change, many children of peasant parents will receive little education at home, and the disparity between urban and rural areas can only increase.

2

The Social Context
of Schooling

In China, as in Western countries, the major work of acquiring literacy is done in school, within a formal education system; in China, even more than in the West, this formal training in school literacy has been historically an important means both of transmitting the cultural values that sustain the political structure and of promoting a degree of mobility within it (Ho 1982; Rawski 1979). The ideological and social functions of school literacy have been a major theme for the past twenty years or so in Western scholarly discussion (see Graff 1979; Street 1984, 1993), and so it made obvious sense to expose the participants in the Nanjing program to some of the literature that has come out of that discussion. As teachers also they would naturally be interested in thinking about what actually goes on in classrooms, about the nature of the interactions between teachers and students, and about how those interactions are affected by outside influences.

The next component of the reading and writing course was, accordingly, one on "Literacy in School." For this component, the participants read two articles about ethnographic studies in U.S. classrooms (Collins 1986; Philips 1972) and one more general review article (Gee 1986) on the development and influence of scholarly theories about literacy. I did not, however, require them to take any of these articles as a model. Instead, I suggested that they might again draw on their own experience, or they might interview primary schoolteachers or examine primary-school textbooks; yet another alternative would be to discuss some broader educational issue and consider how it affected the acquisition of literacy. In the event, the participants produced essays of two types: the first type considered the social context in which Chinese children receive formal literacy instruction; the second focused more narrowly on the writing system itself and the means by which it is taught. This chapter consists of essays of the first type, supplemented by one (Su Xiaojun's "Chinese Examinations in Historical Perspective") that was written in 1992 in response to a more general assignment on Chinese education. Essays of the second type are presented in Chapter Three.

A number of striking points come out from the essays in this chapter. First is the strong sense of history that informs the participants' perceptions of formal schooling: Su Xiaojun, Wu Liangzhe, and Lu Wanying all refer explicitly to the centuries-old Confucian tradition and point out how up until the beginning of the present century, Chinese education was dominated by the study of the Confucian classics. They also assert—in no uncertain terms—that although these classics no longer provide the content for most of the curriculum, the old beliefs about the purposes of study and the most effective methods of teaching still persist; these constitute a straitjacket that constricts both social and individual development.

The mechanism by which these beliefs are maintained is that of examinations. The examination system in China, as Su explains, has its roots in antiquity: The first examinations were set in the third century, and by the seventh they had become a regularly used instrument of the imperial government (see Fairbank 1992; Ho 1982). Their function was to select officials for the bureaucracy, and since high social status depended on a family's having an official among its members (Fairbank 1992), they provided a direct link between literacy on the one hand and power and prestige on the other. Such a link dominates perceptions of literacy in the Western world too (see Goody and Watt 1968), but there its development was of later date, for the feudal lords of early medieval Europe were often illiterate (Clanchy 1993; Graff 1987).

In modern China, a concerted effort to break away from the formal educational tradition was made during the Cultural Revolution, and Su describes in some detail how exams were abolished amid the general condemnation of intellectual activity. His account demonstrates that, despite the harmful effects of exams, the step was a retrograde one. Nothing substantial was put in the place of the examination system, and people were selected for higher education solely on the basis of class background (which, according to Chang [1991] had to be certified by the appropriate officials, giving them ample room for nepotism). The effect, when the political pendulum swung back again in the late 1970s, was to make people welcome with enthusiasm the introduction of the CEE, and this exam has now become the major preoccupation of all senior-secondary-school students. Wu Liangzhe's essay, "The Influence of Confucianism on China's Education," demonstrates from her own experience what a repressive effect it can have on young people.

Nor is it only secondary-school students and their teachers that are affected. Yang Hongqi's essay, "Good Schools and Bad Schools," shows that the exam system dominates education at all levels and that its effects go well beyond what is actually done in class. China's education system is essentially pyramidical in structure, with room for only a small proportion of students at each stage to proceed to the next,[1] and it is by exams that the transition from one stage to another is governed. Moreover, the exams determine not only whether students will be able to continue with their education, but also which schools they will be allowed to attend; again the exams, or rather the proportion of students passing them, provide a ready method of distinguishing between what Yang bluntly describes as "good" and "bad" schools. The judgments based on this criterion seem to be accepted by everyone, and they then become self-fulfilling prophecies: "good" schools attract not only good students, but also good money, for parents will pay for the privilege of getting their children admitted, while government authorities fund the "good" schools more generously than they do those that have less satisfactory pass rates. Another consequence is that Chinese education is characterized by an extreme form of streaming, or tracking, a phenomenon that is seen by many in the West as problematic but seems to be generally accepted in China.

Zhu Xiaowen, in "Problems in Chinese Primary Education," examines the effects of this situation on individual teachers by reporting the experience of one who has worked in both a "good" and a "bad" primary school. Neither provides an ideal environment for learning: the "good" school suffers from overcrowding, the "bad" one from underfunding; in the former the students are overworked, while in the latter they are under-prepared. In addition, the teachers are overworked themselves and, especially in the "bad" school, they are under-compensated and have little incentive to try to encourage the children. All these factors conspire to create a classroom culture that is both teacher-centered and largely devoted to mechanical activities.

Zhao Guangzhu presents yet another aspect of the imbalance between schools, and here she picks up a theme raised in Chapter One—namely, the contrast between urban and rural areas. While it is not true to say that all rural schools are "bad" (indeed, some of them do particularly well in getting their students through the exams), it is true that many of them are poor, and the peasants' children who attend them usually have little preparation for school literacy. Zhao describes a particularly impoverished area in her home province of Liaoning, where the teachers are not even paid a salary and where the children attending school are too few to be divided by age, let alone ability. The acquisition of literacy in these circumstances must be very different from what it is for children in city schools, even though the curriculum followed is the same (Lo 1984).

Lu Wanying, in her essay "Ideological Teaching Through Early School Literacy," considers another issue in which, again, there is a strong link between the past and the present. As Street (1984) has made clear, no kind of literacy can be considered ideologically neutral, but in China, the relationship between literacy and ideology seems to be particularly strong and particularly explicit. The ideology in question has changed, to be sure—in imperial times it was Confucianism,

---

1. According to Cortazzi and Jin (1996), total enrollment in primary schools was 131.95 million in 1995, in junior-secondary schools 47.28 million, in senior-secondary schools 16.53 million, and in tertiary institutions 2.90 million at the undergraduate level.

during the Cultural Revolution it was Maoism, and now it is "Socialism with Chinese characteristics"—but one perception has remained constant, that school literacy should directly support the state. By comparing present-day textbooks (nearly all Chinese primary schools use the same set of books) with those that she herself was brought up on, she shows dramatically how schoolchildren are expected to learn, and accept uncritically, the prevailing political doctrines.

The last two essays consider children themselves and what they experience through the early years of schooling. Qin Haihua describes and criticizes the rigid authoritarianism of the classes in which she was taught, a characteristic also noted by Hudson-Ross and Dong (1990) in their description of classes observed a decade later. Gu Tiexia explores the "heavy burden" imposed on Chinese children by the pressure of exams in school and the expectations of their parents at home; and it is interesting to note that, according to Lee, Stigler, and Stevenson (1986), such high expectations also are held by parents in Taiwan. She also echoes another point made by Lee and his colleagues about the involvement of parents in their children's schooling. It seems that on both sides of the Taiwan Straits, the process of formal schooling depends heavily on the cooperation of parents, not only in seeing that children get to school, but also in easing the teacher's task of checking and correcting the numerous assignments. Such an environment seems to be most effective for teaching elementary literacy, for Lee and his colleagues found that Taiwanese children did considerably better than American children in the reading tests they administered. Mainland Chinese children, one imagines, would do well on such tests too (to my knowledge, no comparable study has been done in China); but Qin and Gu both suggest that the system is so highly pressured as to be unhealthy, and that the repetitive nature of the work stifles children's creativity.

It is evident from these essays that their writers are acutely aware of the problems afflicting China's educational system, many of which, I might add, are recognized in officially sanctioned publications too—*The China Daily,* an English-language newspaper produced for foreigners' consumption, quite frequently prints articles on educational issues under headlines such as "Ray of Hope for Rural Kids" (October 10, 1994, p. 3), "Exam System Put to the Test" (November 10, 1994, p. 5), and "Profitable Firms Should be Taxed to Increase Funds for Education" (November 17, 1994, p. 4). *The China Daily,* of course, presents the problems as being in the process of being solved and, indeed, some of these writers also suggest that change is on the way; note, for instance, the sanguine conclusion to Yang Hongqi's essay. But the weight of the past is great, and such is the competition of the present that few individuals, whether parents, students, or teachers, are prepared to try and break out from under it—at least as far as the teaching of Chinese literacy is concerned. Moreover, they may not altogether want to break out from under it. Discipline is highly valued in China, and social disorder, especially since the Cultural Revolution, is greatly feared (Link 1993). The question is whether the educational system, as presently structured, is indeed the best way of maintaining the one and avoiding the other.

1. Chinese Examinations in Historical Perspective

Su Xiaojun

In ancient times, China had an elaborate examination system to select qualified personnel for its bureaucracy. The earliest record dates back to the Three Kingdoms Period (220–265), when examinations took shape under Cao Cao, one of the most capable rulers in Chinese history. He adopted the system of "evaluation based on nine qualifications." In the Sui Dynasty (581–618), the examination system reached maturity and became fully institutionalized (Fairbank and Reischauer 1979, 103). Over the years, this system was gradually perfected so as to serve as a highly effective tool for the imperial administration. Yet at the same time, it became formalized and ossified to the extent that it shackled the people's minds and constricted the development of social productivity.

Undoubtedly, conflicting ideas would have been detrimental to imperial rule. To govern a country not much smaller than present-day China and to maintain national unity and political stability with the poor transportation and communication services available, imperial courts in ancient China had to resort to an invisible yet most powerful weapon for the preservation of their authority; namely, the examination system. The connection between this system and successful administration seems farfetched, yet it should be kept in mind that this system does not aim so much at the testing of ability or knowledge as at the inculcation of one uniform traditional ideology—Confucianism, which dominated China for more than two thousand years. Even today, in one way or another, Confucius is still with us everywhere and all the time. *The Analects, Mencius, Great Learning, The Doctrine of the Mean*—these were invariably what were tested in imperial China. These four classics are diverse in content, but they all deal with personal cultivation and the handling of interpersonal relations, pragmatic political ideas, and utilitarian philosophical thoughts. Also included in these books are rough biographies of Mencius and Confucius, and their talks with their students as well as the kings and lords of the time. The indoctrination of would-be officials with Confucian ideology ensured that they all subscribed to the same code of conduct and conducted their lives and careers by the same yardstick. It is probably not an exaggeration that the stable unification of China, even the continuity of Chinese history, owes a great deal to this examination system.

In 1906, however, this imperial examination system was abolished by the Empress Dowager, who did it under pressure both from at home and abroad (Fairbank and Reischauer 1979, 393). Given that the system had guaranteed imperial rule for so many centuries, its abolition naturally harbingered the downfall of the imperial government itself. The Chinese bourgeois democratic revolution led by Dr. Sun Yat-sen overthrew the Qing Dynasty in 1911, and so the soil for the imperial examination system was eliminated, once and for all. Ever since then, the use of examinations to select officials has been done away with; however, as a means of testing knowledge, examinations still exist and, by controlling progress through the educational system, they still control access to professional careers.

The founding of the People's Republic in 1949 marked a turning point in China's history, but not in the history of the examination system. It was impossible for the imperial examination system, which had lasted for more than sixteen centuries, not to leave some imprint on people's minds. As a result, the Chinese people still cherish a wholehearted, almost slavish attitude towards examinations, which often lay too much emphasis on mechanical memorization. This was clearly demonstrated in the seventeen years after the founding of the People's Republic. At the time when the Cultural Revolution (1966–1976) began, there were two rival lines in the ruling clique. One emphasized gradualistic, orthodox, even élitist education, which often included over-memorization and strict examinations; the other stressed practical, populist education or, more exactly, training. Mao Zedong was for the second line. Therefore, in 1966, when Mao arrogated all powers to himself, he denounced the other line for having caused the catastrophe of seventeen years and blamed them for all the faults and failures in education since 1949. Thus, on the educational front of the time, there arose a tide of rejecting examinations, and the propaganda organs began to depict the monstrous consequences of examinations in lurid colors. I remember when I was a primary-school pupil, there was a period when all the newspapers and magazines talked about a girl named Zhang Yuqing in Ma Zhen Fu Middle School, Henan Province, who committed suicide because she repeatedly failed her examinations. When Mao heard this, he was shocked and outraged, and this reaction led to his arbitrary and extreme decision that examinations should be abolished altogether.

There were three factors contributing to this decision. First, blind worship of the whole nation had actually turned Mao's head and convinced him that everything he did was bound to be correct and necessary. Second, and more importantly, he was of the belief that everything old must be destroyed to make way for the building of a brand-new China. Third, he recalled his own painful experiences as a young man when he had to take examinations based on the cramming method of teaching and learning; he hated such mechanical memorization. As for his followers, they went to great lengths to prove the absolute necessity and unquestionable soundness of the "epoch-making wise decision." Intellectuals were condemned as "stinking bourgeois" and sent to remote mountainous areas and the countryside to be reeducated by the peasants. A clean family origin—in other words, one that was "red" and proletarian—was of primary importance if one wanted to receive a higher education. There was a popular film at the time called "Spring Seedling," in which an old farmer said, "My qualification for admittance is the calluses on both my hands." The same film also ridiculed education and intellectuals by picturing a professor talking in class about the biological function of a horse tail. Today, people of about thirty years of age can still remember the name Zhang Tiesheng, a young man known to every household at the time, who got zeros on all tests and was admitted to a medical college only because he came from a clean family and had once worked as a worker and peasant.

In 1978, after Deng Xiaoping attained dominant power in the government, he installed the annual, nationwide, highly competitive College Entrance Examination (CEE) system. This was a positive reaction against Mao's policy, and it immediately gained acclamation. Unfortunately, this examination system has become more and more formalized. It has numerous drawbacks, the worst of which is the fact that it can hardly show a student's abilities because examinations of this kind emphasize mechanical memorization rather than creative thinking. It is knowledge, rather than ability, that is tested. Standardized tests modeled on the Test of English as a Foreign Language (TOEFL) have become very popular and have been used to examine almost every subject. They are harmful to the student's imaginative power and proliferative thinking.

Whether we like it or not, this system still exists and will continue to exist, because of both the weight of past tradition and fears, grounded in experience, of the consequences of rejecting it. The question is, can it be modified in such a way as not to force all the teachers and students in China to become examination slaves? That is the challenge that faces all those involved in Chinese education today.

2. The Influence of Confucianism on China's Education

Wu Liangzhe

Over the course of its five thousand years of history, China has created a splendid culture. At the root of this culture is Confucianism, the philosophical and moral system founded by two famous scholars, Confucius and Mencius, during the Spring-and-Autumn period from 722 to 481 BC.

The basic principles of Confucianism are kindness (仁, *rén*), justice (义, *yì*), politeness (礼, *lǐ*), knowledge (智, *zhì*), and prestige (信, *xìn*). Knowledge here means book-learning, acquired through a system of formal education, and its inclusion in the basic principles indicates how fundamental school literacy has always been to Chinese culture.

In feudal[2] times, Confucius' writings themselves formed the main content of Chinese education, and they were the sole basis for the famous 科举, *kējǔ*, exams by which Chinese officials were selected. These exams could be taken by any scholar, regardless of birth, so that Confucian texts provided a way into the aristocratic class for those who were successful. These texts also provided the theoretical basis for government. Chinese monarchs used them to influence their subjects' thought, guide their behavior, and keep them under imperial domination. Even in modern times, Confucianism has a great influence over most people and, by the same token, most people accept without question the importance of education. Even six- or seven-year-old Chinese children can recite Confucius' famous remark, *"Wàn bān jiē xià pǐn, wéi yǒu dú shū gāo,"* which means, "The worth of other pursuits is small; the study of books excels them all."

Since the Cultural Revolution, Chinese people have once again recognized the importance of education and "going to college," which is closely connected to a professional career, has become a hot topic at present. Success or failure in passing the annual CEE has become the only yardstick to measure a person's success in society. So most parents ask their children to try their best to pass the CEE, no matter how much time or money has to be spent. As a daughter of a college professor, I had no choice but to pass the exam when I finished secondary school. "If you don't pass the exam, you will have to work as a textile woman in a factory," my mother often told me, and so, during my school years,

---

2. Fairbank (1992) objects to the use of the word *feudal* for describing Chinese social institutions on the grounds that an essential feature of European and Japanese feudalism, the inalienability of land, was lacking in the Chinese system. His argument is well taken, but I have retained the word in this book because the program participants regularly use it to describe imperial China. (Ed.)

I could not develop any outside interests in life; what I saw, thought, and read were the contents of exam subjects. I even felt that the sky was gray on a sunny day because I was so afraid that my parents might be sneered at by their colleagues, that I might not be able to find a profession, that I might fail the CEE. With these heavy burdens, I had to immerse myself in exercises and sample exam texts. Although in the end I passed the CEE, if I could have the time over again, I would absolutely refuse to undergo such suffering. And what do those students do who fail the CEE? There are often reports in the newspaper of such students committing suicide because of the unbearable pressure. It is not surprising that the CEE is called the modern *kējǔ* exam.

I do not know when China's students will be liberated from the shadow of the CEE. It will be many years, I think, before the influence of Confucianism is reduced and a more effective method than the CEE is found of regulating the educational system and selecting people to staff the professions.

3. Good and Bad Schools

Yang Hongqi

There are many schools in China, but they all may be roughly divided into two categories: good and bad. Here I want to discuss the factors that determine into which category any particular school falls.

First, let us see the distribution of good and bad schools. It is a well-known fact that there are far more good schools in the eastern part of China than in the western part, and there are more good schools in cities or towns than in rural areas. The reason for this is largely economic: The economy of eastern China and of cities is more developed than that of western China and of rural areas, and the development and progress of schools must be based on the local economy. A school is usually funded from three sources: the State Education Commission (SEC), the local office of education, and parents of the school students through fees. None of these sources, however, is able to produce enough funds. Because China is such a large country and government funds are quite limited, the SEC cannot pay for everything necessary to keep a school going; in the under-developed areas of western China and in rural areas, the local offices of education are hardly able to support the number of schools needed; and the fees that parents pay contribute only a small amount to the management of the school, not to mention that in some areas, parents cannot afford to pay fees at all. So schools always have a hard time, and in certain regions there are even no schools because of poverty. The Xiwang (Hope) Project that was launched nationwide a few years ago appeals to people to help those poor areas set up schools (especially primary schools) or to help children of poor families go to school.

Second, the quality of teachers in good and bad schools is different. Schools become good ones, first, because they are well handled and managed, and, second, because they demand a great deal of their teachers while at the same time offering them chances to improve themselves. Local offices of education encourage this pattern, on the basis of inspection and feedback from students and their parents, by appropriating money to schools as a reward for good management and performance. Parents also expect more from teachers in good schools, so that teachers feel obliged to live up to the parents, the students, the schools, and themselves. In bad schools, on the other hand, many teachers are not qualified, and some schools, especially in the countryside, are inadequately staffed so that teachers have to teach more than one subject.

Third, the students themselves make the difference. The experience of literacy before going to school is quite different for children in cities and towns from what it is for children in the countryside. Parents in towns usually find time to teach their children to learn Pinyin and characters, and some even get tutors to teach their children musical instruments, drawing, and so on, which certainly will affect their future education. Children in rural areas, however, seldom have this kind of experience. Another point is the difference in how writing is used in the physical environment. In towns, children can see characters everywhere, on shop signs, posters, and advertisements. In the countryside, such public uses of literacy are less common.

There are many other reasons for the distinction between schools. For example, some schools in China are called "experimental schools." The government, or rather the local office of education, chooses a relatively good school as an "experimental school" and attaches great importance to it. As the name suggests, the school uses the latest teaching materials or new teaching methods to test their suitability; if they prove effective, they will be made universal. As the teaching materials and methods develop, they increasingly improve the education that the school offers, so that the experimental school becomes the best in a particular area.

But how are good and bad schools identified? The factors mentioned so far provide some answer, but it is not enough. In China, we have a very important principle to determine the quality of a school, and that is the proportion of students entering schools of a higher level, especially from primary school to secondary school, and from secondary school to college and university. If a primary school has more students passing the entrance examinations and entering secondary schools than other primary schools, this school will be considered a good one. It will be considered especially good if many of its students get into key secondary schools—that is, schools that have for successive years had a high percentage of students enter institutions of higher learning. Schools that do not have a large number of their students moving on to the next stage, by the same token, are considered bad ones.

This principle is especially important at the secondary-school level. Whether a secondary school is a good one or not is determined by matriculation exams held every July. If over a period of several years a school has a high percentage of students who matriculate successfully and enter colleges or universities, it will enjoy increasing prestige and will be valued by the government and appreciated by eager parents. Thus, it tends to go from good to better. On the other hand, a school that is less successful in the matriculation exams will remain bad if it does not go from bad to worse.

Thus, every school, at primary and secondary level alike, is under great pressure from both authorities and parents. Schools, for their part, shift the burden to teachers; in fact, some schools relate the teachers' pay to their "achievements"—that is, the number of their students who enter schools of a higher level or universities. Teachers then have to put the load on their students, who are required to wade through a sea of exercises and to be buried in books. As a result, students have hardly any spare time for hobbies and entertainment.

Fortunately, Chinese education is now experiencing a great reform, and schools are the first to take action. The *Yangzi Evening Post* reported recently that only four percent of about twelve million Chinese students can enter university; many schools are fully aware of this situation and so are trying to be more realistic. Every school is trying to improve itself. Key schools, which are few in number, still keep their priority and have more students enter universities and colleges than other schools, and common schools also try their best to help students pass the exams. Many of the latter, however, find it difficult to improve in this respect, so they are finding a way out by adding vocational courses to help those who have no hope of passing to learn certain skills in order to make a living.[3] Thus, instead of schools being judged by only one criterion, a school now may be considered weak in one aspect but strong in others.

Whether the reform will be a success or not only time will tell, but one thing is certain: The proportion of students entering schools of a higher grade is becoming less important, and it will probably not be the only criterion in distinguishing between schools as authorities, schools, and parents become more realistic towards education. Nevertheless, as long as there are economic inequalities between east and west and urban and rural areas, there will continue to be good schools and bad schools, no matter how many criteria are used to identify them.

3. See Rosen (1984) for a discussion of vocational education in China. (Ed.)

4. Problems in Chinese Primary Education

Zhu Xiaowen

What is the present situation in Chinese primary-school education? Are conditions favorable to our children in their literacy acquisition? Are parents satisfied with the job schools are doing? What do teachers think about the primary-school education in present-day China?

With these questions, I interviewed Ms. Zhu Jing, a teacher of Chinese from the city of Yangzhou, where I am now working and living. Yangzhou is a city of medium size in the southeastern part of China, which is among the most culturally and economically developed areas. Ms. Zhu, who is thirty-seven years old, is an ordinary primary schoolteacher. She has taught Chinese (as well as some other subjects including moral lessons, handwriting, and general science) in three different primary schools, and has almost seventeen years of teaching experience. Our conversation ranged from the differences in facilities available to schools and the teacher-centered structure of the classroom to the problem of schoolchildren being overworked.

In line with the country's social and economic reform, educational reform has also been carried out over the past two decades. Both the central and local governments have issued policy statements concerning improvements in the educational system. All these policies are meant to better the school conditions and the cultural environment in a way that will be equitable and balanced, yet the reality goes just the opposite way.

According to Ms. Zhu, the Education Bureau of Yangzhou Municipal Government stipulates that each different regional school should enroll only children from its own region, which guarantees the optimal number of students, as well as equal-ability groups in different schools. But people's belief works much more effectively than governmental enforcement. The schools located in the town center, near the government office buildings or institutes of higher learning, are always believed to be better than schools situated in the outskirts of the city. So parents take great trouble to send their children to what they believe to be better schools instead of to the designated schools.

Another fact is that the present economic development has a great influence on primary schools. Ms. Zhu said the better schools were permitted to ask for supportive finance (as much as possible) from the "newborn" entrepreneurs on condition that these schools submit a portion of the money to the Education Bureau; the entrepreneurs were willing to help fund these schools to get the best education possible for their children. With the money, schools can employ better teachers, buy more facilities and equipment, and thus attract the support of more powerful and wealthy families.

Ms. Zhu worked at Yu Cai Primary School, the best one in Yangzhou, before she moved to San Yuan Qiao Primary School, which is one of the lowest rated in the city. She has very different opinions and feelings about the two schools, as well as different experiences in her teaching work there.

Yu Cai Primary School is in the town center, behind the city municipal-government building. When Ms. Zhu was at that school, she began with sixty children in her class; however, at the opening period of each school year, she had to continuously accept newcomers whose parents possibly had paid a much higher fee to the school than what was normally required. Only half of the children in her class were from the designated cachement area for the school; all the rest were from upper- and middle-class families who lived elsewhere. Many of these children had received an excellent literacy education at home and had attended the best kindergartens or preschool classes. Ms. Zhu said that fifty percent of the children performed excellently in her Chinese class, which enabled her to give a little more help to the other fifty percent and make the whole class learn as much as they could. To maintain its prestige, Yu Cai Primary School requires its teachers to work hard and encourages them by paying extra for overtime. Under the supervision of their teachers, the students have to do more work than those of any other school in the city.

By contrast, San Yuan Qiao Primary School, where Ms. Zhu is now working, is in the southwestern part of the city, which is an industrial area. Her fourth-grade class this year has forty-five children, all from working-class families. Although it is not far away from my own institution, I have never heard of any of my colleagues or acquaintances sending their children to that school. Because it is so unattractive to parents, the school facilities have improved little in recent years. Experienced and well-known teachers will not stay there long because, unlike teachers at Yu Cai, they cannot make extra money by working overtime. Ms. Zhu said it is impossible for her to use the teaching methods that she developed at Yu Cai in the circumstances of San Yuan Qiao. Only about five children in her Chinese class can actively respond to her questions; the rest of the class are passive and slow in understanding her instructions. She said it is due to the children's lack of home literacy and explained that many of them never hear their parents telling stories or see them reading books. The children are much less prepared for school education, and the school does little to compensate because the teachers give them only minimal instruction. In addition, the children have fewer after-class activities than do those at Yu Cai.

The result of the discrepancy between the two schools is that each year, Yu Cai sends ninety percent of its students to the best secondary school in the city and San Yuan Qiao sends only ten percent to that school; the great majority go to ordinary secondary schools.

Ms. Zhu said that many researchers believe Chinese children have difficulty in acquiring literacy at primary school because learning Chinese involves much mental work—memorization and analysis of characters—as well as physical work in order to acquire good handwriting. She herself took courses of pedagogical psychology and psycholinguistics before graduation from college, and she occasionally reads research papers on primary-school literacy education or Chinese-language teaching from such magazines as *Middle and Primary School Education* and *Chinese Language Teaching,* or from journals like *Chinese Hanyu Pinyin Weekly*. However, she has great difficulty in applying the theories or methods that she has read about to practical classroom teaching. It is impossible, she said, for a teacher to carry out a game-playing learning activity even at Yu Cai, the best primary school in the city, when there are sixty children in a small, crowded classroom. Traditionally, Chinese educators believe that both teachers and students perform better in a teacher-centered, disciplined classroom atmosphere. Although there is development in the Chinese-language-teaching research field that emphasizes that the teacher is not only a director of children's learning process, but also a participant in it, most teachers feel that they can do nothing but follow traditional teaching principles with the large classes they have to teach and the expectations of their senior colleagues.

Not only do class size and the teacher-centered nature of the classroom make it impossible for both teacher and children to have more interaction and individualized instruction during school time, but also the teachers' heavy workload makes it impossible for them to further their professional development or improve their teaching methods. Ms. Zhu, like almost all other primary schoolteachers, feels her job as a teacher is very, very hard. She is, in the first place, a babysitter, and only in the second place an instructor. She always begins work at 7 a.m., before the children are brought to school by their parents, and she does not finish work until 5 or 6 p.m., after all the children have been taken back home. After eight hours of work at school, she still has a family to look after. Ms. Zhu told me she can seldom find time to work out a more interesting or creative plan for her next day's teaching than the simple, mechanical learning activities that she and the children are used to—reading, reciting, copying, and writing for hours and hours, all of which are easy for teachers to supervise.

On account of these factors, both teachers and children have to cover the school curriculum and achieve their desired goals through intensive work in school and heavy assignments at home. Ms. Zhu asserted that a good relationship between parents and school-teachers is crucial to children's performance in literacy acquisition. Parents are required by teachers to supervise their children doing homework and to sign their names on the top margins of assigned textbook pages. To her pleasure, Ms. Zhu said, most parents usually cooperate with the teachers very well.

Parents object to the heavy burden put on their children by schools because they do not want their children's happy childhood to be ruined by heavy work and no play. But they understand the teachers' difficulties with their enormous classes and heavy workloads, and, moreover, they have great expectations for their children to go to the best schools and universities. Under these pressures, schools, teachers, and parents simply have no alternative but to adapt to and thus maintain the present situation.

5. Literacy at School

Zhao Guangzhu

In China, children often begin their school education at the age of seven. According to the law, they have to be educated for nine years. Before they accept this formal school education, most of those who live in the cities have participated in a preschool training program for ten months, which lays a foundation for the primary-school education. But the situation is quite different in the countryside from what it is in the cities. Children in the countryside never go to kindergarten to learn and play because there are no kindergartens at all. Almost all the children spend their time before going to school in their own families. So there is a great difference in the learning style and the ability of urban and rural children as they use language in school.

In cities, most children have to take a test when they go to school for the first time, which is intended to check their ability. The content of the test is simple, including such activities as counting numbers from one to a hundred, talking about their own families and themselves, telling a story, or reciting a favorite poem. The results are not important for admission to the school, but the marks may be used as a basis for organizing the children into groups— those with high marks in a high group, those with low marks in a low one. Because teachers have different attitudes to the high and low groups, parents want their children to be in the high one. At the primary-school stage, children are not required to go to any particular school, so parents tend to choose schools in which their child will be studying with high-scoring children. Thus, the high groups become larger in size (averaging sixty-five students in a classroom), while the low groups are small (with only about forty students).

Between these groups, the teaching methods used are also different. Teachers who are lucky enough to teach high-group classes treat the students attentively because they want to get a good evaluation based on their hardworking and high-quality students. They prepare their lessons carefully and try hard to conduct them successfully to make students understand. They teach the students not only knowledge, but also learning skills. They encourage them to learn more and to set an aim for study, defining what their goals are and how they plan to achieve them, and they also encourage them to be active in the classroom. By and by, the students get to know how to study well, and a good atmosphere for learning is developed. This is essential to a teacher for conducting classroom activities. After class, the teachers direct children's study and their homework carefully, and they organize all kinds of out-of-class activities, such as competitions in model-making and mathematics, to improve the students' general knowledge and cognitive skills. Competitiveness is fostered, and the combination of students' desire for knowledge and teachers' purposefulness makes such children progress more quickly than others. Thus, the teachers in high-group classes are important directors of the children's education.

The teachers in low-group classes, by contrast, teach their students in a leisurely way and do not worry about whether their teaching is good or bad. They just finish the teaching assignment. This does not mean that these teachers are irresponsible, but maybe the methods are not appropriate or the students are lazy and naughty. At all events, students in these classes show indifference to study. They do not prepare before class or review after it, and they themselves consider that they are not excellent students. By and by, they become worse and worse.[4]

As for education in the countryside, it is quite different from what it is in the cities. Children need not take any test when they go to primary school. In each village there is only one school, and children and teachers are divided into different classes equally. The teacher of each class is in charge of Chinese and maths teaching. In general, there are twenty or thirty students in each class, and the high- and low-level students are in the same classroom. As long as they are in the classroom, the students study hard, but outside class they finish their homework as quickly as possible in order to have time for doing housework. Often their chief extracurricular activity is helping their parents work in the fields.

In some rural areas, for example in the western part of Liaoning Province, the way children are educated is even more different. The living conditions in that part of the country are especially hard and poor. The hills and mountains are bare; there is no field for peasants to plant. People there depend on relief grain for survival. There is not even any electricity in the region. Some people have to leave their hometowns to do odd jobs in the big cities in order to make a living. In each village, only ten to twenty children of different ages can go to school. Because no one likes to work as a teacher in those areas, people have to select one or two villagers whose knowledge is a little more than that of other people to teach the children. These teachers are called "*mínbàn* teachers," which means they are subsidized by local people. They receive no salary at all but, like other peasants in the village, they are paid in *gōngfēn*—that is, they get their reward at the end of the year in grain or a small sum of cash. But those who are chosen as teachers work very hard.

Because of the shortage of teachers in such areas, each school has only one "big" classroom with children of different ages organized together. The teacher has to give lessons of different levels in one classroom simultaneously. Students are arranged in rows: those in the low classes (Primary One and Two) sit in the first two rows, and those in the higher classes sit behind them.

4. For a Western example of such interaction between teachers' expectations and students' achievement, see Collins (1986). (Ed.)

The teacher gives the low classes lessons first, then asks the children to write characters by themselves. Then the teacher concentrates on giving lessons to the higher classes. When the younger students have questions about their lessons, they may ask the older students for help. The results of such learning are not comparable to those of city children, of course. The contrast with situations where even children of the same grade are divided into different levels is a striking one, and it means that the kind of education received in big cities and in poor rural areas is quite different.

The difference in the education received by different social groups lies partly in the attitudes of people to the literacy of their children and partly in the economic situation. In the future, when the living conditions of those poor places change and improve, and when the people who live there perceive the importance of education, they may set up schools where students of different grades have their lessons independently, like city children, without sharing one classroom.[5]

---

5. The high value that Zhao implicitly puts on homogeneity within a school class is in interesting contrast to the North American emphasis on diversity. (Ed.)

6. Ideological Teaching Through Early School Literacy

Lu Wanying

Chinese education always lays equal stress on ability training and ideological teaching. Therefore, early literacy in school always involves much explicit teaching of ideology. This tendency can be traced to early times. Before liberation, the Chinese people who attended old-style private schools (*sīshú*) were taught only to recite famous sayings from Confucius' and Mencius' works or some other ancient books. *The Four Books, The Five Classics,* and *The Three-Character Primer* were the favorite textbooks for old Chinese people, and it was believed that such teaching would promote good conduct: "*Rén zhī chū, xìng běn shàn,*" from *The Three Character Primer,* means "People are born good," and was intended to convince people of the innate good nature of human beings and hence their amenability to good teaching. Many of these sayings concerned personal relationships: one very famous one, for example, was "*Jǐ suǒ bù yù, wù shī yù rén,*" which means, "Don't impose on others what would be an imposition on you." Others referred more explicitly to social status: "*Fù guì bù néng yín*" means "Wealth and noble birth should not make people extravagant and dissipated," while, on the other hand, "*Pín jiàn bù néng yí*" taught that "Poverty and humble origin should not shake people's will." Altogether, these sayings provided a complete set of guidelines for every aspect of social life.

Education in China has changed a great deal since liberation in 1949. However, ideological teaching through school literacy has been kept, though its form and content have changed with the times. As soon as children begin to recognize Chinese characters, they learn some words that can be combined into ideologically meaningful sentences or phrases. First, they usually learn some nouns such as *rénmín,* "people"; *Běijīng,* the capital of China; *wǔ xīng hóng qí,* "the five-starred red flag"; and so on. A little later, they learn some verbs like *rè'ài,* "ardently love"; *àihù,* "take good care of"; and *xuéxí,* "study." After a certain amount of word recognition, they will learn such sentences as "We love our motherland," "We love the five-starred red flag," "We love labor," "Study hard," or "We should take good care of public property." So far as I know, such sentences are included in all the beginners' textbooks of various versions.

In addition to these sentences, the textbooks used in school usually reflect the contemporary social and political situation. In my childhood, for example, when the Cultural Revolution began, our textbooks included much ideological material relevant to political themes. I remember the first lesson of the first volume in our primary-school textbook simply included such sentences as "*Wǒ men rè'ài Máo Zhǔxī,*" "We love Chairman Mao" and "*Wǒ men rè'ài xīn zhōng guó,*" "We love the new China."

My primary schooling coincided with the last four years (1972–1976) of the ten-year Cultural Revolution when class struggle was most emphasized. So our textbook editors used many stories and fables that were intended to teach people to be on guard against bad people, especially class enemies. They adopted a fable from Aesop called "The Farmer and the Snake," which told a story of a farmer who went to market on a cold winter day. He found a frozen snake lying on the road. For pity's sake, he picked up this dying snake and put it in his pocket. When the snake, which was poisonous, regained consciousness from the warmth of the farmer's body, it bit the farmer so that he died. Before his death, the farmer warned people around him, "Don't follow my example. People should never take pity on their enemy." The moral of this fable lies in the last part, and our teacher explained it more clearly by associating it with the social reality of the time. He warned us to be on guard against snakelike class enemies.

Today's primary-school textbooks also choose some fables to be ideological teaching materials. However, the moral of these fables is totally different from what my agemates learned. Take the textbook for Primary One; for example, Volume Two, which was published in October 1993. It contains a fable entitled "Two Lions." It says that a mother lion gave birth to two baby lions, of whom one was diligent and hardworking in practicing its skill, while the other was lazy and said, "My parents are the king and the queen of the forest. Their skill and position will be enough for me to live a happy life." His mother happened to hear him saying this and said to him, "My child, when we get old and are of no use, who will you depend on? You should practice your skill diligently and become a real lion." This fable is intended to teach children of the only-child generation to be self-reliant and not to depend on their parents. The teachers will explain the implication by drawing an analogy between children and baby lions, and so it will be easy for the children to understand.

Helping others is a traditional virtue of the Chinese nation, so it is a constant theme of ideological teaching in school literacy materials. Both my agemates and the only-child generation learned or are learning stories of Lei Feng. Lei Feng was a soldier in the early 1960s who was always ready to help others. He died in an accident when he was still in his early twenties. From the time of his death, he was set up as an example of helping others. His heroic deeds were frequently written as lessons for children to learn. The Lei Feng stories greatly inspired children of my generation to help others. For example, my classmates and I often helped blind people cross streets or old people fetch water. Today's textbooks also have Lei Feng stories, and the content of these stories is more or less the same as what I learned. I believe that such lessons will also have a good influence on the only-child generation.

Patriotism is another constant theme of school literacy. When I was a primary-school student, I only learned some simple sentences on this theme, such as, "We love our motherland" or "I love Beijing, the capital." Today's patriotism lessons, however, are more skillfully designed and therefore easier for children to understand. Here I quote a short poem from the accessory reading book for Primary One children, which was published in May 1994. The title is "To Love Our Motherland":

爱 祖 国
ài zǔ guó

小 燕 子 说 我 们 爱 祖 国 因 为 祖 国 有
xiǎo yàn zi shuō, wǒ men ài zǔ guó yīn wéi zǔ guó yǒu

温 暖 的 泥 窝
wēn nuǎn de ní wō

小 山 羊 说 我 们 爱 祖 国 因 为 祖 国 有
xiǎo shān yáng shuō, wǒ men ài zǔ guó yīn wéi zǔ guó yǒu

长 满 青 草 的 山 坡
zhǎng mǎn qīng cǎo de shān pō

小 蜜 蜂 说 我 们 爱 祖 国 因 为 祖 国 有
xiǎo mì fēng shuō wǒ men ài zǔ guó yīn wéi zǔ guó yǒu

甜 甜 的 花 朵
tián tián de huā duǒ

小 朋 友 说 我 们 爱 祖 国 因 为 祖 国
xiǎo péng yǒu shuō, wǒ men ài zǔ guó yīn wéi zǔ guó

地 大 物 产 多
dì dà wù chǎn duō

我 们 的 生 活 多 快 乐
wǒ men de shēng huó duō kuài lè

The English translation is as follows:

The little swallows say we love our motherland
because she has our warm nests.
The little goats say we love our motherland
because she has green grass-covered hillsides.
The little bees say we love our motherland
because she has fragrant flowers.
The children say we love our motherland
because she is vast and rich
and we live a happy life.

Many of the words, for example, *yǒu, wǒ, pō, duǒ,* and *guó,* are beautifully rhymed in the Chinese, and all sorts of lovely animals are represented. Thus, the poem will be easy for children to recite, and they will understand why people should love their motherland.

What needs a special mention as an ideological theme is the present teaching of plain living. The reason is that one side effect of the open-door policy and the market economy is that young people, including children, have become money-worshipping and extravagant. Some people just waste their money to show off their wealth, and young children blindly compete to show off their fine clothes and expensive toys. That causes old people to feel distressed because they think plain living is a traditional virtue and, above all, our country is still poor. Some complain that this focus on money represents a failure of education, so educators are now advocating the teaching of the virtues of plain living and hard work. Accordingly, the current textbooks include many lessons on such a theme.

Before writing this essay, I carefully examined one Primary Three textbook (Book Six in the series), which was published in October 1993. It includes many lessons such as I have just described. One story, for example, entitled "An Old Coat" tells about Chairman Mao's plain living in the Anti-Japanese War; "In Hard Days" tells about a Red Army man in the civil war who fought bravely against the enemy in very bad conditions. Lessons on the theme of plain living and hard work comprise ten percent of the whole book. Other lessons concern other ideological themes: patriotism, internationalism, sacrificing one's own interests for the sake of others, and sacrificing one's life in the cause of justice. These lessons account for another twenty-nine percent of the whole book.

Ideological teaching through school literacy covers the whole primary-school stage and it continues into junior high school. Because most Chinese primary schools (with some possible exceptions for minorities) use the national textbooks, the influence of such ideological teaching is wide and deep. It is an important means of fostering social consciousness and of promoting specifically Chinese values.

7. Chinese Children in Primary School

Qin Haihua

Throughout the years of school education in China, one of the most important aspects of the experience is discipline. Beginning from primary school, children are trained to obey the rules because everybody believes obedience is a good trait and will benefit people all through their lives.

From my own days in primary school (in the late 1970s to early 1980s), I remember that every year when we went up to a higher class with a new teacher, there would be a seating arrangement. We stood in two rows ranging from short to tall. A pair, often a boy and a girl, of about the same height would sit as neighbors, the short pairs sitting in front and the tall ones behind. So we did not sit with a person we liked but with one who was appointed by the teachers.

The reason why boys and girls were seated together was that little boys and girls did not play together, and so they could be expected not to talk with each other in class. It was funny that there seemed to be such a deep barrier between boys and girls that they had great contempt for each other. Generally speaking, in primary school, girls were more obedient and attentive in class and more hardworking, while boys did not observe the discipline so strictly, and sometimes they deliberately broke the rules to show how brave and carefree they were. In consequence, boys thought that girls were cowardly and pretentious, and girls looked on boys as rude and uncivilized. When I was in primary school, I did not talk with boys. Once I praised a boy for being clever, but my girl companion looked at me so severely and contemptuously that I blushed immediately, thinking myself to be so silly and shameless to say that kind of thing.

The deep barrier between boys and girls kept them from talking to each other. This made it easier for the teacher to control the class.

Besides good class order, teachers expected another outcome: They hoped that the pairs would help each other, because girls often studied better in primary school than boys did. However, this seldom worked. How could teachers expect two totally opposite results from the same seating arrangement? Now I still remember that division line on the desk between my neighbor and me. If one "intruded" on the other's "territory," the other would fight back by giving him/her an elbow and a warning. In such circumstances, it was hard to imagine that the pair could work together peacefully on some difficulties.

As mentioned before, children were not supposed to talk in class, especially when the teacher was talking. Children sat straight, with their hands behind their backs or on their desks, and their eyes fixed upon the teacher. This assured the teacher that nobody was doing anything else except listening attentively. Interruption was not allowed because it was considered impolite. This kind of teaching can be described as exclusively teacher-centered, and it was, in effect, a means of suppressing students' ideas. Children usually view things from a different perspective from adults. When our teachers scolded us for interrupting, they may have extinguished many creative sparks.

As a result, when I first went to college and had classes given by foreign teachers, the mobility, flexibility, and level of activity that they expected were truly "foreign" to us. Things have not changed much now. The experience Chinese students have all through their years of study is that they listen to what is spoken to them and accept passively what is taught in class. Always they are advised to keep silent. In one primary-school textbook, a model class is described in these terms: "The classroom is so silent that the sound of a needle falling to the ground can be heard clearly. All the students are looking at their teacher with the eagerness for knowledge."

I have observed that foreign teachers leave quite a long time for questions and answers at the end of each lesson. However, this does not work well with Chinese students. They are unwilling to ask questions in public, because either they are afraid their question may be a silly one or they are not sure that it is appropriate to ask; or they simply may not realize that it is their turn to speak and are just waiting for something more from the teacher. Actually, most students do not really think about what they are told. I myself, for example, sometimes get lost when listening to the teacher, but I still look at him or her and nod from time to time so that it looks as if I am following.

Another noticeable thing is that our classrooms are always fixed. It never occurred to us when I was in school that desks could be moved into circles or groups. In my primary school, there were students on duty every day who had to clean the classroom after classes were finished. One of the tasks was to arrange the desks in straight lines, this being considered an important sign of classroom orderliness. The fixed-desk arrangement created a serious and isolated atmosphere in class instead of a communicative and cooperative one. Such an atmosphere is especially unsuitable for language classes, in which communication and exchange of information are most important.

All these educational traditions train Chinese children to observe discipline strictly. They have a strong sense of orderliness and tend to take things as they are, without close thinking; they are not capable of questioning. This mode of education will make people's thinking narrow and inflexible. In consequence, many Chinese students are criticized (especially in the newspapers of a few years ago) for having high marks at school but little ability to practice and to innovate. It is difficult for them to adapt to the real world outside school. Given the rapid changes taking place in that world now, it may be vital to bring some mobility and flexibility to what is at present a fixed and rigid educational system.

8. The Heavy Burden of Chinese Children

Gu Tiexia

Chinese parents, especially in the cities, regard their children's progress at school as an important part of their own lives. They hope that their children will have a brighter future than they can expect for themselves. They care much about the grades of their children because only high marks will allow their children to go to key secondary schools, and if children study at such schools, they will have much higher chances of going to college. So parents ask their children to do nothing but study hard. Most students in the cities do not have to help their parents with housework. They are not allowed to go shopping alone, and they are not asked to serve themselves. My sister still helps her son to have a bath, even though he is now twelve years old. Children never do washing or make beds, let alone cook meals. So when they leave their parents, they cannot take care of themselves.

Children are supposed to go to primary school and junior-secondary school near their homes. In some cities, most of the officers in the government, the leading cadres, and some of the intellectuals all live together in one district. The school nearby receives the children from these families. These children have already received more literacy instruction at home than less privileged children do, and their parents pay more attention to their studies once they have started school. In addition, the teachers in these schools are usually the best graduates from teacher-training institutions, and they are expected to work harder than their colleagues elsewhere. Thus, it is not surprising that the children in such schools achieve higher grades than those in other schools, and that is how comparatively good primary schools have come into being. Parents do all they can to see that their children go to better schools. They may pay a lot of money to open "the back door." They may exchange their house for a worse one. As a result, in some of the best primary schools, there are more than seventy children in a class.

Such large classes are bad for training children in literacy skills. Not every child can receive the teacher's care, and they do not have much chance to interact with the teacher individually. Sometimes they answer the teacher's question with "Yes" or "No" spoken in chorus, even though some of the children do not really know whether it is "Yes" or "No." Most children, especially those who sit at the back, only look at and listen to their teacher. When they do not understand, they dare not ask why or beg the teacher to explain the point again.

If teachers want to be regarded as good teachers, the marks of their students are the most important criterion by which they are judged. So teachers do their best to raise the children's marks. In the classroom, children have to read aloud and write what they have learned again and again, no matter whether they like it or not. Teachers think that only in this way can the children remember their lessons. In fact, the speed of lessons is very slow. It seems that the textbook is not very difficult, but the children are assigned many complicated exercises from other books that they cannot do without their parents' help. A lot of time is spent in reviewing old lessons—my nephew told me how he disliked going over the old lessons again and again before the examination.

Children are supposed to sit in the classroom doing morning reading for half an hour. At eight, their class begins and generally they will have four classes in the morning, each of which lasts forty-five minutes. After one and a half hours for lunch, they have to go on with their lessons. At about four in the afternoon, they are dismissed, but some of them cannot go home because they live far away from the school. They have to wait at a certain house (usually the house of an old woman) for their parents to come and fetch them, and their parents will pay the hostess for looking after them.

Then, after supper at home, the parents become the children's tutors. The children have a great deal of homework and often cannot understand what they are required to do, so the parents have to explain to them. The parents check whether the children have mastered what they were taught at school and, if they have not, teach it to them again. Having been examined once by their teachers, the children are examined again by their "tutors" at home. After doing all their assignments, they have little time to read anything for pleasure. Only after final examinations can they be allowed to do what they like; at ordinary times, they are asked to keep the television off except on Saturday evening.

Nowadays, a couple has only one child, so parents ask their children not only to have high marks at school, but also to have other interests and abilities. Children have to spend what little spare time they have in learning other lessons and skills.

My nephew is now in his fifth year at primary school. On Monday and Wednesday, he has to stay at school till half past five to learn about writing. On Tuesday and Thursday, he has to go to a private teacher's to learn English. On Sunday morning, my sister takes him to the Children's Palace to learn drawing. My nephew likes to read Chinese history books, but he has little time to do it. His parents are both ordinary people and feel sorry that they did not go to college, so they hope their son will grasp the chance to build a better future. They believe that it is only as a good student—that is, one who gets high marks at school—that he can realize their dream. My nephew told me he is tired of being burdened with such a heavy task and even of being a good student.

Today in China, it seems that children should have a brighter future than their parents, and that children should realize the dream that their parents did not realize. It seems that all parents consider their children's success as their own. They give up their own hope for the future and place it on their children, no matter whether it is fit for them or not.

The result can sometimes be tragedy. It was reported in the *Anshan Daily* in 1990 that in one small town, a boy was beaten to death by his mother only because he did not get the highest marks in the class. The mother thought that because she could not get a good position in society, her son must do so instead, and she put all her heart into her son's study. She worked hard to create the conditions for him to study, but he had to get high marks for every exam, or he would get a good beating. He was often beaten black and blue by his mother, and he died with this heavy burden. Such extreme cases are rare, but many Chinese children are indeed tired. They need freedom.

3

Learning the Written Language

Despite the increasing openness of China to the outside world, many Westerners still perceive the country and its people as mysterious and inscrutable. A major factor in this perception is undoubtedly the writing system: Although DeFrancis (1984) claims that the spoken language is no more difficult for an English-speaker to learn than French,[1] the written language is infinitely more difficult, with its thousands of characters, many of them so complex that they seem to a Westerner impossible to remember. Nor is it only that the writing system itself appears to be impenetrable. There is a great deal of speculation that because it is so different from the alphabetic system, Chinese people actually may think in some radically different way from Westerners. One writer even goes so far as to say:

> One should . . . expect . . . differences in the thought patterns of societies whose writing systems differ significantly. . . . Chinese and Western alphabetic literacy represent two extremes of writing. The alphabet is used phonetically to visually represent the sound of a word. Chinese characters are used pictographically to represent the idea of a word and hence are less abstract than alphabetic writing. Eastern and Western thought patterns are as polarized as their writing systems. (Logan 1987, 47)

As DeFrancis has pointed out, Logan's characterization of Chinese is "chock-full of misinformation" (DeFrancis 1989, 240)—most Chinese characters, for instance, are not pictographs—and Logan offers no empirical support for his assertions about thought patterns; yet other researchers have found evidence to suggest that different orthographies do affect cognitive processing in certain specific ways. Read, Zhang, Nie, and Ding (1987), for

---

1. I have to point out, however, that this is not my own experience. Chinese, with its lack of cognates with English and its numerous homophones, is to my mind considerably more difficult than French.

example, found that Chinese subjects who had learned Pinyin were more capable of phonemic segmentation than were those who could read only Chinese characters. Scribner and Cole (1981) found that subjects who were literate in Vai (which has a syllabic script) were significantly better at integrating a series of orally presented syllables than were those who were literate only in Arabic or English. Hasuike, Tzeng, and Hung, citing Mann (1984), assert that readers of morphosyllabic scripts such as Chinese may have "an advantage on certain nonverbal tasks requiring visuospatial processing" (1986, 276). Koda (1990) found that Japanese subjects (who could read Chinese Kanji) were significantly less hampered, when doing an English reading task, by the substitution of unknown symbols for certain words than were subjects whose first languages were Arabic or Spanish. Thus, as Koda argues, it seems likely that learners of English who can read Chinese characters will have certain distinctive strategies or abilities that they may bring to bear on their English reading. Moreover, as Hasuike, Tzeng, and Hung (1986) point out, because Chinese characters are so much more complex and numerous than the letters of the alphabet, the process of learning them must of necessity be different; this too, one imagines, must have some effect on second-language learning strategies.

The studies cited previously are all experimental ones and, as such, they all aim to isolate the writing system as an independent variable. In real life, however, writing systems are used and learned in social contexts, and it is the interaction between the system and the context that produces effects on individuals (Olson 1994; Scribner and Cole 1981). The essays in this chapter are particularly illuminating in that they describe such an interaction. It was not possible for the Nanjing program participants to carry out controlled experimental studies, but they could and did consider the question of how Chinese children learn to read and write, drawing on their own familiarity with the writing system and on their own and others' experience of teaching and learning it. In describing the practices of literacy instruction, they show how the complexity of the system combines with the tendency towards centralized forms of discipline (see Chapter Two) to produce a particularly rigorous training for young people, one that is likely to promote strong powers of concentration and highly methodical learning strategies—even while, as Link's (1993) informants complained, it does not encourage students to become independent thinkers.

Chang Qian's "Form, Pronunciation, and Meaning in Chinese Characters" and Xu Ju's "Comprehending Word Meanings in Chinese"[2] constitute an introduction to the system itself from the perspective of those who have been brought up in it. Both emphasize that Chinese characters have three aspects—the form, pronunciation, and meaning of Chang's title. In other words, the

---

2. This piece is an extract from a longer essay called "Chinese Words Acquisition." Unfortunately, space did not allow me to include the whole essay here.

character is not seen simply as a mark on paper but, to use Saussure's terms, as the sign itself, of which the written form is the primary signifier, and the spoken is only secondary. This perception runs through all the essays in this chapter, and it is probably a dominant factor in the way literate Chinese have been taught to think about language.

English words have (written) form, pronunciation, and meaning as well, but their relationships with each other are somewhat differently perceived. First, English speakers, like speakers of other Western languages, tend to think of the spoken form as primary and the written form as the representation of the spoken. Thus, an English speaker will tend to ask, "How do you spell X?", where X is a sound, in contrast to the Chinese speaker's question, "How do you pronounce Y?", where Y is a character. Second, in English, despite many irregularities of spelling, it is generally possible to deduce the pronunciation of a word from the way in which it is written, so there is a direct and fairly easily discernible relationship between written and oral forms. However, in Chinese, although most characters include in their structure a clue as to how they should be pronounced, the clues are not consistently used, and a large minority of characters—including the most frequent ones that children must learn first—contain no such clues at all (it is precisely these characters that are often incorporated into others as pronunciation clues). Thus, for each word, the oral form and the written form have to be learned separately, and then they must be linked together, and a further link must be made with the meaning. Third, while English and Chinese are both characterized by the diversity of regional speech, it can be argued that varieties of Chinese are even more removed from each other than are varieties of English—DeFrancis (1984), for example, claims that Guangdonghua (or Cantonese) is as different from Putonghua (or Mandarin) as Italian is from Spanish. Reading and writing in mainland China, however, is taught in Putonghua, the variety, based on the Beijing dialect, that is spoken by educated people, so learning how to pronounce characters means, in effect, learning a standard language. The point is mentioned in several of these essays, but it is perhaps a reflection of China's highly centralized educational system that this insistence on the standard for literate purposes is not questioned. Nor do the program participants, many of whom speak varieties other than Putonghua themselves, suggest that children who speak such varieties may have particular difficulties in acquiring literacy—though Chang does point out that they have persistent pronunciation problems.

Literacy, of course, is far more than learning the units of the orthographic system and relating those units to individual words of the spoken language. As many writers on English literacy have observed, the key problem for inexperienced readers is to link the sequences of words in a text with the meaning structures, or schemata, that they have already developed from their experiences of life as well as of language (e.g., Goodman 1967; Smith 1982). Some of this linkage occurs at the lexical level: a single word or expression can activate complex cognitive structures and evoke powerful emotions. Xu Ju discusses a particularly interesting aspect of how this works in the case of Chinese idioms.

An idiom in Chinese is not merely a "restricted [collocation] which cannot normally be understood from the literal meaning of the words which make [it] up" (Carter 1987, 58); it is a short sequence of words that calls up a whole story, and literacy in Chinese involves knowing these stories and recognizing the idiomatic references to them. The depth of meaning that the judicious use of such idioms can give to a text is hard for a native speaker of English to appreciate, for it depends both on the exceptionally long history of Chinese as a language in which stories could be preserved in writing and on the remarkable integrity and homogeneity of a culture in which the same stories are taught to everyone.

Most lexical items, however, do not evoke stories by themselves: Stories (or other kinds of text) are formed by the items being placed together in structured sequences, and the task of readers (and listeners) is to perceive how the items are related to each other and to apply the appropriate schemata to their interpretation. In her essay "Step by Step: Reading in Primary School," Wang Jian describes in detail how children are led from the initial stages of character recognition and pronunciation through the interpretation of sentences and paragraphs and, finally, whole texts. She emphasizes that this is a "bottom-up" process, proceeding in a systematic way from the smallest units of the written language to the largest—or, at least, the largest that schoolchildren are expected to deal with. Zhu Minghui, on the other hand, in "How Chinese Children Learn Chinese in School," claims that increasing attention is being paid nowadays to the learning of items in context: At the early stages, for example, children learn basic characters through the medium of songs, and they are also asked to recite and retell stories and to describe material presented in pictures; such oral work is used as a basis for later writing assignments.

Despite the difference of emphasis in the two essays, it is what they have in common that is most striking to a Western reader. First, both document an extraordinarily analytical approach to language, for at every stage they show children identifying the constituents that make up larger units: strokes constitute radicals, radicals characters, characters words, words sentences, sentences paragraphs, and paragraphs texts. The task is to recognize the elements and to perceive how they are combined to form larger wholes until the level of the "main idea" is reached and inferences can be made about implied meanings. Second, both essays reinforce the impression given in the previous chapter of the firmly disciplined way in which Chinese children learn, and they suggest that this discipline may actually be a function of the writing system itself; for when there is so much to be learned, how else is it to be done? Third, the essays present a picture of remarkable success in learning. The success is most striking in the case of Pinyin, which both Wang and Zhu maintain is learned in a matter of months—a claim supported by Ingulsrud and Allen (1992)[3]—and both

---

3. Ingulsrud and Allen point out, however, that given the large classes that teachers must work with and the short time in which they are expected to teach Pinyin, the difficulties experienced by children may simply not be detected.

accounts also indicate steady progress in the acquisition of characters so that by the end of primary school, everyone should know the two thousand or so considered necessary for basic literacy. Of course, we must be careful in generalizing from this information, for although it comes from different writers, both of them come from the relatively "advanced" eastern region of China, both are now living in urban areas, and both, of course, are highly educated themselves; they are not in a position to describe those situations where the pedagogy of Chinese literacy fails. Nevertheless, the methods of teaching and learning that they describe are evidently widespread, and we can expect them to have significant effects on the ways in which literate Chinese learn English.

Wang Kui, in her essay on "Reading Aloud in Learning Chinese," focuses on one of the themes brought up by Zhu Minghui; namely, the use of recitation to foster the growth of literacy. She points out that this, like so much in Chinese education, is an ancient practice; students were taught in prerevolutionary times to "chant" whole texts as a way of understanding their meaning and learning how to produce such texts themselves. Such practices have now been largely rejected in native English-speaking countries, but they are still widely used in China at every stage of literacy acquisition. Wang argues convincingly, from her own experience, that they can be a powerful aid to children in reaching a more holistic understanding of their reading materials and a full appreciation of their literary heritage; again, her essay suggests that literate Chinese have well-developed strategies for appreciation and memorization that they could well turn to the purposes of learning English (cf. Erbaugh 1990).

The final essay of the chapter is Wu Lili's "Classical Chinese Reading in Junior-Secondary School." This looks beyond the basic literacy that is learned in primary school to the study of Chinese at the secondary stage, a study that in some ways is more similar to learning Latin in an English-speaking environment than it is to learning English. For classical Chinese is, as Wu points out, significantly different from vernacular Chinese, in both grammar and vocabulary, and the approach to learning it is, again, highly analytical: Students are asked to paraphrase and punctuate classical texts and to identify particular characters that have changed in meaning and/or pronunciation since classical times. Her account suggests powerfully how much there is to learn in Chinese, how totally absorbing it can be, and how richly rewarding.

Taken as a whole, this set of essays reiterates a theme that came up in Chapter One; namely, the powerful ways in which the Chinese writing system, and the literature that is enshrined in it, connects those who learn it with the past. This is not to say that there have been no changes, for the characters themselves have been revised from time to time, most recently with the introduction of simplified characters on the mainland since the 1950s.[4] The use of a phonetic writing system to help in the learning of characters is also a twentieth-century

---

4. A second scheme of character simplification was introduced at the end of the 1970s, but it was quickly aborted (Gu Yongqi, personal information, August 1995).

innovation, and the development of Pinyin, in particular, is an achievement of the Communist administration (DeFrancis 1984; Ramsey 1987). The way in which Pinyin is used is also in a process of change, for primary-school text-books now print Pinyin representations of characters to a much later stage than they used to in the past. We can expect Pinyin to be used increasingly in public life as more foreigners visit China and as more Chinese learn English. DeFrancis, indeed, argues that characters should be abandoned altogether, for other than ceremonial or scholarly purposes, on the grounds that it is only on the basis of a simpler writing system that universal literacy can be achieved (1984, 286–7).

In the light of the essays presented here, however, such a radical change seems hardly likely to happen. On the one hand, it is clear that these writers, and presumably most other educated Chinese, feel tremendous devotion towards their writing system—how could they feel otherwise, having spent so much time and effort on learning it?—and they frequently express pride in its beauty and expressiveness. On the other hand, the system is considered by many to be a significant factor in maintaining political unity. The Chinese people are much more diverse than outsiders commonly recognize, and this diversity is reflected most powerfully in the variety of speech forms. At the same time, Chinese political unity is highly valued and, as the period of war-lord rule after the 1911 revolution showed, it cannot be taken for granted. Many fear that to move to a writing system that captures pronunciation dif-ferences would be to break the nation up, and no Chinese would wish to take responsibility for that. Thus, the writing system is likely to remain as one of the most important symbols of national identity and, incidentally, it will continue to constitute a peculiarly rigorous form of intellectual discipline for those children that succeed in learning it.

1. Form, Pronunciation, and Meaning in Chinese Characters

Chang Qian

The first two years of primary education are perhaps the most important, because that is the period when children transfer their knowledge of the spoken language to written material, and it is the preparatory stage of knowledge-learning. Written material is the record of knowledge and experience people have accumulated from practice and thinking through thousands of years. In the course of becoming literate, children not only learn the characters of Chinese, but also use the characters as the medium to comprehend the whole world.

Since children cannot develop spontaneously from spoken language to written language, it is the teacher's task to guide the way. Actually, when we talk about school literacy, we cannot make a general introduction without analyzing the features of Chinese characters. Chinese characters are the combination of pronunciation, form, and meaning. In the process of learning how to read, children learn to connect these three components with one another in respect of each character. So, here I will briefly introduce school literacy in China by analyzing how each component is grasped.

The Grasp of Form

Teachers must understand that children learn to read on the basis of having a preliminary grasp of the spoken language. English words are made up of letters, and insofar as students have some knowledge about the rules of pronunciation, they can pronounce or even write the words. Unlike English, Chinese characters are made up of strokes, and one cannot write a character on the basis of its pronunciation.

How easy a character is to learn depends on three factors. The first of these is the strokes of which the character is composed. The simplest strokes in Chinese characters are the horizontal and vertical strokes. It is easier for children to accept those characters that are made up of these two strokes, such as 田, *tián,* "field"; 口, *kǒu,* "mouth"; 日, *rì,* "sun"; and 目, *mù,* "eye." Secondly, the structure of a character affects how easy it is to grasp. Let us have a look at the characters 双, *shuāng,* "a pair"; and 林, *lín,* "forest." They are symmetrical and so are appealing to children and can be easily perceived. The third factor has something to do with the children themselves. Generally speaking, the more characters they grasp, the easier they find it to learn new ones. Their ability to distinguish the structure develops with the analysis and comparison of different characters. For example, 越, *yuè,* "cross" or "bypass"; 篮, *lán,* "basket"; and 稻, *dào,* "rice" are extremely difficult for children in the low grades. These characters are made up of many complicated strokes and are asymmetrical and irregular. Students in the higher grades are found to grasp them better; as they learn larger numbers of characters, they become more familiar with the component parts and understand better the principles on which the parts are combined. For example, the meaning carried by the radical in a character is usually reflected in the meaning of the character itself. Thus, the radical 禾, *hé,* means "grain," so many of the characters that include this character also have something to do with grain: 种, *zhǒng,* for example, means "seed," and 秧, *yāng,* means "seedling."

The Grasp of Pronunciation

The structure of a character cannot express the pronunciation in itself. To pronounce a character correctly, children must learn Pinyin as the most important tool, both for learning new characters and for going over characters that have already been learned.

Learning how to pronounce characters can be quite difficult. Children are most likely to confuse the prenasal consonant and the postnasal consonant. For example, they cannot distinguish *eng* from *en* and *in* from *ing.* Also it is difficult for them to pronounce the double vowel *ou* correctly, while *a* is easy for them.

There are many dialects in Chinese. Many children grow up in a dialect-speaking environment, and their way of pronouncing a word does not follow the Pinyin system. Later, when they are learning Putonghua, their dialect interferes greatly with the standard pronunciation and it is hard to correct. There are students from southeastern China, for example, who can never distinguish *n* from *l.*

The Grasp of Meaning

While it is quite easy for children to remember the meanings of characters that represent words they already know orally, there are still some difficulties in grasping meaning, apart from the obvious one of learning words that are completely new.

Because a single Chinese character does not necessarily have a fixed meaning, there is a unique phrase in Chinese called 组词, *zǔ cí,* which means to combine one character with another or other characters to form new meaning. Here is an example to illustrate this point. 太, *tài,* is originally an abstract word meaning "too much." But 太阳, *tài yáng,* means "the sun," while 太平洋, *tài píng yáng,* means "the Pacific Ocean."

Another phenomenon that teachers must pay attention to is that there is a large number of characters that are similar in form but totally different in meaning. Examples are 熟练, *shú liàn,* "skilled," and 锻炼, *duàn liàn,* "exercise." Children tend to write them as 熟炼 and 锻练.

To teach the students the characters, we realize the union of pronunciation, form, and meaning in two ways. One is to establish a new relationship between form and the already known connection of pronunciation and meaning. The other way is to form the relationship between pronunciation and meaning for those words that are unfamiliar and abstract and then to relate this combination to the form of the character. Whichever approach is taken, students cannot be said to know a character (or word) until all three components are firmly linked in their minds.

2. Comprehending Word Meanings in Chinese

Xu Ju

Chinese vocabulary, like that of English, is composed of three interdependent and interactive elements: sound, form, and meaning. In this essay, I would like to explore the relationship between form and meaning and discuss the regular patterns that can be used in learning new words. I shall also discuss idioms, which are peculiarly characteristic of Chinese, being related to background knowledge that is remote and strange to modern learners.

An important feature of Chinese orthography is the use of radicals, *piān páng bù shǒu*. Radicals are not whole characters, but many are themselves meaningful. For instance, the radicals 氵, 石, 衤, 艹, 心, 钅, 目, and 竹 are respectively related to "water," "stone," "clothing," "grass," "heart," "metal," "eyes," and "bamboo." The meaning of a word composed of a radical of this kind and a root is usually closely related to the meaning of the radical. So we can roughly guess the meaning of a word just from the radical, even if the word is completely new to us. For example, 汗, *hàn*, means "sweat," which has a relation to the meaning of its radical 氵, "water."

Many two-character Chinese words are word groups, or compound words, that are made up from individual words, each of which has its own meaning. The relationships between the two individual words have been generalized into four types. They can be illustrated as follows:

1. Consisting of a subject and a predicate, for example:
   目送, *mù sòng*, "eyes send off," hence "gaze after."
   民用, *mín yòng*, "civilians use," hence "civil."

2. Consisting of a verb and an object:
   命名, *mìng míng*, "assign a name."
   唱歌, *chàng gē*, "sing a song."

3. Consisting of a modifier and a head noun:
   寝室, *qǐn shì*, "sleep room," hence "bedroom."
   素描, *sù miáo*, "plain drawing," hence "sketch."

4. Consisting of two one-character words of the same meaning:
   来临, *lái lín*, "come arrive," meaning "arrive" or "come."
   重新, *chóng xīn*, "again anew," meaning "anew" or "afresh."

From these examples, we can see that Chinese compounds are skillfully and regularly constructed. It is possible to guess their rough meanings from the meanings of their components, the two individual words.

As in English, most Chinese words have more than one meaning. An important skill to be acquired is to define the exact meaning from context clues. Here is an example of a word with multiple meanings:

深, *shēn*:　这课书很深, *zhè kè shū hěn shēn:* "This lesson is <u>abstruse</u>."

那条河很深, *nà tiáo hé hěn shēn:* "That river is <u>deep</u>."

Like the sounds / tiə / and / tɛə / for the same form *tear,*[5] Chinese vocabulary also includes words that have more than one sound. For example, the character 长 may be pronounced *cháng* and mean "long," or it may be pronounced *zhǎng* and mean "grow." Students are instructed to distinguish the different meanings and sounds by considering the context in which the character appears. For example:

长短, *cháng duǎn,* "long and short"

成长, *chéng zhǎng,* "grow up"

Chinese teachers have devised many kinds of practice for their students to acquire the meanings of words. These include making up sentences or writing a paragraph using the given words; categorizing words on the basis of their meanings; drawing analogies between pairs of words; and analyzing and comparing synonyms, antonyms, and parts of speech. However, no method is superior to learning meanings through contexts. Word meanings studied in isolation are easily forgotten, but when they are studied in context, they can be acquired on the basis of comprehension.

Compared with the usual words, Chinese idioms are unique not only because most of them are four-character words, but also because behind each of them there is a lively classical allusion. These allusions were initially recorded in certain classical works such as *Records of the Historian* by Sima Qian of the Han Dynasty, and *History of the Three Kingdoms* by Chen Shou of the Northern and Southern Dynasties. Later writers mentioned the stories again in their own works by using words that could summarize the key points and that, frequently, are combinations of four characters. People of later generations appreciated the allusions, as well as the expressions describing them, and repeated them time and again in their own speech and writing. Thus, idioms came into being. Most of them have been handed down for generations. They are regarded as the cream of the Chinese language.

---

5. It will be noticed that Xu uses British pronunciation as the basis for her phonetic transcription, reflecting the strong British influence on English-language teaching in China. (Ed.)

Yè gōng hào lóng, "the man Ye loved dragons," is an example of a Chinese idiom that is used to describe a professed love of what one really fears, just like Ye Zigao's love for dragons. The story was first recorded in *New Preface: Miscellaneous Affairs,* which was written by Liu Xiang of the Han Dynasty. The original words can be translated as follows:

> Ye Zigao was a man who loved dragons. He drew dragons, carved dragons, and described dragons in the essay that was carved on the wall of his room. And then the dragon of heaven heard of it and dropped down, popping its head in from the window and looking about while extending its tail into the central room. As soon as Ye saw this, he was scared out of his wits and fled in panic. That man Ye did not love dragons at all! What he loved was the representations of dragons but not real ones.

Later on, Chen Shou, of the Northern and Southern Dynasties, cited the story in *History of the Three Kingdoms: Biography of Qinmi,* and commented:

> In the past, Ye Zigao . . . loved dragons. But when the magical dragon really dropped down, his love for the unreal things was demonstrated and made known to God and to mortal people as well.

From then on, the fixed four-character word *yè gōng hào lóng* was transmitted from generation to generation and gradually became a widely used idiom.

Utilizing idioms in speech and writing is considered a skill, but students are not encouraged to overdo it because it will distract readers from the content. In spite of that, Chinese idioms can be regarded as a succinct language expressing rich ideas in few characters. The acquisition of full literacy in Chinese includes learning to comprehend and use the idioms.

The process of acquiring Chinese literacy is a long one, but learners, if they devote themselves to it, can find that it is both delightful and fruitful because the forms of Chinese words are so unique and follow such distinct rules, while the meanings that the words bear are so impressive and interesting. By the time they finish secondary school, average students have probably acquired about ten thousand Chinese words, and they will continue to acquire more through reading by themselves or, if they have the chance to enter university, through the development of specialized knowledge of a particular subject area.

3. Step by Step: Reading in Primary School

Wang Jian

In China, children nowadays begin school at the age of six and spend six years in primary school. Once they enter school, their Chinese study begins and continues throughout the six years. Although Chinese lessons cover training in all the language skills, I would like to focus here on how children's reading ability is developed. To me, primary-school reading is a bottom-up learning, which goes from Pinyin to character; then to word, sentence, paragraph; and finally a complete essay. Every link in this chain of study is carefully planned so that it prepares students for the next stage of learning. By examining the focus of learning of each grade and the Chinese textbooks for primary-school students, I hope to demonstrate how children develop their reading in this bottom-up learning process.

To get a general idea of the paced learning, the following is an outline of the objectives of teaching of each year in primary school (the information was provided during an interview by Ms. Liu, a teacher of Chinese at Nanjing Pei Jia Qiao Primary School in Nanjing):

Primary One: Pinyin, a limited number of characters

Primary Two: characters, words, the use of the dictionary

Primary Three: comprehension of words and sentences, main idea of a paragraph

Primary Four: outline of an essay, main idea of each part of an essay

Primary Five: theme/main idea of an essay

Primary Six: implications of a sentence

Please note that two seemingly confusing terms are used here, *character* and *word*. In the Chinese language, the character is the smallest unit in written form. One character always represents one syllable. Unlike a word, which always has a meaning, a Chinese character may not have any meaning on its own and must be used together with another character to form a word. Some characters, however, have their own meanings; therefore, they are also words.

Another term used in this essay is *Pinyin*. It consists of all the twenty-six letters in the English alphabet and is the phonetic transcription of Chinese characters. With Pinyin, people can learn how to pronounce a character in standard Chinese.

Primary One

Learning in the first year is focused on Pinyin and a small number of characters (i.e., 160 in the first term and 280 in the second). Children spend their first month in school learning Pinyin. More than one third of *Book One* of the textbook series is devoted to the teaching of Pinyin only. Children's knowledge of Pinyin is consolidated throughout their first two years in school, with frequent exercises in various forms; every character in the four books for use in these two years is printed under its Pinyin representation.

After Pinyin, learning goes into the second stage: character study. To arouse interest in learning, simple characters are introduced in the beginning with colorful pictures of the objects described and of the writing of the characters in primitive times to show how the writing came into being. In learning characters, students' attention is often directed to the right order of writing strokes of a character, from top to bottom, from left to right, or from outside to inside. To demonstrate the right order of writing, a teacher usually turns his/her back to the students and writes in the air. The children follow the teacher and write in the air too. Children's attention is also called to radicals and their meanings. For example, 晴, *qíng,* which means "sunny," and 晒, *shài,* which means "to dry," share the same radical, 日. A Chinese teacher will explain to the class that 日 means "the sun" and that those two characters share the same radical because what is meant by each of them is related to the sun. Typical exercises for students at this stage include pointing out the radical of a given character, providing a character that is formed with a given radical, and providing an analytical writing of a given character, as shown in Figure 3-1, so the teacher can see if a student has got the right order of strokes.

The study of Pinyin, strokes, and radicals prepares children for learning in the second year, as well as for future study. Although not emphasized, there are other exercises such as sentence-making and thinking of a word that includes a given character. These exercises also help to get students ready for the next year's study when they are going to learn a lot of new words and will be asked to make up more sentences.

Primary Two

Teaching in the second year is centered on the use of dictionaries and command of a large vocabulary (i.e., an average of 370 characters each term). Children are required to learn how to find a character in a dictionary in two ways. Since all the characters are arranged in alphabetical order according to their Pinyin spelling, Pinyin is certainly one of the methods students can now use to look up words in dictionaries. This method is applied when students are given either the pronunciation or the Pinyin of a character that they do not know how to write. The other method is to find a character by referring to its radical; that is, finding a dictionary's section for that radical and then search-

Figure 3-1
Analytical writing of a Chinese character

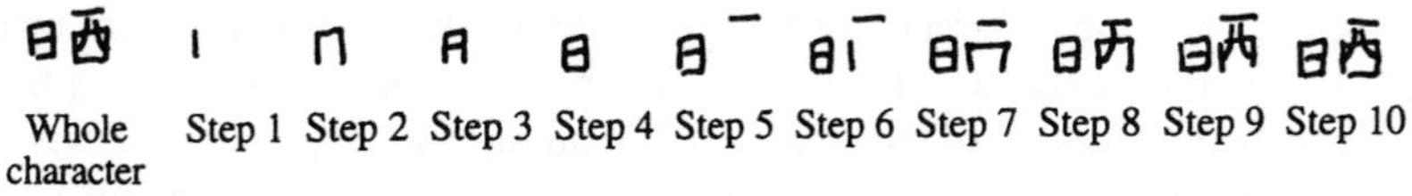

日西   ।   冂   円   日   日⁻   日ᵢ   日ᵣ̄   日ᵣ̃   日ᵣ̃   日西

Whole   Step 1 Step 2 Step 3 Step 4 Step 5 Step 6 Step 7 Step 8 Step 9 Step 10
character

---

ing the section for the character by counting the number of strokes left when the radical is taken from it. (All the characters sharing the same radical are arranged within the section according to the number of strokes, not including the strokes of the radical itself.) This method is usually used when students come across new characters in reading and do not know their pronunciations and/or meanings.

So from these two methods of using a dictionary, we can see clearly how children's first year of study paves the way for what they learn in the second year. The study of characters and words at this stage is conducted at a higher level than in the first year. Exercises usually require children to explain word meanings, to provide synonyms and/or antonyms for given words, to distinguish characters that are similar in writing, to recognize different pronunciations of a character, or to make up sentences with a given character, word, or expression.

By the end of their second year in primary school, children have gone through the fundamental stages of their reading development and are ready to take up more advanced reading challenges. From now on, they will not be asked frequently about the Pinyin of a character, the meaning of a word, or the number of strokes. Such exercises may still appear sometimes, but they are meant to be revision exercises.

Primary Three

The goal of the third year of teaching is to train students to summarize the main idea of a paragraph. Most teachers find this is a crucial, difficult part of primary-school learning. The third-year study is a transition from relatively simple study of characters and words to the more challenging task of comprehension of reading materials, which requires thinking and analyzing on the part of students. So two types of training are carried out simultaneously in the third year: paced learning offered in the two textbooks, and supplementary training designed by the teacher.

The textbook for use in the first term consists of eight units, each unit composed of three or four lessons. A short reading guidance precedes each unit, pointing out the focus of learning, and a reading-writing review at the end of the unit sums up, or repeats, the major points and shows students how to apply their learning in this unit in their own writing. Understanding word meaning is the focus of attention in the first two units—Unit One introducing the idea and Unit Two reinforcing it. Unit Three is centered on understanding word meaning with the help of dictionaries or the context in which a word is used. Unit Four is a general review of the previous three units. Looking up a new character or word in a dictionary does not require much thinking on the students' part, but the training in judging word meaning from the context initiates students' thinking in reading. Unit Five further develops children's ability to analyze, with more exercises in figuring out word meaning from the context, preparing them for study of the next two units. In Units Six and Seven, the reading-comprehension requirement is broadened from understanding individual words to understanding a complete sentence. The last unit in the book reviews the material learned in Units Five through Seven.

Learning in the second term can be divided into two parts: sentence study and paragraph study. In the first half of the term, teaching concentrates on sentence study. In addition to the meaning of each sentence in a paragraph, children are required to understand the relationship between these sentences and in what order they are organized; that is, how the paragraph is developed. To make the point clear, a typical exercise at this stage asks students in what order the writer describes an object or an event in a paragraph, in the order of time or space, and so on. The latter half of the second term focuses on paragraph study. Now children are told that by understanding the relationship between sentences and how they are organized, they can see that all the sentences in a paragraph point to something in common—the main idea of a paragraph.

Most teachers think that paragraph study begins late in the textbook and that children's analytical ability is not strong enough for study in the fourth year by the time they finish the carefully planned learning process discussed previously. To make up for this drawback, the idea that every paragraph has a focus, the main idea, is introduced to children at the very beginning of the third year. At the beginning, the teacher selects a paragraph from a text and raises a series of questions to lead students to arrive at the main idea of a paragraph. Gradually, the teacher provides fewer hints or suggestions, while students rely more on themselves in getting the main idea.

Throughout the third year, word study continues to be an important part of learning. It is considered a crucial, indispensable link in the bottom-up learning process. At this stage, children learn an average of 280 characters each term.

Primary Four

When the development of children's analytical ability is initiated in Primary Three and they can summarize the main idea of a paragraph, they are ready for a greater challenge: understanding the organization of a reading text and identifying the main idea of each part.

In the beginning, teachers of Primary Four give students a lot of help in the form of hints, suggestions, and questions to lead them to understand how a text is organized and what paragraphs go together under what topic. Gradually, less help is offered and children become more independent in fulfilling the task.

In the first few lessons, the textbook provides the outline of a text and children are asked to divide all the paragraphs into parts according to the outline. Then the task becomes more difficult. Given a set of expressions or sentences, students are expected to organize them in the right order so that an outline of the text is formed. Then the children should divide the text into parts according to the outline. Gradually, questions in the book become more straightforward with few hints, and children depend on themselves to recognize paragraphs that belong together under a subtitle and to come up with the main ideas of a text.

Less emphasis is placed on study of new vocabulary. Children learn 163 characters in the first term and 131 in the second.

Primary Five

The focus of teaching in the fifth year is on understanding the main idea of a text. This is also a difficult part of primary-school learning because students are often confused as to what is the central concern of a text when they are faced with the main ideas of different parts of it.

To solve this problem, teachers capitalize on what has been learnt in the fourth year. After a review of getting the main idea of each part of a text, children's attention is directed towards the relationship between these parts and the idea on which they are centered. Then children are asked to explain what is emphasized in the text and what is not, what is described in detail and what is described generally, and why. From these exercises, children learn to recognize the important points of a text and to summarize the main idea. To help students get a better understanding, teachers also show them that—like sentences in a paragraph that are organized in an order and revolve around the main idea of the paragraph—all the parts of a text are organized in some order and lead to the theme, the main idea of the text. It is explained to the students that a piece of writing can roughly be divided into three parts: the beginning, in which the thesis is established; the middle, in which the thesis is developed; and the end, in which the conclusion is reached; and that the beginning and the concluding paragraphs resonate with each other.

Because learning in Primary Five is closely linked with what has been learned in Primary Four, exercises on the study of organization of a text and main ideas of different parts continue to comprise an important part of learning in the fifth year. As to the study of vocabulary, children learn 121 characters in the first term and 110 in the second.

Primary Six

Study in the last year of primary school is mainly a revision of what has been taught over the past five years. Most of the exercises in the two books are on word study, sentence study, summary of main ideas and outline of a text, and summary of the theme of a text.

However, an important part of learning is drawing inferences, although it does not take up a large proportion of the exercises. Training in making inferences actually starts in Primary Two, when students are given pairs of sentences, one of which has descriptive adjectives and/or adverbs and the other does not, and are asked how the sentences in each pair are different and what those adjectives and/or adverbs tell about the writer or people in the text. From Primary Three to Primary Five, some challenging questions appear now and then in the textbooks asking students to explain—by drawing on their understanding of words, sentences, and paragraphs—what is implied in the writing or what can be inferred about the writer's or a character's feelings, opinions, likes, and dislikes. In Primary Six, more emphasis and practice are given to the training of this reading skill.

A small vocabulary is learned in the last year of primary school: ninety-one characters in the first term and eighty-two in the second.

Conclusion

Primary-school learning is the foundation of one's education. Without this solid foundation, one's future education and development will undoubtedly be hindered. The bottom-up learning process in reading class in Chinese primary schools leads children, step by step, to take greater challenges in reading, to do more advanced study. By the time children leave primary school, equipped with basic reading skills, they are ready for higher learning in secondary school.

Study in secondary school is much more difficult than in primary school. Students are expected to understand texts beyond their literal meanings and to read between the lines. Less emphasis is placed on vocabulary study. Although there is a continued study of main ideas of paragraphs and the outline of a text and its theme, exercises such as making inferences, working out the author's implied message in a text, and examining writing styles appear more frequently than in primary school. Moreover, the study of classical literature (see Wu Lili's essay in this chapter) is part of secondary-school learning. Such study is quite difficult because the writing is highly condensed and rigid in form. In reading these classical works, an analytical approach is used. Attention is given first to understanding of vocabulary items so as to achieve understanding of a sentence, then of a paragraph, and last of a text; thus, the bottom-up method of learning, which has brought children to the point of being able to read vernacular texts as wholes, is recycled once more in respect to classical literature.

4. How Chinese Children Learn Chinese in School

Zhu Minghui

There have been arguments whether Chinese is learned by a bottom-up or top-down method. Some people maintain that children are taught to learn Chinese in a bottom-up way and, therefore, their reading strategies will also tend to be bottom-up. Is this opinion true? To answer this question, let us take a look at how Chinese children are taught to read Chinese in primary school nowadays.

Character Learning

The four fundamental elements that learners of Chinese characters must work on are: Pinyin, basic characters (i.e., characters that cannot be divided into radicals), radicals, and the sequence of strokes. The first thing that children are taught in school, therefore, is Pinyin, the phonetic system that represents the sound of Chinese characters. In Chinese, each character is read as a syllable that is composed of three parts: *shēngmǔ, yùnmǔ,* and *shēngdiào.*

Shēngmǔ refers to the beginning consonant in a syllable; for example, *h* is a *shēngmǔ* in *hǎo,* 好, which means "good." Some syllables have no beginning consonant; for example, *ài,* 爱, which means "love." Syllables of this kind are called zero syllables. In Chinese, the following consonants are *shēngmǔ* (presented in the order in which they are initially taught): *b, p, m, f, d, t, n, l, g, k, h, j, q, x, sh, ch, sh, r, z, c, s, y, w.* However, we cannot say that *shēngmǔ* means "consonant" in Chinese, because the word is not used for the consonants *n* and *ng* when used at the end of a syllable.

Yùnmǔ refers to the part in a syllable that follows the starting consonant, such as *ao* in the syllable *hǎo.* Syllables having zero *shēngmǔ* are composed of only *yùnmǔ.* Nor is *yùnmǔ* equivalent to "vowel." Some *yùnmǔ* are composed of vowels only; namely, *a, o, e, i, u, ü, ai, ei, ao, ie, ue, ou,* and *iu,* but some are composed of vowels and nasals, namely, *an, en, in, un, ün, ang, eng, ing,* and *ong.* For example, 年, which means "year," is pronounced as *nián,* in which the end of the syllable is a nasal.

Shēngdiào, or tone, refers to pitch variations that may contribute to distinguishing between different characters. Syllables having different tones may have different meaning in the characters they represent. For example, *fān, fán, fǎn,* and *fàn* have different meanings: "turn over," "annoying," "opposite," and "meal" (but there are other possible interpretations, because a Pinyin spelling, even with the same tone, often represents more than one character; for example, there are four characters that are pronounced *fān* with the first tone).

79

Traditionally, there are four tones in Chinese, namely *yīnpíng,* the first tone; *yángpíng,* the second tone; *shàngshēng,* the third tone; and *qùshēng,* the fourth tone. We use the four diacritic symbols ˉ, ´, ˇ, and ` to represent the four tones, respectively. There is also another tone called the weak tone, which is indicated by the absence of a diacritic.

When learning Pinyin, children first learn single vowels. They practice these vowels in different tones, such as *ā, á, ǎ, à, ō, ó, ǒ, ò.* When they learn consonants, they spell them with the single vowels they have learned, also with different tones, such as *bā, bá, bǎ, bà.* Beside each meaningful spelling in their textbook, there is a colorful picture indicating the meaning of the character that the syllable represents. Then they learn the more complicated *yùnmǔ.*

The study of Pinyin usually takes children about one month, because many of them have learned a bit about it either at home or in kindergarten. They do not learn Pinyin according to alphabetical order until the beginning of Primary Two. When we were children, we did not learn alphabetical order at all, so it sounded strange to me when I heard a child recite the alphabet for the first time.

After one month's study, children can use Pinyin to represent any character or word they hear. In the first section of the textbook used by students of Primary One, there are no characters at all. For example, on page thirty-three of *Chinese Book One,* there is a picture of ten animals, and the name of each animal is represented in Pinyin. At the bottom of the page there is a direction: *"Shuō shuo nǐ xǐ huān nǎ xiē dòng wù,"* which means,"Please point out the animals you like." At this stage, though children do not know any characters (or are presumed not to know any), they can read with the aid of Pinyin.

Since Pinyin is only the phonetic spelling system used to pronounce characters, the second stage is character study. As a beginning, children learn to read and write the characters, 一, 二, 三, 四, 五, 六, 七, 八, 九, 十, which mean "one, two, three . . . ten," by studying the song:

yī	*qù*	*èr*	*sān*	*lǐ,*
一		二	三	
shān	*cūn*	*sì*	*wǔ*	*jiā,*
		四	五	
ér	*tóng*	*liù*	*qī*	*gè,*
		六	七	
bā	*jiǔ*	*shí*	*zhī*	*huā.*
八	九	十		

The rough meaning of this song is:

> One walk, two or three li covered,
> There are four or five families in a mountain village.
> There are six or seven children playing,
> And eight, nine, or ten flowers around.

In this song, the ten characters that the children are expected to learn are written beneath the Pinyin. The other words are given in Pinyin only.

Following these numbers, children learn some simple pictograms; that is, characters that reflect traces of pictorial origin. For example, 山, *shān*, which means "mountain," comes from the picture 𝗠 and 牛, *niú*, which means "cow," comes from this representation of a cow: 𝕐. The number of characters derived from pictograms is not large, and they are relatively easy to grasp.

After learning some characters of this kind, children will learn other simple characters that have something to do with their daily life. In Lesson Seven of *Chinese Book One*, the text is given like this:

> *zhuàn bǐ dāo, huā qiān bǐ,*
> *hóng chǐ zi, bái xiàng pí,*
> *wén jù hé lǐ bǎi zhěng qí.*
> *xiǎo xué shēng, ài xué xí,*
> *shǐ yòng wén jù yào ài xī.*

This song means:

> Pencil sharpener and colorful pencils,
> Red ruler and white eraser,
> Are put orderly in the pencil box.
> Pupils love studying,
> And should take care of the stationery too.

From the two songs quoted here, we can see clearly that the characters students will learn are put in a certain context. Children are expected to understand the main meaning of the song or text before they learn to read and write individual characters. In each lesson, no more than seven characters are taught in the first half of Primary One and up to eleven in the second half of the same year. By the end of primary school, children are supposed to learn around twenty-five hundred characters, with a larger number of words (because not all characters are words and not all words are single characters). Among the twenty-five hundred characters, the twelve hundred most commonly used ones are taught in Primary One and Two. These characters are learned and reviewed through a large amount of reading material.

After some work on simple characters, children will begin to learn characters that have radicals. For example, in the character 灯, *dēng*, which means "light," the radical is 火, which indicates "fire." Such radicals will help them to remember the meaning of a character. Knowing radicals will also help people look up characters in a Chinese dictionary.

Apart from all this, the correct sequence of strokes is emphasized too. The basic rules of sequence are as follows:

1. First horizontal stroke, then vertical stroke, as in 十, *shí,* which means "ten": 一 is written first and then 丨.

2. First left-falling stroke, then right-falling stroke, as in 人, *rén,* which means "person": 丿, is written first and then 乀.

3. From up to down, as in 芳, *fāng,* which means "sweet-smelling": first the upper part, 艹, then the lower part, 方, is written.

4. From left to right, as in 恨, *hèn,* which means "hate": first, 忄, then 艮 is written.

5. From outer to inner part, as in 同, *tóng,* which means "the same" or "similar": first the frame 冂 is written, then the inner part 口.

As mentioned previously, children are not expected to learn characters separately. Characters are put in a certain context and together with words that they can form. For example, in *Zhuàn bǐ dáo* quoted previously, 生, *shēng,* is a simple character and is given in the song together with 学, *xué.* Although the children know neither of these characters, they are familiar with the pronunciation of the word 学生, and they know the word means "student." After they have acquired quite a lot of characters, they learn more complicated ones together with those they already know. For example, when the character 国, *guó,* "country," is taught, the teacher will say: "It is *guó* as in *guó jiā*"(*guó jiā* meaning "nation" or "country"). In this word, 家, *jiā,* which also means "home," is not new to students.

When children are in Primary Two, they begin to learn new characters and words in a more complicated way. They are asked to make sentences with the new words from texts. For example, when they learn the word 高兴, *gāoxìng,* which means "happy," "be pleased," or "glad," they can make sentences such as:

今 天 老 师 表 扬 了 我 我 很 高 兴

jīn tiān lǎo shī biǎo yáng le wǒ. wǒ hěn gāo xìng.

This means, "I am very glad that the teacher praised me today."

Other Training Methods

While students learn and review characters by reading and understanding a large amount of materials, the aim of learning characters is to enable students to speak and write in a more standard way and to read more quickly. To achieve this purpose, the first step is story-retelling. Children begin story-retelling by reciting songs for children and very short stories. At the same time, they are asked to use their own words to describe a picture or several pictures that tell the whole procedure of an event. In this way, they learn to describe things explicitly.

In addition to such oral work, they are asked to provide explicit descriptions in writing; for example, they may be told to observe something in their life and then write down the observation. This is the beginning of composition. It usually begins in Primary Three and in some schools as early as Primary Two.

One more important exercise relating to both storytelling and composition is reading comprehension. A large amount of reading material is provided in the textbooks to improve students' reading ability and to widen their range of knowledge. Some of this material is to be read intensively, some extensively, and some by children on their own.

Conclusion

When I was a child (I began schooling in 1974), I was taught Chinese in a way that was more bottom-up: We first learned separate characters, then words formed by these characters, then sentences, and then whole passages. Even nowadays, many people who learn Chinese as a foreign language are still taught in this way. As a result, many people have the view that learning Chinese must be by a bottom-up strategy, but this is certainly not quite right.

The situation is quite different for primary-school children today because the Chinese textbooks used by children are completely different from those we used. They are compiled according to different reading strategies. Chinese students are expected to acquire characters together with the words they can form, and the characters are presented in specific contexts. In other words, characters are not read and practiced separately. Before learning single characters, children first grasp the main meaning of the context in which they come across them.

Children are provided with much more reading material than in the past in order to learn and review characters. Thus, to my mind, learning Chinese need not necessarily be in a bottom-up way; instead, we can do it by a top-down strategy. More people have realized this now and are trying their best to teach Chinese by a top-down method. The phenomenon that we cannot avoid seeing is that there are still many teachers who teach Chinese in the bottom-up way; but we cannot say that Chinese education is a total failure just because of this phenomenon. Changes have already taken place in primary-school teaching of Chinese and there is good reason to hope that more changes will take place in the future.

5. Reading Aloud in Learning Chinese

Wang Kui

Reading aloud has always been a traditional and effective method in children's learning of Chinese, and it is now still often applied in Chinese classrooms in primary and secondary schools.

In ancient China, educators attached great importance to the use of reading aloud in their teaching. They insisted that readers must read every word clearly and loudly without making any mistake; after reading a text in this way several times, readers naturally read fluently and remembered the content of the material for a long time. So they asked children to read ancient poems or essays with correct pronunciation, pauses, and the four tones of Mandarin Chinese. While reading aloud, children had to show corresponding feelings and facial expressions too. In Chinese understanding, this was not reading the poems or articles aloud, but actually chanting them. A famous scholar of classical Chinese in the Qing Dynasty named Yao Ding said, "All the pupils studying classical Chinese writings must read aloud, first quickly, then slowly. As time goes by, they will certainly understand the writings. If they can only read the materials silently, they will be laymen of classical Chinese writing all their life." Educators at that time believed that by reading aloud, students would deeply understand the material, and thus they could acquire some sense of writing poems and essays themselves, just as described in the old saying, "If one could read aloud the three hundred famous Tang Dynasty poems and remember them, he would have no problem writing poems himself." Many famous Chinese writers in our literary history, such as Lu Xun, have described the chanting of materials they did in their early school life and claimed they benefited greatly from it.

Reading aloud is still widely used in Chinese classrooms. Children in the first year of primary school begin to use this method of learning under the guidance of their teachers. When they start to learn Pinyin at the very beginning, they must read aloud the separate Pinyin letters and then their combinations. When it comes to the study of characters and words, reading aloud helps them to get correct pronunciation and intonation. For example, in some Primary One classrooms, the teachers ask students to read the following three groups of characters to practice their tones: 妈, 麻, 马, 骂, *mā, má, mǎ, mà;* 麦, 埋, 买, 卖, *māi, mái, mǎi, mài;* 汤, 糖, 躺, 烫, *tāng, táng, tǎng, tàng,* meaning "mother, hemp, horse, scold"; "wheat, bury, buy, sell"; "soup, sugar, lie, hot." In addition, teachers ask students to read the new characters they are learning aloud and at the same time, memorize their strokes and structure, and try to relate the characters and phrases to what they know in life. Later, when students learn sentences, they chant the sentences in their textbooks and try to grasp their sense and grammatical structure. Reading aloud becomes more necessary when students begin to deal with whole passages. Take, for example, a short text from Lesson Eleven of *Chinese Book 1* (used for Primary One pupils). The whole text is printed on a colorful picture of a little girl sitting on the golden moon looking at the stars. The general idea of the text is presented as follows:

The Small Boat

The crescent moon looks like a small curved boat.
The small boat has two bending ends.
I am sitting in the small boat.
I can only see the blue sky and the twinkling stars.

Exercise:

1. Read the text according to the Pinyin above each word and answer questions:
   a.   What does the small boat look like?
   b.   What do I see while sitting in the small boat?
2. Fill in the blanks:
   a.   crescent (   )
   b.   (   ) boat
3. Copy the new words printed below the directions for Exercise Four.
4. Read the text aloud and recite it.

   头   里   船   坐   星
   (end)   (in)   (boat) (sit) (star)

To deal with this lesson, the teacher usually explains the new words first and leads the students to read the words in chorus. Then the teacher tells them the main idea of each sentence, relating the content to the picture. After that, the teacher leads the students to chant the text in unison, sentence by sentence. When the students have no difficulty reading each sentence, they are asked to read the whole passage together, with the teacher beginning the first phrase and saying, "One, two, start." The teacher usually will remind the students to imagine, while they are reading, the beautiful things described. This whole process can take forty-five minutes or longer; after class, the students have to read the text several more times, according to the directions for Exercise One. Such practice goes on as the texts become increasingly complex. When students are in the first year of junior-secondary school, their Chinese textbooks begin to consist of contemporary poems and prose and many writings in classical Chinese; at this stage, too, students use chanting as a means of understanding and appreciating the materials.

Reading aloud does not always mean the same thing; it depends on why it is done. First, the characteristics of Chinese and Chinese characters decide the importance of this method of learning. Chinese characters have different meanings in different contexts and different usages in different sentence structures. What is more, Chinese words do not change their form when used for different grammatical functions. The grammatical means of indicating the structure of a sentence is not inflections, but rather word order together with function words. Reading aloud may stimulate students and help comprehension and analysis of the material, because the readers have to judge where the sense group stops in order to pause appropriately and decide what tones and intonation to use. They should read slowly according to the sense groups, analyzing the relationship between words and sense groups in the mind at the same time, and trying to construct a complete outline of the whole passage. Thus, they understand the meaning of words and structures better. For example, in *The Analects of Confucius,* one of *The Four Books* of ancient China, the word 仁, *rén,* whose basic meaning is "benevolence" and "kindness," appears frequently. When readers read the passages containing this word aloud many times, they will gradually remember the contexts of the word in different parts, so they can get the basic sense about its meaning and uses.

Second, China has an abundant literary heritage, and literary appreciation is an important component of learning Chinese. Reading aloud is beneficial to this part of learning as well. To achieve this purpose, learners have to read aloud, using appropriate facial expressions to show the theme, feelings, and images of the material as well as they can. This kind of reading involves the senses of sight and hearing and the skill of speaking at the same time; it sets up a connection between the eye and the ear, the mouth and the brain, which helps to internalize the writing system and contributes to the full appreciation of the materials. Chairman Mao used to adopt the method of reading aloud in his learning when he was young. Whenever he started to learn a prose passage, he would chant it repeatedly, trying to catch the theme, feelings, and rhythm. We ourselves also have such experience. I can still remember some famous literary pieces that I chanted time and time again and even recited by heart when I was in secondary school. One of these was Zhu Ziqing's "Spring," which describes a beautiful spring scene; another was the Tang poet Du Mu's poem, "On Epang Palace," which describes the palace's magnificent architecture. While reading these pieces aloud, I imagined myself to be in the scenes described and tried to convey my love and appreciation for their beauty. Sometimes I was moved to tears when I read aloud, so strong was the emotion that I felt.

Reading aloud can also be used to help readers improve their writing. In writing an essay, one has to choose meaningful words and use function words to combine them according to their possible combinations, as well as one's intended meaning. Reading aloud from model essays presented in learners' textbooks or from other sources familiarizes students with the rules for combining words into sentences and at last into whole essays. Moreover, they can master the style and the soul of the written texts and get some sense of their composition and artistic conception. The aesthetic patterns absorbed from a lot of reading will work their way naturally into students' writing. For Chinese learners in our schools, whose chief goal in learning Chinese is to master the written language, reading aloud is a very important method.

6. Classical Chinese Reading in Junior-Secondary School

Wu Lili

Any Chinese student, when proceeding to junior-secondary school at the age of thirteen or so, has to encounter the task of reading classical Chinese—that is, reading some ancient Chinese works or selections from them. Meanwhile, vernacular Chinese reading remains as important a reading task as it was in primary school.

In primary school, the reading texts are mainly simple prose narratives, such as short stories, fairy tales, tales of travel, and fables, as well as children's songs and ballads, all of which are written in vernacular Chinese. Even a few ancient Chinese poems included in the textbooks are so deliberately chosen that the language of the verses is similar to vernacular Chinese. In this case, most young children, provided they have learned a certain number of Chinese characters, can easily refer to everyday spoken Chinese when performing their reading tasks, because vernacular Chinese is the same as or similar to the Chinese used in ordinary speech (i.e., the standard dialect, which is used for school teaching; it is not, of course, the same as the other dialects).

However, students can no longer take advantage of their spoken language when they are required to read classical Chinese in junior-secondary school. Some reading skills founded on modern Chinese grammar may not work or may even mislead the readers. My mother is a Chinese teacher in secondary school and is enthusiastic about research in classical Chinese teaching. In helping her analyze test papers, I too have become interested in the problems that arise for students in classical-reading tests.

Most of the tests are composed of three parts: paraphrase in vernacular Chinese, identification of *tōngjiǎzì*, and punctuation. The testing materials may be extracted from either texts or other materials that are not presented for students, and both are discussed later in this essay. The textbooks used from 1987 to 1990 are consulted for reference.

Paraphrase in Vernacular

Errors in this part of the test typically reflect how students' classical Chinese reading is influenced by their vernacular reading. These errors can be classified into three kinds, which correspond to three distinctions between classical and vernacular Chinese.

First, the meanings of many characters in classical Chinese have undergone a great change. Students who are not so alert to that change may misparaphrase a given sentence. In the following example, an original phrase in classical Chinese is given with both incorrect and correct paraphrases, and an English translation is provided for each word and phrase.

Original:	说	之	以	厚	利
	shuì	*zhī*	*yǐ*	*hòu*	*lì*
	persuade	him	with	a lot of	gains

Incorrect paraphrase:	和	他	谈 论	优 厚 的 利 益	
	hé	*tā*	*tán lùn*	*yōu hòu de lì yì*	
	with	him	talk about	a lot of	gains

"to talk with him about a lot of gains"

Correct paraphrase:	用	优 厚 的	利 益	来	说 服	他
	yòng	*yōu hòu de*	*lì yì*	*lái*	*shuō fú*	*tā*
	with	a lot of	gains	to	persuade	him

"to persuade him with a lot of gains"

The Book of Hanfeizi

Contrasting the two paraphrases, we can see that the error results from the misunderstanding of 说, which, in its classical Chinese context, is pronounced *shuì* and means "to persuade," instead of *shuō,* which means "to speak" or "talk" in vernacular Chinese.

Another cause of frequent misparaphrase is the different syntax of classical Chinese. For example, classical Chinese and vernacular Chinese usually employ different sentence patterns to express the same meaning. Instinctively turning to their knowledge of modern Chinese syntax, students may run into pitfalls, as in the following example:

Original:	人	莫	乐	于	闲
	rén	*mò*	*lè*	*yú*	*xián*
	people	not	delightful	than	leisure

Incorrect paraphrase:	人	不要	陶 醉	在 空 闲 之 中		
	rén	*bú yào*	*táo zuì*	*zài kòng xián zhī zhōng*		
	people	should not	find pleasure	in	leisure	

"People should not find pleasure in leisure."

Correct paraphrase:	人	最	快乐的	莫	过 于	空 闲
	rén	*zuì*	*kuài lè de*	*mò*	*guò yú*	*kòng xián*
	people	most	delightful	not	than	leisure

"To people, nothing is more delightful than leisure."

You Meng Ying, by Zhang Chao

In this example, the students fail to comprehend the particular sentence pattern in the original and just paraphrase it through a word-for-word correspondence, as shown previously. To get the correct paraphrase, one should first interpret the original pattern in this way:

Original	莫		于	
translation:	*mò*	adjective	*yú*	noun
	not		than	

"nothing is more (adjective) than (noun)"

Paraphrase:	最		莫 过 于	
	zuì	adjective	*mò guò yú*	noun
	the most		not than	

"nothing is more (adjective) than (noun)"

Once the pattern is correctly interpreted, students are more likely to decide on the right paraphrases of polysemous characters, such as the two in the previous examples: 乐, *lè,* "delightful" or "to find pleasure," and 于, *yú,* "than" or "in."

Omission in classical Chinese is one more cause of misparaphrase. One kind of omission is of general referring nouns such as 人, *rén,* "a person, people"; and pronouns such as 其, *qí,* and 之, *zhī,* both of which mean "he/she, him/her, it, one, somebody, or something," and 此, *cǐ,* meaning "this, it." Another kind is of conjunctions and conjunctive adverbs, such as 而后, *ér hòu,* and 然后, *rán hòu,* both meaning "then"; 如, *rú,* or 若, *ruò,* meaning "if"; 时, *shí,* "when"; and 纵, *zòng,* "even." Both kinds of omission are found in the following example; for clarity, the omitted words are printed here in brackets:

Original:	[纵]	[其]	穷	[时]	则	独	善	其	身
	[zòng]	*[qí]*	*qióng*	*[shí]*	*zé*	*dú*	*shàn*	*qí*	*shēn*
	even	he	unsuccessful	when	then	only	better	his	character

Incorrect	穷 人	就	只 能	善 待	自己
paraphrase:	*qióng rén*	*jiù*	*zhī néng*	*shàn dài*	*zì jǐ*
	a poor man	then	can only	be kind	to himself

"A poor man can only earn his own living."

Correct paraphrase:	即使	一	个	圣	人	不	得	志	时
	jí shǐ	*yī*	*gè*	*shèng*	*rén*	*bù*	*dé*	*zhì*	*shí*
	even		a saint			when unsuccessful			

还	能	改 善	自 身 的	修 养
hái	*néng*	*gǎi shàn*	*zì shēn de*	*xiū yǎng*
still	can	improve	his own	character

"Even when he is not successful in his career,
a saint can still cultivate his own character."

Original:	[其]	达	[时]	则	兼	善	天	下
	[qí]	*dá*	*[shí]*	*zé*	*jiān*	*shàn*	*tiān*	*xià*
	he	successful	when	then	also	better	the	world

Incorrect paraphrase:	发达的人	就	还 能	善 待	世 人
	fā dá de rén	*jiù*	*hái néng*	*shàn dài*	*shì rén*
	a rich man	then	can also	be kind to	people in the world

"But a rich man can also be generous to other people."

Correct paraphrase:	[他]	得 志	[时]	就	还 能	造 福 于 世 人
	[tā]	*dé zhì*	*[shí]*	*jiù*	*hái néng*	*zào fú yú shì rén*
	he	successful	when	then	can also	benefit the world

"When he achieves his ambition, he can benefit the world as well."

The Book of Mencius

By comparing the incorrect and the correct paraphrases, we can presume that if the students are aware of what is omitted in the original, they will see that the two clauses are dealing with two cases of one subject (a saint) and pick out the correct meaning of the two polysemants, 穷, *qióng,* "unsuccessful" or "poor," and 达, *dá,* "successful" or "rich."

In most cases, a piece of classical Chinese contains more than one distinctive feature; therefore, the different kinds of errors may combine or overlap in the students' production of a paraphrase.

Identification of Tōngjiǎzì

Tōngjiǎzì refers to a group of characters, each of which corresponds to a different character in a vernacular Chinese paraphrase; but *tōngjiǎzì* are still used in vernacular Chinese, only with different meanings from their classical meanings and sometimes with different pronunciations as well. The character 见,

xiàn, "appear" in the following piece of classical writing may serve as an example of *tōngjiǎzì:*

Original:

图	穷	而	匕	见
tú	qióng	ér	bì	xiàn
map	end	then	dagger	appear

Paraphrase:

地图	展 到 尽 头	就	出 现 了 一 把 匕 首
dì tú	zhǎn dào jìn tóu	jiù	chū xiàn le yī bǎ bì shǒu
map	unfolded to the end	then	appear a dagger

"The map was unfolded to the end and a dagger appeared."

Intrigues of the Warring States

When the meaning of 见, *xiàn,* as used in classical Chinese, is expressed in the vernacular, the character 现, *xiàn,* must be used. However, 见 is also used in vernacular Chinese, but then it is pronounced as *jiàn,* and it means not "to appear" but "to see." Thus, 见 is a different character from 现, and 见, meaning "to appear," is termed a *tōngjiǎzì.* More examples are as follows:

Tōngjiǎzì:	简	还	女
Classical pronunciation	jiǎn	xuán	nǚ
Classical meaning	select	turn	you
Vernacular pronunciation	jiǎn	huán/hái	nǚ
Vernacular meaning	simple	return/also	woman/daughter
Vernacular Substitutes:	拣	旋	汝
Pronunciation	jiǎn	xuán	nǚ
Meaning	select	turn around	you

In summary, a *tōngjiǎzì* means a different thing or idea in classical Chinese from what it means in vernacular Chinese. Sometimes it is also pronounced differently in these two varieties of Chinese. Neglect of this characteristic of the classical language may lead to errors in either pronunciation or comprehension.

Punctuation

In analyzing this part of the test, it should be pointed out first that original classical Chinese works were written in vertical lines without punctuation. When included in modern textbooks, all are punctuated and printed horizontally. In a punctuation test, the marks are deleted and a paragraph consisting only of characters is left for the students to repunctuate. It is commonly agreed by both teachers and students that punctuation should be based on comprehension. If students fail to comprehend, they can only punctuate by guesswork. Consequently, the errors in this part of the exam are too varied to be classified in any simple way.

There is, however, one exception to this rule that deeply impresses me. It seems that some classical Chinese writings themselves may provide students with some clues as to how they should be punctuated. First, some characters may actually function as punctuation marks, even though in other contexts they have meanings and so can function also as words. For example, 耳, *ěr,* means "ear," and 也, *yě,* means "also," but either may be used simply to indicate a full stop. Similarly, 乎, *hū,* may suggest a question mark when used at the end of a sentence, and 哉, *zāi,* an exclamation mark, or a question mark when used with an interrogative word. Second, the repetition of the same sentence pattern may indicate a pair of antithetical phrases or a string of parallel clauses separated by commas. Moreover, some conjunctions may suggest continuation, such as 与, *yú,* "and," and 而, *ér,* "then" or "but." All of these clues will work significantly in the following example:

Original:	惟	江	上	之	清	风	
	wéi	*jiāng*	*shàng*	*zhī*	*qīng*	*fēng*	
	only	river	on	of	cool	breeze	
	与	山	间	之	明	月	
	yú	*shān*	*jiān*	*zhī*	*míng*	*yuè*	
	and	mountain	in	of	bright	moon	
	耳	得	之	而	为	声	
	ěr	*dé*	*zhī*	*ér*	*wéi*	*shēng*	
	ear	catch	it	then	become	sound	
	目	遇	之	而	成	色	也
	mù	*yù*	*zhī*	*ér*	*chéng*	*sè*	*yě*
	eye	meet	it	then	become	color	.
	取	之	不	尽			
	qǔ	*zhī*	*bù*	*jìn,*			
	take	it	not	end			
	用	之	不	竭			
	yòng	*zhī*	*bù*	*jié,*			
	consume	it	not	end			

是	造物	之	无尽藏	也
shì	*zào wù*	*zhī*	*wú jìn zàng*	<u>*yě.*</u>
this	nature	of	inexhaustible treasure	

(Function words, repeated sentence patterns, and conjunctions are underlined.)

Translation:

> Only the cool breeze on the river,
> the sound you can catch with your ears,
> and the bright moon in the mountains,
> the brilliance you catch with your eyes.
> You take it, it lasts forever,
> forever filling with wonder,
> the inexhaustible treasure that nature freely bestows.[6]

Fù on the Red Cliff,[7] by Su Shi

Instead of first comprehending and then punctuating, many students first punctuate passages like this one and then use the punctuation for the purpose of comprehension. However, one should not think that the punctuation of classical Chinese is rigid. As a matter of fact, classical Chinese enjoys a greater flexibility of punctuation than vernacular Chinese, associated with more flexible interpretation. For example, in one of the annual Chinese contests for junior-secondary students in the city of Huangshan, there was this question: On the top of a pottery teapot are engraved five characters in a ring, as shown in Figure 3-2.

Participants are asked to punctuate the sequence of characters with a full stop to get as many meaningful readings as possible. Full scores are given to the following performance:

1.

[其]	可	以	清	心	也
[qí]	*kě*	*yǐ*	*qīng*	*xīn*	*yě*
it	can		clear	mind	

"It can clear the mind."

---

6. This is my own translation, adapted from Su Xiaojun's. In her original essay, Wu Lili translated only the first and last lines of the poem. (Ed.)

7. A *fù* is a particular poetic form that can be translated as "prose poem" or "rhapsody." I am grateful to Su Xiaojun for this information. (Ed.)

Figure 3-2
An exercise in punctuating classical Chinese

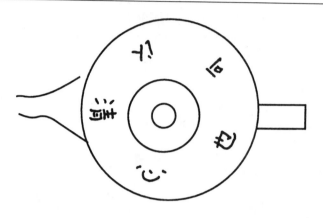

2.

以	[之]	清	心	也	可
yǐ	*[zhī]*	*qīng*	*xīn*	*yě*	*kě*
with	it	clear	mind	also	possible

"It is also possible to clear the mind with it."

3.

清	心	也	可	以
qīng	*xīn*	*yě*	*kě*	*yǐ*
clear	mind	also	possible	

"To clear the mind is also possible."

4.

心	也	可	以	清
xīn	*yě*	*kě*	*yǐ*	*qīng*
mind	also	can		clear

"The mind can also be cleared."

5.

也	可	以	[之]	清	心
yě	*kě*	*yǐ*	*zhī*	*qīng*	*xīn*
also	can	with	it	clear	mind

"It can also be used to clear the mind."

Sentences 1, 2, and 5 would be considered incomplete by a vernacular Chinese reader, as the omitted words are required in vernacular Chinese. The syntax of classical Chinese, however, allows such omission, and thus allows greater flexibility in punctuation and hence in interpretation.

Although I enjoy reading classical Chinese, I used to doubt its practical value in modern life. Once I argued with my mother and her colleagues about whether it was reasonable to include classical Chinese in textbooks, but I was convinced by a series of facts. First, classical Chinese is still used in some formal speeches and writing, such as invitations, memorial speeches, messages of congratulation, antithetical couplets, and epitaphs, all of which are associated with traditional Chinese culture and customs. Second, the classical Chinese reading materials that are used in schools are either literary or philosophical works. For example, *Composed by a Little Pool of Stones,* by Liu Zongyuan, is an enjoyable tale of travel, and *Hanfeizi* is a collection of comments and fables that illustrate the philosophical view of Hanfeizi, the ancient thinker. Reading such works helps cultivate the character as well as imparting knowledge. On the one hand, students may be positively influenced in forming their outlook on life and in developing their value systems; on the other, they may learn important language skills that they can employ in their own writing. A good Chinese writer tends to refer to the concise language, refined choice of words, and antithetical sentence patterns of classical Chinese; all these make his composition more polished as well as elegant, more convincing as well as appealing.

Part Two

The English Language in China

4

The Social Meaning of English

Whereas the previous chapters in this book have explored the background in first-language literacy from which Chinese students approach English, the present and subsequent chapters examine Chinese experience of English itself. That experience is considered first in a broad perspective, in terms of the social functions of English and social attitudes towards it.

Sociolinguistic studies in other parts of the world have demonstrated that English, as an imperial language (Phillipson 1992), evokes conflicting responses, often within the same individuals. The Sri Lankan students that Canagarajah (1993) describes, for example, declared a strong desire to learn English and even spent hard-earned money on extra tuition for it. At the same time, however, their responses to English classes and English textbooks demonstrated considerable resistance to the language and the culture that it represents. In broader terms, Kachru (1992) shows that while English must be regarded as an Indian language, given its role in Indian national life and the numbers of people that use it, it is nevertheless an "other tongue," expressing an ideology that is alien to indigenous Indian cultures. Similar contradictions are found in Anglophone-African experiences of English; there is constant tension between the desire to acquire and use it as a matter of practical necessity and the desire to reject it as an expression of foreign hegemony (Parry 1992; Schmied 1991).

It was such ambivalence that I attempted to bring to the attention of the Nanjing program participants as we began the unit on "Approaching English." Accordingly, I gave them for the first reading assignment Widdowson's article on "The Ownership of English" (1994), which questions the native speaker's assumed right to determine questions of usage and methodology, and three chapters from Masani's *Indian Tales of the Raj* (1987, 71–98), in which he reports Indian informants' feelings about the English language and the cultural values that they learned with it under British colonial rule. A week later, the participants read Canagarajah's article together with a critical response to it by Braine (1994). Finally, in the third week of the unit, they read an article about English-language teaching in China by Campbell and Zhao (1993). In response to these readings, the participants produced a diverse set of essays: some examined the changing social position of English in China, others reminisced about their own experiences of learning the language, while still others looked more specifically at how English is taught in Chinese schools. In this chapter, essays of the first two types are presented; essays of the third type are represented in Chapter Five.

As it happens, the first essay to be presented here is by a writer who did not read the materials just mentioned, for Liu Yuanyan was one of the participants in the 1992–93 program. Nevertheless, her essay suggests more strongly than any of them that many Chinese are indeed sensitive to the notion that English is an imperial language. She explains this sensitivity in terms of traditional perceptions of foreigners, which long predate Western colonial expansion. In the Confucian scheme of things, Liu maintains, relationships were necessarily hierarchical; thus, in encounters between nations, one had to be superior to the other, and it seemed obvious in all foreign contacts up to the nineteenth century that China was the superior party. Furthermore, according to Liu, the Chinese polity traditionally was perceived as a closed unit, sheltered behind the Great Wall, just as the ideal extended family lived at peace within itself inside a walled compound. To this kind of mentality, any outside influence, linguistic or otherwise, was considered a threat. Given this perspective, it is easy to understand why, as Liu points out, the nineteenth-century Western intrusion upon China should have been regarded as a terrible violation, and while the experience prompted some Chinese to study English in order to draw on Western technical expertise, it was with deep feelings of inferiority and consequent hostility. Such an analysis certainly explains the viciousness of Chinese reactions against English after 1949, especially during the Cultural Revolution, when, as is indicated in several of the essays, anyone who knew the language was regarded as a traitor.

In the next two essays, Chen Ting's "English in China" and Zhu Minghui's "Why Chinese People Learn English Now," the association of English with British colonialism and subsequent American cultural influence is explored in more detail. Both present the study of English in China as having grown out of the need for self-defense in the aftermath of the opium wars; but Zhu, in particular, points out that the originally limited aim of being able to understand treaties written in English was soon extended to being able to understand Western science and technology. Thus, English came to be sought after, not for its literature or for the values it represented, but for its practical usefulness. Both Chen and Zhu explain how this perception of the language strengthened in the first decades of the twentieth century, as Western commercial activity increased in China and as more opportunities became available for Chinese to learn English. A tension developed similar to that described in former British colonies: English was to be rejected because it was humiliating, but it was to be welcomed because it was useful and offered economic advancement.

It is this idea that English is useful that has become dominant since 1979; the language is associated with well-paid jobs and lucrative foreign trade, and this perception has brought thousands if not millions of Chinese to night schools to learn it. It has been embraced, moreover, in official government policy. Since the late 1970s, English has been a mandatory secondary-school course, and since 1983, it has been given as much weight as Chinese in determining who should be admitted to college. Similarly, a mandatory college-English exam (i.e., the College English Test Band 4) was instituted in 1987, and there is even an English exam for the promotion of those who work in public institutions. Most Chinese, therefore, who are learning English now are learning it for purely instrumental reasons, often limited to the passing of exams, and the lack of any real interest in English-speaking culture is expressed in the frequent assertion that English is "only a tool."

For some Chinese, reservations about the desirability of Western cultural influence may strengthen into actual hostility when English is forced on them in this way. In "The Present Craze for English: Negative Aspects," Du Qunhua suggests that secondary-school English classes are filled with students who can see no point in learning the language and do so only under compulsion; similarly, those adults who must demonstrate apparent proficiency in English to be promoted will use whatever strategies they can to get through the exam with a minimum of actual learning. Given such resentment on the part of millions of Chinese, coupled with the history of imperialist intrusion, it might not be difficult for a political leader who wanted to do so to provoke a renewed xenophobic reaction against the language.

Even now, when the Chinese authorities are actively promoting the teaching and learning of English, they are manifestly afraid of certain kinds of Western influence—witness their attempts to limit the impact of the 1995 United Nations conference in Beijing and of the accompanying nongovernmental organizations' conference in Huairou. The assertion that "English is only a tool" expresses well their apparently limited view of language learning, for they surely do not want the language to be sufficiently internalized for many Chinese to become deeply involved in English discourse. As one of the participants said in her response to the article by Campbell and Zhao, "They [the authorities] thought that [it]'s enough for Chinese to read in English. It's not necessary to know foreign culture and context as well as exchange thoughts with foreigner[s]. It can only cause trouble." But linguistic tools, even when only partially mastered, will inevitably open the way to cultural influence. This point is suggested by Wu Lili in her essay on "English Loan Words in Chinese," where she discusses how English enables people to express attitudes and manifest behavior that they would not normally express or manifest in their own language. The examples that she provides may seem trivial, yet they show the subtle ways in which learning a new language may cause or at least enable people to change. Thus, to revert to Liu Yuanyan's image, the language can be seen as a means of escaping the enclosed courtyard of the traditional Chinese community.

That English has intrinsic interest for at least some Chinese is amply demonstrated in the next three essays, which are personal accounts of the writers' own experience with the language. He Yue, the writer of "My Experience of Learning English," is the oldest of the participants in the 1994–95 program and, as such, is able to remember the persecution to which English speakers were subject during the Cultural Revolution. She describes vividly how children at the time were taught to equate interest in English with treachery. Yet only a few years later, English was reintroduced into the secondary schools, and teachers were sought out among those who had learned the language before 1949 and who had suffered for that knowledge during the past two decades. He Yue paints a moving picture of the dedication of her teacher despite what he had been through, and it is hard to believe that such teachers did not think that what they were doing was intrinsically worthwhile. That this is He's own attitude is clearly evident when she writes of her desire to see or read in the original films and novels that she had encountered in translation, and when she describes her excitement on finding that her present students are able to communicate with foreigners in English.

Sun Wenjing, who is eight or nine years younger than He, describes in "Why Do We Study a Foreign Language?" how she began to learn English at home before going to secondary school, being encouraged by her parents and inspired by the story of *Jane Eyre,* which her father had read to her in translation. She presents a charming picture of her childish delight in and wonder at a language that had only twenty-six characters, yet was able to express so much variety and meaning; her account of how she found herself able as a college student to use her English to communicate with foreigners is equally charming. She ends her essay with a reference to the Nanjing program itself, making explicit what we, the foreign teachers in the program, had inferred from the participants' behavior in class—that, despite the unhappy history of English in China, and despite the widespread and officially supported idea that the language should be regarded only as a means of gaining immediate practical advantages, they themselves found that learning it was an enriching and liberating experience.

The final essay of the chapter, Qin Haihua's "What Is English?," is interesting because in it Qin articulates the conflict between her own feelings about the language and currently prevailing attitudes. As one of the youngest in the 1994–95 group, she grew up at a time when English was more widely and better taught, and she was able to specialize in it as an undergraduate at one of the country's best universities. She writes warmly of the experiences to which this study of English exposed her, but is evidently worried about her recent decision to be a college English teacher. This is the only career, she says, that will allow her to pursue fully her interest in the language and the culture it represents, but the protests of her friends and relatives force her to question the wisdom of "sticking to English" because teaching is such a low-paying job.

In expressing this ambivalence, Qin demonstrates the main point of this chapter: Although China never experienced colonial rule, and although the status of Chinese (i.e., Putonghua) as its dominant language has never been questioned, the social meaning of English is as complex in China as it is in some former colonial countries. It includes a number of contradictory strands, and individual attitudes and motivation may be correspondingly ambivalent. But it is also clear from these essays that attitudes can and do change and, as will be suggested in Chapters Five and Seven, a significant factor in causing them to do so may be the influence of teachers. It is accordingly important that teachers, like those participating in the Nanjing program, should be encouraged and helped to think about such questions as are examined here, for it is only with a well-developed sense of the social context in which they are teaching the language that they can fully understand and adjust to their students' needs.

1. Chinese Attitudes Towards English

Liu Yuanyan

Chinese attitudes towards English, generally speaking, are based on feelings of superiority and inferiority combined. These feelings are sensitive, complicated, and subtle, and they have permeated Chinese relationships with other countries, the process of accepting or rejecting exotic ideas, Chinese concepts of social status, and many other social areas. Talking about Chinese attitudes towards English is actually talking about attitudes towards the nations where the language is used, towards the culture it carries, and towards the thoughts it reflects. The language itself does not matter that much.

If a topic involves culture, thought, and consciousness, we cannot talk about it in a Chinese context without talking about Confucianism, which has permeated every level of Chinese society and dominated people's thinking ever since its glorification after the death of its founder in 479 BC. What is more, the ingrained influence of Confucianism continues to be passed from generation to generation even now. The essence of Confucianism is obedience and respect: at the level of country, subjects obey and defer to the ruler; at the level of family, women obey and defer to men, sons to their fathers, and the young to the old. Through each imperial dynasty, this ideology inevitably maintained a society of rigid hierarchy and a government of centralism. Each member of society found himself or herself an appropriate and more or less stable position within a pyramidical structure, as superior to some people and inferior to others. At the top of the pyramid was the ruler. Of course, except for the ruler, the system meant that everyone experienced the two contradictory feelings of superiority and inferiority. This, according to Confucius, was how social order was established and maintained, and it was this concept of the order of society that was extended to the order of the world by the Chinese rulers themselves. Unfortunately, they put China on the top of the pyramid, and this led directly to ethnocentrism.

The other property of Confucianism is Confucius' image of the ideal community—united, peaceful, and harmonious. The idea is reflected in the Chinese notion of a happy family. Family reunion is the most common way of celebrating holidays, festivals, or any other occasion; the mid-autumn festival, for example, is set up specifically as a time for family reunion. Although the nuclear family is becoming popular in cities, the big family of four generations is still considered an enviable model. For the Chinese, unity, harmony, and peace—apparent or actual—are what they seek, what they take pride in, and what they treasure. The traditional Chinese building style expresses the same

106

idea: all the houses for one family, no matter how big the family is and how many members it has, are built within the same four walls for protection. What can be seen from outside are walls and a big gate that is always closed, with a small door in it big enough to admit one person. Similarly, the Great Wall functioned as the protecting wall for the big "family" of China. Although in Chinese history there has been no lack of warfare, every ruler had to bear in mind the idea that the Chinese people hated separatism and chaos. Within the wall, the Chinese wanted to maintain and enjoy peace and security and the ideas they set up as long as possible, and they had no wish to go outside. Even at the high point of Chinese history, during the Tang Dynasty (618–907), there are few records of China's invading other countries or making any expeditions to new lands.

Now it is time to consider these two properties of Confucianism together. The ideal of union, harmony, and peace within the walls, so treasured by the Chinese, and the concept of the necessarily hierarchical relationship between individuals and communities eventually combined to become a hotbed of ethnocentrism.

The greatness of China was proved in the Tang Dynasty. The capital Chang An, which is called Xi'an today, was a cosmopolitan city inhabited by a million people. The thriving economy, the advanced techniques, and the flourishing culture of Tang China were spread out to the world and, at the same time, attracted vassals, merchants, missionaries, and visitors from other countries. Unfortunately, the sense of superiority engendered at this time was carried on through the generations, till in the Qing Dynasty (1646–1911) it was shattered to pieces by the gunpowder that had been originally invented by the Chinese but was used by the European countries. Confronted with foreign cannons and opium, the Chinese government appeared cowardly and incompetent, and the Chinese people, seeing their country now as being almost at the bottom of the pyramid, automatically found a corresponding position for themselves.

The sense of humiliation and inferiority prodded the Chinese to go out to learn from the West and reform China. This was the first time the Chinese government sent students abroad to study and the first time many Chinese people went abroad by themselves to learn rather than to teach. Thus, when the door was forced open, the Chinese were put in an inferior position, both in their motherland and in other countries. When the reforms intended to strengthen China proved fruitless, what had once been the greatest and strongest empire was reduced to a semi-colonial and semi-feudal country. The Chinese people had no chance to know what superiority tasted like. They hated those foreign invaders, but in the meanwhile, they felt inferior to them and afraid of them. These feelings of hatred and fear have come down to us with history, and today people over seventy still carry such feelings with them.

After liberation in 1949, China closed its door to the West or, more precisely, to Capitalist society. By recalling the glorious history and culture of five thousand years and believing that communism, the most advanced society in human history, was what they were going to carry out, the Chinese people recovered part of their feeling of superiority. However, when China reopened its door to the West in 1980, the Chinese sense of superiority was hurt once again as people automatically repositioned themselves on the pyramid.

The combined feelings of inferiority and superiority have a new manifestation now, which is directly and obviously reflected in people's attitude towards the language, English. The one who knows English and the one who does not are put in certain positions on the pyramid. Compared with the ones who are confined within the invisible wall built up by the language barrier, those who know about English feel superior because English brings them closer to modern life, to advanced technology, and to the scientific and economic development of the world. On the other hand, when they encounter foreigners who come from developed countries, both those Chinese who know English and those who do not feel inferior, more or less. This feeling of inferiority is hard to accept and admit, whereas when Chinese stay within the wall, using only their own language and looking back over their own culture and history, all of them can feel proud.

However, we must face the fact that China is backward in economy, technology, and science, and it is only through learning English that we will be able to catch up. The feeling of inferiority may make us reluctant to go outside our linguistic wall, but we have no choice, at least not now.

2. English in China

Chen Ting

The position of English in Chinese social life is affected directly by the relation between China and the Western world; accordingly, English, as a tool and medium of communication, has experienced several ups and downs in recent Chinese history.

In the old days, during the period of feudalism,[1] China was a completely closed society. The emperors claimed that they were the dragons who were the sons of heaven, and everything they did and every word they said were the orders of heaven. The common people should simply follow and obey them. To stabilize their power, the emperors and their ranking officials pursued a policy of obscurantism. They kept the people in ignorance and tried their best to prevent the common people from getting in touch with new and advanced things. During the whole period of feudalism, most Chinese people led a life of "husband farming and wife weaving" (nán gēng nǚ zhī). The country maintained a self-sufficient economic system, so few people knew that the outside world even existed; Western languages, including English, were completely unknown.

It was in the late Qing Dynasty that groups of Chinese people began to know and study English as a tool. In the middle of the nineteenth century, world imperialism was developing quickly, and Great Britain took the lead in penetrating the Chinese market, using opium and guns as a stepping-stone into the country. With the ending of the First Opium War in 1842, the British set foot on the soil of China and, together with opium and guns, they of course brought their language. Because of their defeat in the First Opium War, the rulers of the Qing Dynasty realized that there was need for them to understand those people from the other side of the world and to know the guns in their hands and the boats sailing on the sea. Some enlightened officials began to study English, the language used by those foreigners.

Formal English-teaching in China began in the latter half of the nineteenth century. A group of high-ranking officials, led by Li Hongzhang, initiated a Westernization Movement that aimed to introduce the techniques of Capitalist production to China and to catch up with the world, while preserving the feudal rule of the Qing Government.[2] They set up a school and offered courses

---

1. See Chapter Two, Note 2. (Ed.)
2. This movement was known as the Self-strengthening Movement. For further information, see Fairbank (1992, 217–21) and Spence (1990, 218–20). (Ed.)

about the new information from Western countries. But compared with the obstinate power of feudalism, the influence of this group of people was weak. Few people could get the chance to attend this school, and English remained little known in China.

With the coming of the twentieth century, the imperialists entered much deeper into the country. They opened banks, set up new factories, and also built many mission schools. So in the first half of the twentieth century, English began to be associated with good jobs, rich salaries, and high social position.

My father was born in 1934. He once told me that he received all his pre-college education in mission schools, beginning with a kindergarten run by foreigners and graduating from a mission secondary school. He began to learn English when he was in the sixth year of primary school, and English was an important course at secondary level, "because," he said, "you had to know English if you wanted to get a good job after you graduated from school." In those days positions in banks, railroads, and postal services were regarded as the best and most stable ones—but most of those places were in the control of foreigners at that time, so you had to know English if you wanted to get a good position and quick promotion. That was why many youngsters were sent to the schools held by foreigners. Also, because not all schools could offer English courses and only children from fairly rich families could be sent to school (especially to the better schools), mastery of English became a symbol of a privileged family background.

From the end of the 1930s to 1945, the War of Resistance against Japan made the life of Chinese people miserable. Then, just when the Chinese wanted to enjoy the ending of the war, the Guomindang government, supported by America, provoked the Civil War, and the Chinese Communist Party started the War of Liberation. After Liberation in 1949, the Americans were also involved in the Korean War until 1953. These events caused English to be associated in Chinese people's minds with American imperialism.[3]

In the 1960s, the Chinese people fell into an even more confusing situation. All the things that were connected with new and old hostile elements became symbols of evil. English was regarded as the language of American imperialism, and it certainly could not be learned by revolutionary people. Those people who knew English were criticized and denounced as spies of imperialism, instead of being respected as they had been in the past.

Then, after about twenty years of confusion, Chinese people woke up again. In the late 1970s, Chinese leaders became aware of and impressed Chinese people with the gap between the Chinese economy and that of the Western world. They knew they needed new information and modernization.

---

3. Throughout the 1950s, the official policy was to "learn from the Soviet Union," and not from the West, so Russian became the foreign language of choice, and many former English teachers were now required to learn and teach Russian. See Dzau (1990a). (Ed.)

So the open-door policy was initiated. The policy again put English in a prominent position.

I remember that I began to learn English in 1977 when I was in the fifth year of primary school. At that time, English was not offered in primary school yet. My parents encouraged me to follow English lessons broadcast on the radio every day. I did not understand why my parents did so at that time. Later, I knew that they had realized that the English language would be useful and popular again as a tool in Chinese society, and they are proved right now.

In the past twenty years, English has become a bridge to the new modern techniques and the latest information. More and more people who know English are needed by the society, and more and more good jobs are waiting for those who know English. But this time, Chinese people use the language in a more active way than did those in the first half of the twentieth century. People who now try to master English want not only to look for a good job in a factory controlled by foreigners but also to organize their business, their life, and their country according to their own will. Take my father, for example: He strengthened his English in the 1980s and led a group of young people in his factory to learn English, because he wanted to communicate with some people from English-speaking countries in order to import technology and equipment and develop and improve the production of the factory.

Although English has had different meanings in China at different periods, it has never lost its basic purpose, which is to be a medium of communication. Its position has gone up and down with the change in relations between China and the Western world. But, however important the position it may hold, it can never take the place of Chinese in China, for China has her own traditional culture, after all, and Chinese is also a beautiful and systematic language. So English is and will be only a means to serve this country, and I think it always will be popular among the better-educated Chinese.

3. Why Chinese People Learn English Now

Zhu Minghui

After work, in the evening, people from every direction swarm into class-rooms to learn foreign languages, and most people learn English. Those who go to night schools are mainly workers, and some are students who are still at school. The latter can again be divided into two types. Some are just beginning to learn English at full-time school and come to night school to learn more; others are going to graduate soon and come to relearn English because they have not learned it well. So why is English so important and so popular? In China, interest in English has risen and fallen like the tide. The country is now witnessing its third tide of English learning, so before explaining the present one, I shall first describe the other two.

The first tide of English studying in China was after 1860. In 1842, China, being too poor and weak to defend itself, was forced to "open" its "door" by some Western countries' guns. It was forced to sign several unfair Sino-foreign treaties. From 1862, these treaties were all written in English, so the Qing government needed English translators badly. In this year, the government decided to set up an institution named *Tóng Wén Guǎn* ("Same Knowledge School") to train translators of English.[4]

Unexpectedly, translators who were originally trained to serve the Qing government by translating treaties into Chinese and helping Qing officials to communicate with officials from other countries, also introduced and spread physical science from abroad, such as chemistry, maths, physics, electricity, acoustics, optics, geography, hydrology, botany, and many other subjects. A course in general knowledge of physical science was offered in the institution so that translators could have a wider range of knowledge. Some young people were even sent abroad to study English. There, they learned not only the language, but also knowledge that they thought was useful in developing a country's economy and defense. Many people realized that only when China was strong and rich enough to defend itself would it not be bullied by other countries.

In the first tide of English learning, people paid much attention to intro-ducing the knowledge of technology. It was in the second tide that new trends of thought were emphasized. The second tide was around 1920. After the Bourgeois Revolution in 1911, the monarchy was overturned and the Republic

---

4. Cf. the account given by Ross (1992). (Ed.)

of China was founded. In the following several years, China was in tremendous confusion; some people with military power governed their own regions, and one of them even wanted to become emperor.[5] At this time, Chinese intellectuals launched a movement called "the New Cultural Movement." In this movement, they called on people to reject the negative aspects of Chinese feudalism and try to accept the ways some developed countries used to develop their economy. They advocated individualism and naturalism in the arts and upheld peace in society and democracy in politics. In their opinion, China should follow the same way as Britain, the United States, and Japan so that it could develop in both economy and defense. To learn more, many young people went abroad to study. When they came back, they brought with them not only new technical knowledge and new thoughts, but also different ways of living that were new to traditional Chinese people. However, only some young people from rich families could afford to go abroad, and later some promising young men (some of them from poor families) who were sent abroad by the government to study. Their numbers were small; more people learned English in China.

Each of the tides of English learning rose when China was in difficulty and needed fresh air and energy. The third tide came under this condition too. This tide began in 1979.

Only eleven years after Liberation in 1949, the country ran into difficulties. Chinese people were told that because socialism had already been set up, communism was not far away, and they thought they could enter communism by living in such a way that people shared everything. People were poor then, having just been through several wars, and now that they were told they could share, ordinary people of course took and ate as much as they could. The country's productivity was not sufficient to sustain consumption, and the situation was made worse by the three-year-long natural calamity that began in 1961.[6] Then the ten-year Cultural Revolution began, during which the slogan "The poorer, the more revolutionary!" was popular. The years from 1958 to 1976 did not bring China any development. On the contrary, the national economy was on the brink of collapse and people were very poor.

In any society, it is impossible for people to have spiritual life when their material needs are not met. The Chinese leader Deng Xiaoping realized this. So after he came to power in the late 1970s, we Chinese people "opened" our "door" once more, and at the same time opened our mind. People began to talk about money openly and to work hard in order to improve their material life.

At the beginning of the open policy, there were not enough opportunities for many people to become rich quickly at the same time. So some people

5. This is a reference to Yuan Shikai, the first substantive president of Republican China. See Spence (1990, 286). (Ed.)
6. The famine referred to here is described eloquently in Chang (1991). Chang, however, questions whether the calamity was "natural." (Ed.)

thought of going abroad. Among those who went abroad after 1979, some were sent by the Chinese government to learn advanced science and technology so that when they came back they could serve our country better. Other people went abroad at their own expense also to study, but they had to work very hard to support themselves. Most of them got not only knowledge, but also some money, which was nothing compared to what people had in developed countries, but compared to the resources of people in China, the amounts were significant. The success of these people made others dream of earning money abroad, and knowledge of English was the most important ticket they needed to make this dream come true. Increasingly large numbers of Chinese registered to take the TOEFL to have formal evidence of their proficiency.

In the past couple of years, however, the number of people taking the TOEFL is decreasing dramatically: in Jiangsu province, for example, seventy-two hundred people took it in 1988, whereas in 1994, only about two thousand took it.[7] Among the people who wanted to go abroad previously, some wanted to learn more, some wanted to make money, and some, especially people with much knowledge, valued the condition for their research and chances to give free rein to their ability. But now, because China is more open, there are many such chances in China too! So more people choose to stay, and we are now in the second phase of the third tide of English learning.

Now, Sino-foreign trade is increasing and communication with people from other countries is becoming important within China. This means that there should be more people who know English working in Chinese foreign-trade institutions. People who work in these institutions get higher salaries than ordinary people, as well as more chances to go abroad on business, so the competition for such jobs is keen—and the criterion by which employees are selected is their command of English.

Similarly, as China becomes more open, people from different countries come to run factories and companies in China. These enterprises need a large number of managerial personnel who can manage the enterprises and communicate with foreign bosses at the same time. Working in joint ventures also means higher salaries. If people know English, they have better chances to work there than those who do not know it. There are often advertisements in newspapers for managers, secretaries, and skilled workers. These advertisements say those who have both English and other needed knowledge and abilities will be considered first. This urges people, many of whom have already worked for many years, to go back to the classroom to learn English.

There is another phenomenon that should not be neglected. China is a country with an ancient civilization, and it has many interesting and historic places that are worth seeing. Nowadays, many people from other countries come to visit and travel in China, so the tourist industry is growing rapidly.

---

7. This information was provided by Yang Zhizhong, chief administrator of the TOEFL in Jiangsu Province. (Ed.)

The related trades, such as the hotel and restaurant business, are growing too. These trades also need more people who speak English; it is no surprise to see and hear taxi drivers, waiters, and waitresses say one or two English words or sentences.

I have outlined several reasons why more people are learning English now, all of which have something to do with money. There are also people who study English hard but not for money. They are from academic circles. This phenomenon has two aspects. On the one hand, academics, especially scientists, need to read articles about advanced technology in other countries; such articles are mostly written in English. If scholars know English, they can get the information quickly and conveniently without translation. It is always important and helpful for them to be informed of the latest developments in their own fields. On the other hand, there are some subjects in which Chinese scientists have made progress and English can help them to be known by the world. They need to be able to use English in order to communicate with scientists in other countries.

There are still other aspects to be considered. Of traditional Chinese knowledge, some is really advanced, such as traditional Chinese medicine. If people from other countries want to know China well, they must know something about this aspect of Chinese culture. Similarly, people from abroad will not understand China completely if they know nothing of Confucianism and its influence on Chinese people. And since foreigners have great difficulty in learning Chinese, Chinese people who know English are needed to bridge the gap.

Some other people study English just because they want to lead a life different from what they have now. They probably know something about Western lifestyles from films, television programs, magazines, and novels. As a result of English learning, many people, either consciously or unconsciously, will be influenced by English culture. Most Chinese who learn English, however, will not completely reject Chinese culture in favor of English. They have the ability to control what they take; that is, to retain what is good in Chinese culture and take what they see as positive from the West.

Although the Earth is the same one people inhabited several hundred years ago, we feel it is becoming smaller and smaller now, because transportation is more convenient and people can communicate more efficiently. The Earth has become a global village, with different countries being different families living in it. We should work hard to develop and protect this village together and, in order to achieve this, we have to communicate with each other. So we must have one language that most of us can understand, and English is serving as such a language; it functions as a tool to unite these families. China, as one of the families, cannot avoid communicating with others. We must learn from the advanced knowledge in other families and let other families share what we have. In order to get along well with others, we also should let them know what we are thinking. In this way we can protect and develop ourselves.

All these factors require us to learn English and to use it freely. More and more Chinese have realized that English can help us connect ourselves with the outside world. As the proverb goes, "Necessity is the mother of invention." The need to develop our economy connects Chinese people with people from other countries, and the need to communicate forces us to learn English.

4. The Present Craze for English: Negative Aspects

Du Qunhua

With the downfall of the "Gang of Four," the introduction of the open-door policy, and increasingly frequent contact with people from foreign countries, many people in China have come to realize the importance of mastering English. They think that it will help to promote friendship between Chinese people and people all over the world, and that through English they can learn about events outside our country and about foreign achievements in advanced science and technology. Almost overnight, English books, dictionaries, television programs, tapes, and training classes have prevailed in all parts of China. In short, English is booming, especially in the cities.

However, everything has both positive and negative features. As English is becoming more important, both secondary schools and universities have made it an indispensable part of the curriculum. So students have to study English, whether they like it or not, for otherwise they will not be able to get their diplomas.

The situation is especially serious for secondary-school students: whether they specialize in science or arts subjects, they cannot expect to be admitted to colleges, institutes, or universities unless they have passed the English exams. This situation leads to a number of problems. Those students who are weak in all subjects think that, as they have little chance of entering university, English is of no use; they attend English classes, but only passively. They haven't the slightest inclination for studying English, so the period is really a hard and unbearable time for them. Those students who do well in subjects other than English usually have some hope: once they have improved their position in English, they will perhaps be able to enter university. They usually exert greater effort and spend more time on English than on any other subject. Unfortunately, not all of them can achieve their aim. Despite their efforts, some still fail the English exam, thus losing the chance to enter university to develop their strong subjects such as physics, chemistry, or maths, and this is really unfair to them.

Students in university have different attitudes towards the study of English. Some have a personal purpose in learning the language; for example, to go abroad or get a good job in a big company. Others, however, have no ambition other than to pass the Band 4 exam. The former kind of students usually have greater motivation to study than the latter kind. The latter ones will be satisfied if their score is only sixty, which is the passing point for Band 4. Because of the nature of the exam, they expect grammar-oriented instruction

117

from their teacher, which they believe will be of great practical use to them in answering the questions. As speaking is not included in the exam, it is often neglected by both teachers and students. They usually think it is a waste of time to do any activities intended to practice their spoken English. Once they have passed Band 4, they put all their English books aside and feel as if they have finished something great; by the time they graduate from college, nearly everything they have learned will have faded from their memory.

Besides the required English exams in secondary school and university, those who work in public institutions are also required to take part in an English exam, one designed specifically for those who want to get promoted. This kind of exam is frowned upon and regarded as unrealistic by many people, for most of those who take it are already in their thirties or forties, and some are even in their fifties. It is hard for them to refresh their memory, since the English they learned in school or university has been long forgotten. The only thing that they can remember is the twenty-six letters of the English alphabet and everyday conversational phrases like "Good morning," "Good-bye," and "How are you?" What should they do if they have to pass the exam in such a short time, since they usually have only a few months in which to prepare? In such circumstances, the teachers assigned to coach them usually tell them what to review or, rather, give them some hint as to which paragraph in which book will probably be dealt with in the exam—for some of these teachers are testmakers themselves. Then the test-takers copy that particular paragraph down beforehand and learn the Chinese translation by heart. If the passage they have memorized happens to appear in the exam paper, they have got it and, without looking through the original paragraph, they write down the translation from memory. Such an exam cannot really be called an exam. It is not as serious as the exams taken by secondary-school and university students; it is a mere matter of form and can never show the test-takers' real ability in English. From the point of view of the test-takers, this kind of test is of little value and should be canceled, because it is a waste of their time and energy.

So learning English has its negative features, especially for those whose work has nothing to do with English and for those who have no intention of mastering the language. It is really unnecessary to set up a testing authority for them, because they can probably do well in their own sphere without knowing English. A teacher of Chinese does not need English to give vivid lessons to his or her students, nor does a teacher of fine arts need it to draw good pictures, nor yet a bank clerk to do calculations; for all such people, the time and energy spent preparing for English exams should be spent on things in which they feel interested, so that they will have more pleasure and enjoyment and will do their own work much better.

5. English Loan Words in Chinese

Wu Lili

Nowadays, English is popular in China, and more Chinese are showing their enthusiasm for learning it. When asked why they like it, those learners will scarcely hesitate in listing dozens of benefits that it offers: English is required to exchange culture and science with the rest of the world, English is important in foreign trade, English is helpful to further one's education. These are the reasons why most Chinese are learning the language. However, English has one other advantage, too minor to be considered a purpose of learning, that tends to be neglected although it is really appealing to many Chinese. That is, English, through its loan words, complements one's communication even in Chinese.

Now that China is open to the outside world, the Chinese language is also open to international communication. Many English loan words, instead of being translated into Chinese words as in the past, are directly inserted in Chinese speech. What is more noticeable, the loan words are no longer confined to professional jargon; everyday expressions like "Okay," "Hi," "Excuse me," and "Bye bye" frequently appear in ordinary communication. People, even those who favor those loan words, tend to regard their use as merely a kind of fashion or simply showing off. But, in fact, the prohibition of the loan words would make some speakers find it difficult to express themselves efficiently. In other words, some loan words are becoming fundamental rather than ornamental.

Why should this happen? Long as I have been interested in the insertion of English loan words in Chinese, I am not sure of the definite answer, but I am on the way to approaching it. I suppose the following classification of English loan words will illustrate something about why and how Chinese people choose to borrow English words.

One source of loan words is professional jargon. Technical terms from English used to be translated into Chinese according to either their meaning or their pronunciation. The translation of pronunciation (i.e., transliteration), in which the English syllables are rendered by similar-sounding Chinese characters, used to be considered the more convenient way and thus was employed in most cases. It would take some time, however, for the authorities to decide on one transliteration because there are so many homophonous characters in Chinese. Now, when there are so many English technical terms pouring into Chinese in a short period, transliteration is just lagging far behind. Even those terms that do have their transliterations tend to be used in the original forms for the sake of both authenticity and precision.

The other sort of loan words are everyday expressions, which—though outnumbered by the professional jargon—are more outstanding for their high frequency of use. They can be further subdivided into several groups according to the reasons why Chinese people use them in Chinese communication.

One group can be represented by the English expression "Okay." Chinese speakers use it in rising tone to solicit opinions and confirmation, in falling tone to show agreement and offer confirmation, and even as a hesitation sound to indicate an intention of negotiation or a hint of suspicion. That is not to say that the Chinese language does not have expressions for those concepts. A person who has never learned English may express those ideas quite clearly with Chinese expressions, which are, however, more complicated than "Okay." For example, in order to show a slight suspicion, one may say in Chinese *Shì zhēn de ma?*, "Be, real?" or *Shì zhè yàng a?*, "Be, this way?", but I suspect that those who favor English loan words would doubt their exact equivalence. They would argue that the Chinese expressions are likely to sound more suspicious and accordingly not so tactful, while "Okay" indicates more agreement or magnanimity than suspicion. As a result, it is believed that the insertion of "Okay" in Chinese speech could make the communication more concise and subtle. Other expressions like "Hi" and "All right" are used for similar reasons.

The expression "I love you" is another typical case. Although it does have a literal Chinese translation, that translation is seldom used in the spoken language to express one's affection, especially to the opposite sex. The Chinese expressions like *Wǒ xiǎng hé nǐ jiāo ge péng you,* "I want with you make friends" and *Wǒ xiǎng hé nǐ cháng qī jiāo wǎng,* "I want with you keep a long contact" are either too implicit to be to the taste of modern people or too ambiguous to be told from the Chinese equivalent of "I like you." For this reason, English learners in China appreciate "I love you" for its concise words and comprehensive meaning. But the most significant element of "I love you," I suppose, is the frankness and boldness it conveys by showing one's affection directly and overtly, qualities that are not traditionally characteristic of Chinese people. Other expressions associated with sex or marriage, such as *husband/wife, boyfriend/girlfriend, pregnant,* and *prostitute,* are used for similar reasons. What is particularly interesting, but not surprising given the conventions of Chinese women's behavior, is that Chinese women use them more frequently, for they are not expected to talk about marriage or sex openly. To sum up, this group of expressions seems to enable Chinese people to speak out what they need but are too ashamed to say.

Another group of loan words, by contrast, make Chinese people say what they have not wanted to say or at least have said less frequently. One representative example is "Excuse me," which corresponds to its Chinese equivalents *Láo jià, Jiè guāng,* and *Duì bu qǐ* . Usually, the Chinese equivalents are not considered necessary when one causes a slight disturbance or inconvenience to others, for example, by coughing when talking or passing by in front of somebody. If one persists in saying them in those situations, one would be regarded as being conspicuously polite; the convention is that, on the contrary, other people should show their concern for the one who coughs by either stopping speaking or saying (in Chinese) something like, "Oh, you're coughing. Did you choke on that hot coffee?" So those who are always concerned with their manners will find "Excuse me" a suitable way of expressing their slight apology. Similarly, instead of conventionally showing modesty, a few Chinese people are getting accustomed to expressing an overt acceptance and appreciation of a compliment by saying "Thank you," whereas the Chinese equivalent *Xiè xie* is considered only appropriate for expressing gratitude for a favor.

In short, more English loan words are coming into Chinese for various reasons, including those beyond my present knowledge. In spite of the argument about whether or not they are playing a positive role in Chinese communication, their use in Chinese speech indicates that, in some respects, Chinese patterns of behavior are being modified as a result of contact with the West. These modifications are reflected in the particular words that Chinese people choose to borrow from English.

6. My Experience of Learning English

He Yue

I began to study English formally after I entered university. Although my subject was English, I had to learn it from ABC since I knew little about it before I went to college. Most of my classmates were the same as me.

Just as I began primary school in 1966, the Cultural Revolution took place. My parents were teachers of foreign languages, but they did not intend to let me or my younger brother learn any foreign language, for at that time many people who knew such languages were suspected of having illicit relations with foreign countries and being inclined to betray our country. In that situation, my parents never taught us any foreign language, not even one word. I myself was afraid of learning English because my classmates or the other children would call me "little spy" if I knew English or Russian. The children, of course, were influenced by their parents who were not quite sure what the truth was, because truth and falsehood were confused during those years. My classmates often spoke about it like this: "Traitor, traitor, little traitor, betray our country and please the foreigner." (I once did the same thing with them.) None of us wanted to be a "little traitor" because we heard some adults had been arrested for being "traitors." So we took care not to talk at all about foreign things. I remember that two of my classmates were cursed sarcastically just because they said "Goodbye" to each other one day.

By the time I went to secondary school, the political situation had changed. English began once more to be taught in secondary schools, but English teachers were very few. I was still afraid of learning English, but as the school arranged to teach this course, I just studied it. Anyway, if something serious happened, I was not the only one concerned.

We once had an old man, who was sixty then, to teach us English when I was in junior-secondary school. He was my first English teacher. He had been declared a "Rightist"—that is, a conservative and reactionary who was opposed to the political revolution—by mistake and had been in prison for seventeen years.[8] He had just come out to teach English in our school. He was a kind old man who wore a pair of glasses with thick lenses because of his short sight. His English pronunciation and intonation were somewhat funny, and most of the boys in our class were always imitating him. But he was extremely earnest in his teaching and was never impatient with the sixty-four

---

8. For information about the anti-rightist campaign of 1957, see Spence (1990, 572–3). (Ed.)

of us. He even taught us to recite the patterns one by one after class. The pattern drills we practiced most at that time were: "What's this? What's that? This is a door. That is a window. These are desks. These are chairs." Unfortunately, after two months, our teacher died of lung cancer. Hearing of his death, most of us were very sad, and I was especially so, for I had just come to be interested in English and had just been made English study monitor in my class (although I did nothing more than collect and hand out the exercise books). But later, I thought, I would not have a chance to deal with English anyway because I would have to do physical work in the distant area of Inner Mongolia for the rest of my life.

I learned very little English in secondary school. The only thing I remember learning, apart from the drills, was the song "I Love Beijing Tian An Men," which was translated from the Chinese song. It goes like this:

I love Beijing Tian An Men.
The sun rises over Tian An Men.
Our great leader Chairman Mao
Leads us forward.

That was the first song in English I learned and also the one I remember clearly after twenty years.

I began to touch English again in Inner Mongolia in 1977 after I had been there for two years; like many secondary-school graduates, I had answered our Party's call to go to the remote countryside to do physical work and be taught by the peasants.

During the Cultural Revolution, youngsters whose parents did intellectual work and were regarded as *Chòu Lǎo Jiǔ,* "the Stinking Ninth,"[9] would not be easily allowed to study in colleges or universities. As the Gang of Four was driven from the political stage, our country resumed entrance examinations for college in 1977. So I had, after all, an opportunity to attend the exams— including the English exam, in which I got only thirty-six points, mostly by guesswork—and to enter the university.

From 1977, our country began to progress rapidly and seemed to have a bright future since the setting up of the open-door policy. My parents realized that English would be emphasized in China as it is in many other countries, so they hoped that I would learn English. As for myself, I had no special reason to choose English as my professional course. I had wanted to be a teacher from my childhood, probably because my parents were teachers. Since I hated mathematics and physics, I chose literature (either Chinese or English) and

9. During the Yuan Dynasty (1271–1368), the rulers divided society into ranks. From the top to the bottom were (1) officers, (2) officials, (3) Buddhist monks, (4) Taoist priests, (5) doctors, (6) workers, (7) craftsmen, (8) prostitutes, (9) Confucian scholars, and (10) beggars. In the Cultural Revolution, "Confucian scholars" were taken to refer to intellectuals, who had no high position then.

expected to teach it later. I liked literature very much in those years. I often saw Western films and read Western novels in Chinese, and I wished to see or read the original ones someday. I thought that if I had a chance to learn English, my wish would be realized. But the fact was that I had only learned a little English in secondary school and my vocabulary then was no more than thirty words (I tried to go over the book I had used in secondary school and found that I only remembered thirty of the sixty-two words learned). Therefore, I did not think I could be lucky enough to be chosen to enter any English Department of any school. Thus, I made Chinese literature my first choice and English my second; either Chinese or English literature would satisfy me.

For the first two years after the reintroduction of entrance examinations to college, it did not matter whether one's English exam grade was high or not. Most examinees were those who had been doing physical work and staying in the countryside for two to ten years. They had either learned some English in secondary school but had forgotten most of it after many years of laboring, or they had learned no English at all. Therefore, those whose Chinese exam grades were high and whose total grades were above the norm were given a chance to be admitted to learn English on the basis of an additional oral test (in which they had to imitate the examiner's pronunciation and repeat some English words). I was asked to take the oral test and chanced to be chosen to study in the English Department. I never thought that I would be so lucky because I had received very low scores in the written English test. As soon as I heard that I was admitted to the English Department, I made up my mind to learn the language well and decided to be an English teacher in the future.

I was quite lucky that my dream of becoming an English teacher came true. I have now been teaching English for about ten years, and the longer I teach it, the more I like it. I find it really interesting and significant work to do. Whenever I realize that my students can communicate with foreigners and with each other in English, I feel very excited. But it is a pity that there are still many gaps in my own knowledge of English, so that I often have more problems in teaching than those who went to university later, including my classmates in the United Board program now—I took fewer courses than they did. Although I have been teaching English for so many years, I am still not a fully qualified teacher, and I am always worried about my ability. I think it is essential for me to learn continuously, for otherwise I will not keep up with the developing society, the progress of the new generation, and the increasingly needed English-teaching profession.

7. Why Do We Study a Foreign Language?

Sun Wenjing

There are many different reasons for learning a language, but basically they all boil down to one thing: We learn a language to communicate with other people, and we learn a foreign language to communicate with people who speak or write a language that is different from our own.

English is an international language: More than half of the world's scientific and technical journals, as well as newspapers, are printed in English, and English is the language of three-fifths of the world's radio stations. There are more than three thousand languages in the world today, but the one that has had the most amazing, rapid, and widespread growth is unquestionably English. Chinese people study English to understand the world and, on the other hand, we use English to introduce our country and to enable the world to understand China.

Here I will tell you why I myself study English and how I first came to know about the language. During the Cultural Revolution, there were not enough books to read, especially in Western literature. One day in 1972, my father borrowed from one of his friends a Chinese translation of a novel called *Jane Eyre*. He read this novel to my mother and me every evening, since at that time we had no television set. Although I could not really understand it, I knew Jane Eyre had a poor childhood, she had a hateful aunt, and she was a teacher when she grew up. The novel made me ask many questions: "Is Jane Eyre a Chinese girl?", "Does she speak Chinese?", and "Why does she only teach one student?" My parents told me Jane Eyre was a British girl and she spoke English. "But where is Britain?" and "Do British people look like Chinese people?" My mother bought a small terrestrial globe, showed me where Britain was, and told me what kind of language they spoke. So when I was eight years old, I came to know there was another language in the world, which was English. And when I learned that my parents could not speak English, you cannot imagine how disappointed I was.

In 1973, when I was nine years old, there was a broadcast program that would teach English from ABC. My parents bought the teaching materials for that program—*English* written by Cheng Lin. I opened the book and thought, "Ah, English words are just the same as my parents told me. They look like Pinyin." From that time, I had my first English teacher—the radio. I remember at the beginning they said, "Good morning, comrades. Long live Chairman Mao! Long live Marxism-Leninism and Mao Zedong Thought!" After I learned the twenty-six letters, I realized that English words were all made up of combinations of these letters. How interesting English was! It only had twenty-six letters, but these twenty-six letters could express a person's feelings and thought. And people use English for international trade, international scholarship, and scientific research. . . . Now I still think English is a very interesting language.

I studied English for two years on the radio. I could read simple texts by myself and I could make simple sentences. I learned some grammar, such as tenses, yes/no questions, and question words. In our country at that time, students only began to study a foreign language when they reached secondary school. I, however, studied English for two years by myself before I went to secondary school. So two years later, when I entered the secondary school, I studied English from ABC once again. I remember one day my teacher asked me to read sentences: "This is a map. That is a map of the world. This is a map of China." After I read them, she was surprised. When she discovered that I had been learning English for two years, she said, "You are my teacher." But, unfortunately, the radio program was finished. So my parents borrowed some English textbooks for me to continue learning by myself.

Of course, studying English is no royal road, and there are no shortcuts. When I worked on it by myself, I felt I was not improving much. I would have liked to have given up, but I did not because my mother told me, "To begin is easy enough, to continue is tough, but to go on to the end of the road requires courage and effort."

When I was a college student, I read some English novels: *Gone with the Wind, Jane Eyre, Love Story,* and so on. I loved these novels, especially *Jane Eyre,* now that I could read it in the original. I also learned to speak English a little. One day I met some foreign friends who were visiting Qinghai, but they did not understand Chinese, and they were looking so anxious. I came up and asked them, "Can I help you?" I will never forget their happy faces. I told them how to get to the hotel and how to find many scenic spots in Qinghai. "If you go to Qinghai you should look at Qinghai Lake, because it's the biggest salt lake in China. On the way, you will see Sun-Moon Mountain and the famous river Daotanghe. And there is a well-known Bird Island near Qinghai Lake. If you like, you can get a ship to go to Haixin Mountain in the middle of Qinghai Lake. And another place is Taer Lamasery. If you don't go there, you may regret it later. . . ." I felt so happy after they said "Thank you." I suddenly realized that if you know another language, you will find the world becoming small.

I think that if you study a foreign language, you will escape the world of your own language and people. You will be able to detach yourself and see your own world in perspective. In mastering a foreign language, you will become rich, not in a material sense, but in feelings; for you will make friends in a new world, just as now, in this program, we are sharing thoughts, ideas, and emotions with our foreign teachers through English. In China there is a wise saying: To find a friend is to find a treasure. So if you want to make friends all over the world, please study English because English is an international language.

8. What Is English?

Qin Haihua

English is becoming increasingly popular these days. With China's "open-door policy," there have emerged so many joint ventures and the foreign-trade businesses have become so prosperous that people find themselves out of the lot without English. Learning English has become a craze. It is time we stopped and asked ourselves the question: What is English?

To me, English means something new, something out of my reach that I would like to know about. In secondary school, English was my favorite and best subject. I was a science student at that time, and university English departments are usually only open to arts students. However, in 1990, the English Department of the University of Nanjing began to enroll science students. So I chose this department without hesitation. I majored in English language and literature. I have to say that I am not qualified to be called an English-literature major, because the literature I have read is too limited; but all the same, English has brought me a new world.

With the study of English, I have access to something foreign, something new to me that I have never known before. For example, there are so many interesting foreign customs. Valentine's is such a beautiful day, not only for lovers, but also for friends and relatives. And I will never forget the Christmas Eve of 1991 when we ten girls, in white, stood in a row, holding candles in our hands and singing "Silent night, holy night." The lights were all out, the audience so quiet; I was lost in the calm and peaceful night and felt such a soothing feeling I have never felt before. When I read *The Gadfly,* I burst into tears when Arthur and his girlfriend bade each other farewell. In *A Passage to India,* my mind went along with Aziz's uncontrolled emotions of warmth and friendliness and coldness and hatred. There is so much flavor that I could not know if I did not know English. Nor would I have had a friendly conversation with an old Australian lady about the chrysanthemums in the warm sunshine.

However, realistic people should not stick to English, because for most Chinese English is only a tool. I was warned by many people, including my father and some of my English teachers in college, that the language was no more than that. They concede that English is connected with "foreign," which surely means a good job with a high salary and good working conditions, a job with bright prospects. However, for practical use, it is not the English language itself that is valued, but the information and knowledge the language conveys. The ultimate goal of knowing the language is to get the target information and make use of it, while the language itself is nothing more than the connecting part, the conveyance. English alone is nothing, as far as practical considerations are concerned.

That is why I felt so diffident when I had to apply for a job at the end of my university career, even though Nanjing University is one of the top universities in China and I was not a bad student in my field. My problem was that I had learned nothing besides the language of English, and no company needs pure English.

Knowing that now I am a college-English teacher, many people say to me, "College is good, very peaceful. It's suitable for you girls. But why didn't you try for a better job?" I know what they mean. I could have got a job in a foreign-trade company in my hometown with a much higher salary, but I know that that would mean my four years of English study would be almost useless except as an entrance ticket to a well-paid job. I would regret this.

Many of my former college classmates are now working in foreign trade companies, banks, insurance companies, and so on. They are making money because these are all profitable jobs. But I don't think they are using much English except for some simple business correspondence. What is the point of spending four years studying and then giving up English almost completely after graduation? My classmates have abandoned their specialization, nor are they well qualified in the fields in which they are now working because they did not study them when they were in university.

Maybe I am quite wrong to be thinking this way. If English is no more than a tool, why should I stick to it and become a tool of a tool? One should be clever enough to make use of it. Now that the chief criterion for success is how much money a person can earn, I clearly belong to the unsuccessful group. Maybe I should drop teaching English and go for a job that will make me "successful." But I always hold the idea that English is a friend I cannot easily desert, one that has opened a new and attractive world for me. Many people disagree, and it is difficult to say which of us is right, for we clearly have different standards of judgment.

5

English in the Chinese Classroom

The astonishing spread of English across the globe has resulted in new perceptions not only of the language, but also of what is involved in language teaching. Traditionally, in the Western world, foreign languages were taught by the grammar-translation method: students learned vocabulary lists and grammatical paradigms and applied this knowledge to translation exercises both out of and into the foreign language. Similar methods were found in East Asia too: Hino (1992) reports that Chinese was taught in just this way in Japan, and so was Dutch, at a later date. But such methods were not feasible in classrooms where English was taught as a second language by teachers who did not know their students' mother tongues, nor were they appropriate when students needed to acquire oral fluency. In the immigrant countries of North America and Australasia, and also in the British Empire (and later Commonwealth), teachers had, perforce, to teach English through English and, as the profession of TESOL (i.e., teaching English to speakers of other languages) grew, these methods developed so dramatically that many described the field as having undergone at least one "paradigm shift" (Raimes 1983).

The starting point of this shift was the behaviorist view of language as a complex set of conditioned responses. In accordance with this theory, teachers in the 1950s and 1960s tried to condition their students appropriately by using grammatical drills and substitution exercises, and they carefully controlled any productive use of language lest mistakes should become established. The theory, however, was undermined by the work of Chomsky (1957, 1965), who argued that children learning their first language were not simply learning a set of predetermined responses but were developing an innate, uniquely human, and essentially creative capacity for thinking and expressing thought through syntactic structures. This development led to a more imaginative approach to

English-language teaching: Students were encouraged to hypothesize about grammatical rules and to test their hypotheses by constructing their own sentences. With the development of theories of interlanguage (Selinker 1972), mistakes came to be regarded in a more positive light, as indicating natural stages in the acquisition of a new grammatical system.

However, language is not only a matter of individual cognition, it is also a social phenomenon, as was emphasized by Hymes (1974) in the development of his theory of communicative competence. To know a language, Hymes argued, implies not only knowing vocabulary and a set of grammatical rules, but also knowing the social conventions that govern the use of particular forms in particular circumstances. This model of competence has led to more emphasis in English-language teaching on the appropriate expression of social relationships, whether between listeners and speakers or between readers and writers. It has also led to greater attention being paid to the sociocultural context in which language is used and a desire to work with materials that are both meaningful and authentic (e.g., Cathcart 1989).

With the increasing emphasis on social relationships, there has been a growing tendency to question those relationships themselves. In many Western classrooms, this has meant a reexamination of the role of teachers and, to some extent, an abdication of teachers' authority in favor of students' initiative (Hill 1994). In such classrooms, teachers make great efforts not to tell students, as writers, what they are to say (Reid 1994). They encourage them, as readers, to engage actively in the construction of meaning (Zamel 1992), and they ask them, as language learners, to explore and develop their own learning strategies (Oxford 1990; Scarcella and Oxford 1992). All this has led to a radical restructuring of classroom activity: students sit in circles or in groups, they talk as much as they listen, and they are expected to learn as much from each other as they do from their teachers.

Such changes, however, have been by no means universal in the Western world and they are distinctly unusual elsewhere. In many African and Asian countries, most classrooms, including English ones, look much the same as they did half a century ago: The students sit in straight rows facing the teacher, the teacher does most of the talking, and where students and teacher share a common first language, the talking tends not to be in English. There are many reasons for the maintenance of this pattern: Classes are usually large and therefore difficult to organize in any other way; teachers are insecure in their own English and so, even if they speak it, are unwilling to allow any unplanned discussion; both colleagues and students exert pressure on teachers to assert their status as sources of authority; and there is an exam to be worked for, the demands of which seem incompatible with more communicative styles of teaching. All these factors combine with natural conservatism to create powerful resistance to change.

On an international scale, therefore, English-language teaching is characterized, at the end of the twentieth century, by a growing disparity between "modern" and "traditional" methods. This disparity all too frequently parallels such politically charged distinctions as between "European" and "non-European" cultures and between "developed" and "developing" countries. Like the language itself, then, English-teaching methodology has its political overtones: Native-speaking teachers and teacher-trainers who sally forth to Africa and Asia to promote better methods of teaching can all too easily be accused of linguistic imperialism (Phillipson 1992), on the grounds not only that English itself is an imperial language, but also that the methods they use constitute an imposition of Western cultural values. Western professional experts have begun to articulate and examine this problem (Widdowson 1994; Edge 1996), but it has so far been little explored from the perspective of non-native-speaking teachers who are teaching English in their own country.

This problem, therefore, was a major theme underlying our work in Nanjing, and we encountered it at various levels. First, my American colleague and I naturally used teaching methods that we had developed elsewhere and believed to be most effective. We expected the program participants in their role as students to speak in class, both to us and to each other; we frequently asked them to work in groups or pairs; and we rarely told them the "right" answer to a question, but rather opened it up for discussion. Such methods were new to many of the group, and some of them admitted later to having been quite uncomfortable at first. Second, in both the linguistics and the methodology courses, as well as in the reading and writing course that is represented here, the participants were learning much of the theory that underlies this approach. They read about language learning, for example, as part of a broader process of socialization (Bruner 1993); they considered language in general, and writing in particular, in relation to its communicative functions (Chaika 1994; Katz 1993); and they discussed the importance of motivation in language learning and its relation to perceived communicative goals (Brown 1994; Heny 1994). These ideas challenged not only the classroom practices to which the participants were accustomed, but also more fundamental perceptions of language and social relationships, both within the classroom and outside it. Third, the participants saw, in a demonstration class given by my colleague, how the principles of communicative language teaching could be put into practice with Chinese students, and when it came to teaching practice, they were encouraged to experiment with such methods themselves. In doing so, they were not only taking in new ideas, but also were making these ideas manifest in their own behavior. This meant convincing their students, as well as themselves, that the ideas were sound and would produce more effective teaching and learning.

The papers in this chapter, then, constitute a commentary on established methods of teaching in China, informed by the participants' experience in the program. As such, they reflect some skepticism regarding the applicability of Western ways to the Chinese situation and an acute awareness of the institutional and social constraints on effecting change; but they also show a growing spirit of criticism and a sense—which apparently is felt well beyond this particular group—of an urgent need for reform.

The first two papers are essays written by Rao Zhiren and Zheng Guolong in response to the third of the first term's assignments, "Approaching English." Rao presents a gloomy picture of a class devoted to rote memorization and mechanical exercises. He makes no bones about the fact that he found English dull (indeed, in an earlier draft, he suggested that he still does), but it is clear that at the time he did not question the methods used and that he, indeed, appreciated the large amount of time spent on exam practice. Zheng, on the other hand, in his essay on "Two Teachers," describes what seems to have been an exceptional individual who, long before "communicative-language teaching" was widely talked of in China, taught most of the time in English and encouraged his students to infer meaning from pictures and gestures. Zheng and his classmates evidently loved this teacher (indeed, he must have been a remarkable man), but unfortunately they were to spend only one year with him. Their teacher in the second year was, as Zheng says, much more "traditional," and in describing his methods, Zheng presents another picture of unrelieved boredom.

Rao's and Zheng's papers refer to secondary-school teaching as they experienced it in the 1980s; Bao Jingying brings the account up to date by describing two secondary-school classes that she observed during the program in 1995. This and subsequent papers in this chapter were written in response to the research assignment during the second term. As such, they are interesting not only for the data they present, but also for the evidence they provide of the participants' initiation into the principles of empirical observation and of the degree to which, by the second term, they had come to subscribe to the ideas encountered in the first. In their original form, some of these papers included substantial discussion of the issues outlined in this introduction; I have had to cut out most of this discussion, in the interest of saving space.

In "Problems of English-Teaching in Secondary School," Bao describes two classes in what is reputed to be an extremely good school; it is ranked highest of the senior-secondary schools in Nanjing (hence its designation as a "key" institution), and Nanjing is one of the most educationally advanced cities in the country. One of the classes was, moreover, a demonstration class, presented as a model for other teachers to follow. It is a measure then, of the distance between Chinese and Western perceptions of "good teaching" that Bao found even the demonstration class inadequate in its communicative use of English, while the regular class seems remarkably similar to those described by Rao and Zheng.

In the next paper, "English-Language Teaching in China: The Gap Between Secondary School and College," Gu Tiexia also reports on classes that she observed, but these include a college class, as well as two senior-secondary-school ones, and her focus is on the relationship between them. The secondary-school classes follow the same patterns reported in the previous papers; in the college class, Gu describes a teacher who seems to be trying valiantly to teach in English but with little success. Gu's description shows all too clearly how it is possible for Chinese students to sit through years of English lessons and emerge quite unable to speak the language. It argues again for more extensive orientation of teachers not only at secondary school, but also at college level—if, indeed, as the participants assert, it is competence in spoken English that is now most needed.

He Yue, in "Traditional and Communicative Approaches in China's College English Teaching," reports more extensive observation of college English classes, as well as interviews with a large number of teachers and students, and she addresses directly the question of why communicative-language teaching is being taken up so slowly in China. The classes she observed largely followed the grammar-translation method; although there was some variation in the amount of English used, in all cases, the focus was on either explaining the text or checking whether exercises had been done correctly. As for the interviews, the teachers (especially those who had worked in the Nanjing program) showed some interest in communicative-language teaching, but also some skepticism with regard to its practicability, while the students seemed to think that it might be fun, but it could not be relied upon to get them through the exams. He Yue concludes that neither Chinese teachers nor students are ready to adopt a wholly communicative approach nor, she suggests, is it desirable for them to do so. The traditional method has some real merits in the discipline that it imposes and the firm knowledge base that it establishes; so she argues that elements of grammar-translation should be retained even while more communicative activities are introduced.

Through all these papers, as in earlier chapters of this book, a major theme is the effect the exam system has in inhibiting change. The chapter ends, therefore, with a paper by Du Qunhua on "The College Entrance Exam and College English Test Band 4: Effects on English Teaching." Du provides an overview of both of the major national English exams and then analyzes samples of their reading components in some detail. She shows clearly how these reading components, like those in other examination systems (Hill and Parry 1992), militate against any holistic and integrative approach to language. In addition, she provides data from a small survey of secondary-school and college teachers to show that their teaching is so directed by the exam that the requirements of its tasks are particularly influential. Real reform in China's teaching of English, she concludes, depends on change in the exams, although she also argues that even within the constraints of the system, teachers can do much to make their teaching more lively and communicative.

The picture of English-language teaching that emerges from these papers is one of remarkable uniformity. China is an enormous country, and the writers of the papers in this chapter come from various parts of it—Rao from Guangxi in the south, Zheng from Heilongjiang in the north, Bao and He from the east-central province of Jiangsu, Gu from Liaoning in the north, and Du from the central province of Hubei—yet the classroom practices that they report are virtually the same; where there is variety, it is clearly a function of the personal qualities of individual teachers. Of course, in assessing how representative these accounts are, the urban bias of the program participants must be remembered (see Introduction, p. xi). However, given the relative lack of resources in the countryside, one can only suppose that the tendencies remarked here are, if anything, more pronounced in rural schools.

A second feature of the picture is the evident conservatism in how English is taught. This conservatism can be explained in terms of more or less universal features of foreign-language teaching: Where the language is not needed for immediate communication and there are few sources of input outside the classroom, it is a common tendency for teachers to teach about the language rather than through it, and it is equally common for them to use their own and the students' first language for the purpose. These tendencies, however, may be exaggerated in the Chinese situation. It was only quite recently that English-language teaching was reintroduced after the Cultural Revolution (see Chapter Four), so that the teachers of today's teachers necessarily used the methods of a previous era; and today's teachers naturally tend to teach in the way they were taught themselves. Furthermore, the grammar-translation method so prominent in the descriptions given here is entirely congruent with the methods of teaching Chinese described in Chapter Three. There is the same emphasis on individual lexical items as in the initial teaching of Chinese characters, and there is the same analytical approach to grammar as Wu Lili describes in her essay on classical Chinese (see pp. 89–97)—though the use of oral reading of whole texts, as described by Wang Kui (see pp. 85–88), is conspicuously absent.

A third and most striking feature is the way in which English-language teaching, as conducted in China, reflects Chinese patterns of authority. The education system, like the political system as a whole, is both centralized and hierarchical (see Chapter Two); the means of maintaining the central authority, as well as all the gradations beneath it, are exams, backed up by prescribed textbooks. English teaching is as dominated by the exams as is any other subject—indeed, more so, because the score in English in the CEE is now considered the most decisive factor in determining whether a student is successful;[1] it is these exams that justify teachers' authority and ensure students' discipline. It seems, then, that the English exam has come to play in modern times the part that the *kējǔ*, or imperial examination essay, played in the past (see the essays by Su Xiaojun and Wu Liangzhe in Chapter Two).

Yet there is a difference, for English is a foreign language, and a living one at that, which provides opportunities, for some Chinese at least, of communication with people with quite different perspectives from their own. The difference is particularly apparent in professional discourse about language

---

1. I was given this information in June 1996 by Donald Snow, who, in his work for a Chinese nongovernmental organization, the Amity Foundation, had been interviewing teachers in rural teacher-training institutions in Jiangsu and neighboring provinces.

teaching, and it is the very question of authority that is at issue. As the papers in this chapter show, the participants in the Nanjing program were increasingly questioning the authority of traditional teaching methods and of the exam system to which teaching is directed; they were reconsidering, too, the nature of their own authority in the classroom. This does not mean, however, that they were simply accepting as an alternative orthodoxy what my colleague and I were telling them. As He Yue's paper shows, they were using the program to examine their own ideas about language and language teaching, asserting what they thought to be good in the Chinese system and becoming increasingly critical of what they thought to be bad. In this way, we hoped, they would become more autonomous as teachers and would acquire sufficient confidence to allow their students more autonomy too. It is ironical that the encouraging of such autonomy should appear as a manifestation of linguistic imperialism.

1. Approaching English

Rao Zhiren

The first time I encountered English was when I enrolled in junior-secondary school in the early 1980s. The language attracted me deeply. It sounded beautiful, and my teacher told me that we had to master it because China had begun her reform and opening to the outside world, and urgently needed people who could speak it. Chinese people with English-language proficiency would act as a kind of bridge between Chinese and English speakers, getting information, interacting, and coming and going with each other. I realized that English was the main means of access to the outside world, so I made up my mind to do well in it.

But English proved a long and difficult way for me to walk. It required much painstaking work and was boring and dull. Each lesson in our textbook consisted of an English text, words and expressions with Chinese explanations and notes, comprehension questions, and translation questions. In class, what I did first of all was to follow my teacher reading the new words and expressions by rote again and again, until we felt exhausted and couldn't stand it. Then my teacher explained the new words one by one. Many examples about the word usage and grammar rules would be given on the blackboard so that I had to take notes. We were forced to learn the notes by heart out of class and then recite them before the teacher. This kind of teaching turned us into bookworms. Many of us could read and understand English, but it was difficult for us to speak and listen to it. It was a case of inculcation rather than interaction, of being fed unwillingly rather than learning through practice. I spent much time memorizing isolated words and idioms; book in hand, I muttered incantations while comprehension and context eluded me.

Actually, I was encouraged to learn English in context, since my teacher often gave us background information and asked us to learn more about it, but if I had not memorized anything it was impossible for me to understand. Class was always in Chinese: my teacher hardly spoke English at all; neither did I. If, on occasion, the teacher spoke a few words of English, the subject seemed to me to be more difficult than ever because, since I couldn't speak it, I found it difficult to listen to. In any case, my teacher advised us to recite more English words and idioms and told us that our English acquisition would be in direct proportion to our English vocabulary size. If we had a large vocabulary, he said, we would learn English well and easily, but I don't think now that he was right.

As for exercises, my teacher emphasized grammar rules, reading comprehension, and word usage. There were no oral exercises or listening exercises, nor any interactive work for me. I spent much of my time in doing test papers and none in writing responses and book reports. These test papers consisted of multiple-choice and cloze questions, and at the time I thought them most useful to learning, because questions of that kind accounted for most of the marks on the exam. Here is an example of the kind of phonetic exercise that we did:

> In each item, choose from (a), (b), (c), or (d) the word of which the underlined part sounds the same as the part underlined in the word given:
>
> 1. brush   (a) build   (b) busy   (c) judge   (d) refuse
> 2. food   (a) foot   (b) book   (c) cool   (d) look

The following is an example of a vocabulary exercise:

> Choose from (a), (b), (c), or (d) the best word to fill the blank:
>
> He has been offered a _____ job in Paris.
>
> (a) plum   (b) nutty
> (c) seedy   (d) apple-pie

It was the same with reading comprehension. After reading a given text, I was asked to finish the multiple-choice questions about the text. There was no listening and speaking class for us. I didn't hear a native speaker speaking English during the whole period of secondary school. What I did was to prepare for the different examinations, which was the most urgent thing for me to do.

My way of approaching English was difficult for me, yet no matter what I encounter in approaching English, I am sure I will go on in the future. On the other hand, I will adapt myself to new teaching methods, when I will be as a learner in the classroom. I think there is no short way to English acquisition but hard work, and serious study is the only successful way to English acquisition. "Knowledge is indefinite," and "To live is to learn."

2. Two Teachers

Zheng Guolong

Secondary-school students are required to learn a foreign language in China, and English is the favorite option. I chose English as my second language when I was enrolled in secondary school in 1986. Here I would like to discuss my own learning experience in the first couple of years.

Because it was the first time for me to study English, I felt quite excited at first and began my learning with great curiosity. Our teacher then was a graduate from Heilongjiang University, where he had majored in English. He was one of the most interesting and humorous men I've ever met. He taught us with brand-new teaching methods, which made both him and his class attractive to us. I can still remember clearly the lessons he gave.

Unlike other English teachers in our school, he seldom spoke Chinese in class but used signs and pictures to make students understand the meaning of words, phrases, and sentences. The textbooks were grammar-centered, but our teacher tried to teach us to learn words in context. Every class, the teacher brought with him many colorful pictures that he collected by himself, under which he wrote the words we had learned. He asked questions while pointing at one of the pictures. For example, there was a picture in which there was a car. The teacher asked, "What is this?" The students might answer, "This (it) is a car." Then the teacher showed us other pictures and kept on with the question, "What is this?" and the students would go on with the answer, "This (it) is a _____ ." Sometimes the teacher would put one of the pictures on the window; then he would stand near the door, pointing at the picture and asking, "What is that?," and the students would answer "That (it) is a pen." Over a period of practicing, we came to know what the words *that* and *this* meant, even though the teacher didn't speak a Chinese word.

It is quite difficult for English beginners to learn tense. I can still remember our teacher taught us the future, present progressive, and past tenses with a comparison. He wrote down three sentences on the blackboard, which were like the following:

1.   I will take the book off the table.
2.   I am taking the book off the table.
3.   I took the book off the table.

These three sentences are the same with different verb forms. He made a chart on the blackboard like this:

The teacher demonstrated actions to make us realize the difference between the three tenses. Such teaching made us gradually acquire the abilities of comparison, analysis, and induction in English learning.

At that time, English classes were so attractive that I was eager to attend them. Our class got better grades than the other classes in the final exam at the end of the school year. All was changed, however, when we moved to the next year's work and a new teacher took over. He taught the second volume of the same textbook with the traditional teaching method. That is to say, he talked throughout the whole class time, mostly in Chinese, and seldom offered opportunities for students to speak. He asked us to memorize endless words and grammar rules in isolation. When we read texts, he asked us to focus on grammar rather than content. We spent a lot of time trying to memorize grammar rules, such as the following:

1. Present continuous indicates what is in progress or is happening at present time.

2. It is formed by "am (is, are)" + present participle.

3. Present participle is formed by adding "-ing" at the end of the verb.

4. The negative of it is formed by adding "not" between "am (is, are)" and present participle.

At that time, we all felt English was so boring that we couldn't stand it.

These two teachers were both university graduates who had majored in English. Roughly speaking, they were at the same level of English proficiency, but their teaching results were dramatically different. One of the most important factors was that they referred to different teaching methods. Our first teacher tried to make English learning dynamic and offered opportunities for students to speak; our second taught us a static knowledge of English, and we were just like bystanders.

There is a saying that goes, "Interest is the best teacher of all." As English teachers, we should try our best to arouse students' interest in English. We should make use of teaching methods more flexibly and let students have their say in class. If students are the actors of a class, they will find English interesting and they can make improvement quickly.

3. Problems of English Teaching in Secondary School

Bao Jingying

Although there has been much discussion about English teaching in Chinese colleges and universities, secondary-school teaching of English has been neglected. But it is in the secondary school that a Chinese first begins to study English and where the methods of teaching have a great influence on how most people learn the language. So how is English taught in secondary schools in China now? What is the teaching method? How effective is it as preparation for students when they go on with their further English study in college or university?

Most students in China begin to learn English when they enter secondary school at the age of thirteen. When they enroll in college or university, they "have had four to six years of English . . . [and] acquired a vocabulary of fifteen hundred to two thousand most frequently used words [and] a basic knowledge of English grammar " (Dzau 1990b, 42). Much time and effort have been put by students into learning English, yet only "about ten percent of the students can learn it well and use English as a real tool" (Tang 1988, 15). In college or university, the students always complain that they cannot interact with their teacher in English and cannot keep up if their teacher speaks English all the time in class.

So how can we deal with these problems? To answer this question, we need to know exactly what happens in secondary school. This study presents my observation of two secondary-school classes; discussion of these observations will lead to some suggestions as to what we, as college English teachers, can do to help our students.

Method

My research was carried out at Nanjing Number One Middle School,[2] which is one of the key schools in Nanjing, with a high proportion of students entering colleges or universities after taking the national CEE. On March 17, 1995, I went there with my tape-recorder to visit two classes, of which one is a regular class (Section Two) in Senior Two,[3] consisting of forty students, and the other

---

2. The term "middle school" is a literal translation of the Chinese *zhōng xué*, secondary school. It is opposed to *xiǎo xué,* or "little school"—i.e., primary school—and *dà xué,* "big school"—i.e., university. (Ed.)

3. Chinese secondary school is divided into two levels, junior and senior, each taking three years to complete. I have used the terms Junior One, etc., and Senior One, etc., to designate the classes within each level in order to avoid using either the American "grade" or the British "form." (Ed.)

is a special class (Section Three) in Senior One, consisting of forty-three students. In this class, an excellent English teacher demonstrated how she taught the text. Each period of class time lasted forty-five minutes. In each class, I sat there keeping track of what happened, and at the same time I recorded everything. After class, I had a free talk with the teacher and the students in Senior Two (Section Two). I asked the students questions such as the following: "Do you like your English teacher speaking English all the time in class?", "Is it good for you or not?", "What is your teacher's method in teaching?", and "Do you like that teaching method?" The questions I asked the teacher were similar: "Do you speak English in class all the time?" and "What do you think is the best way to teach English?"

Findings

The answers that I got from both the teacher and the students were somewhat disappointing. The purpose of learning English for almost every student and the purpose of teaching English for the teacher was exactly the same—to pass the national CEE. For the same purpose, the students prefer their teacher to speak Chinese in English class so that they can understand what the teacher says better, although they do acknowledge that speaking English in class is good for their listening ability. Similarly, the teacher understands the advantage of speaking English in class, yet she does not actually insist on doing so. As a result, the teacher spends most of class time talking Chinese and the students learn English through the medium of their mother tongue.

The Senior Two class I observed was for vocabulary teaching. It was the first lesson of Unit Five, entitled "The Gift" in *English Book III*. There are altogether forty-six new words and expressions in the list after the text. The teacher covered all of them within forty-five minutes. The students told me that the lesson was conducted according to the usual procedures. The teacher presented the new words in the following steps:

Step 1: The teacher read aloud each new word with correct pronunciation and the students read aloud, imitating the teacher.

Step 2: The teacher explained the definition of the new words in English and then illustrated their usage by taking examples from the dictionary.

Step 3: The teacher gave students several Chinese sentences in which the equivalent of the new English word was used and asked students to translate orally.

Step 4: All the students tried to translate these sentences into English and spoke out orally in chorus.

Step 5: After learning forty-six new words, the students read all the new words and expressions aloud once again and tried to remember them.

An example of how the words were handled individually is the teaching of the word *income:*

T: The next word *income* should not be pronounced as [in'kʌm]. For instance, how can we say: "*Nǐ yī gè yué ná duō shao qián*"?

Ss: How much—income—do you have?

T: Yes, you can say "How much income do you have every month?" or "How much income do you have a month?"

The teacher repeated the two sentences while writing them down on the board.

T: Now, pay attention to this question. You should not ask a foreigner at first, understand?

Ss: Yes.

T: You should not ask a foreigner, "How much income do you have every month?" I think it is very impolite. Right? It is very impolite. Now, when you ask some questions to a foreigner, what question, which question should be first?

Ss: The date, *tiān qì* [weather].

T: Good. Weather, then *shénme*? [what?] *dì fāng, huán jìng* [place, surrounding]; e.g., "*Nǐ xǐ huān zhè ge chéng shì ma?*" *Rán hòu, shú xī qǐ lái yǐ hòu kě wèn duì fāng de shēntǐ qíng kuàng děng.* ["Do you like this city?" Then when you get familiar with each other, you can ask about his or her health, etc.]

Here the teacher gave the students some information in Chinese about customs in Western countries.

T: Okay, how can we say "*Wǒ yǒu yí gè xiāng dāng kě guān de shōu rù*"?

Ss: I have a—good income.

T: Yes. We can say, "I have a good income."

The teacher did the same as before, writing the translation on the board while repeating the sentence.

T: Then how about the phrase "*gè rén suǒ dé shuì*"?

Ss: Tax—income.

T: Yes. That is "tax on income." Okay, the next word, *expense* . . .

The rest of the lesson went on like this. The work on *income* took three minutes. Three or four minutes were spent on learning each of the words that were on the syllabus, while the students just read aloud those words that were not on it. The teacher spent five minutes explaining the subtle difference between some similar words or phrases, such as *be worth doing something* and *be worthy of something,* or *expense* and *expensive.*

The Senior One class I observed was having a special lesson in which an excellent English teacher demonstrated how she taught the text. It is the second lesson of Unit Eleven, entitled "At the Tailor's Shop." The lesson procedures were carried out as follows:

Step 1:   The students spent five minutes reading aloud all the new words and phrases listed after the text.

Step 2:   The teacher introduced background information about the text by asking the students: "Do you know who the story was written by?"

Step 3:   The students listened to a tape-recording of the text and did comprehension exercises by asking and answering questions on it. Both teacher and students spoke in English.

Step 4:   The teacher went on with comprehension exercises by asking the students to fill in the blanks according to the text.

Step 5:   The teacher gave key words from the text and asked several students to retell the main idea of the text.

Step 6:   The teacher related the text to the students' life by asking questions in English. The students answered these questions with their own thoughts individually.

Step 7:   The teacher assigned homework.

Discussion

My observation of the regular class shows that throughout the whole teaching process, for a large portion of the class time, the teacher was talking and explaining; the teacher dominated the classroom while the students listened passively and engaged in exercises on command. Almost no time was spent on real communication between the teacher and the students or among the students themselves. The classroom was teacher-centered, not student-centered.

The demonstration lesson was much better than the first one because the teacher in the demonstration class spoke English all the time and more activities were introduced. However, even in the demonstration lesson, there was no communicative-language teaching at all.

Communicative-language teaching is a method in which the goals are developing communicative competence and developing exercises that emphasize the interaction between language users and their environment (Li 1990). On the contrary, the teacher and the students here were interested in getting knowledge about the English language rather than in developing communicative competence and habits of correct use. It was obvious that what the teacher wanted the students to do in class was mimicry—memorizing the language form and storing it in their brain for later use. Little time or attention was given to practice in developing students' ability to express their own thoughts in normal conversation. Especially in the regular lesson, there was too heavy a load of vocabulary learning divorced from the context that would show the students how the words were used. This means that what the students really learned was the Chinese translation of each English word. This may result in difficulties in reading comprehension, as well as in listening and speaking.

Conclusion

From what I have described, you can see that in China today, especially at the beginning stage in secondary school, English-teaching methods still remain traditional. Teachers use the "forced-feed duck" method of talking, while students listen and take notes passively. The "product" of this method can be compared to a computer: the students operate only according to command without any creative thinking. It is true that, compared to those years when I was in secondary school, much progress has been made, for there are more interactive exercises between the teacher and the students than there used to be. But the progress is too little and too slow to meet the demands of our rapidly developing society.

4. English-Language Teaching in China: The Gap Between Secondary School and College

Gu Tiexia

It is well known in China that only a small minority of college-age students can go to college. In Anshan,[4] where I teach, only nine percent of the junior-secondary-school students can pass the examination to key senior-secondary school and study there. About fifty to sixty percent of the students from key senior-secondary schools have an opportunity to become college students. Their English scores in the CEE range from about sixty to eighty. It is possible for the examinees whose scores reach sixty to seventy usually to enter ordinary colleges or university, and those whose scores are about seventy-five to eighty enter key universities.

Those students, therefore, should have achieved a fair measure of proficiency in English. According to the syllabus for secondary-school English issued by the government in December 1986, the purpose of English teaching is to train the students in English learning, speaking, reading, and writing; to foster the ability of using oral and written English; and to put emphasis on reading in order to lay solid foundations for use and further study. They are expected by the time they reach college to have command of all the basic grammatical structures and to know about fifteen hundred to two thousand English words. Thus, they should not only be able to interact with teachers in English in the class, some of them should even be able to communicate simply with native speakers.

However, if we look at the real situation of the students, especially freshmen, in college, we will find that secondary schoolteachers and students have not accomplished the object of the syllabus. Most freshmen in college find it difficult to follow teachers who speak English in class, except for those students who come from big cities such as Beijing, Shanghai, Guangzhou, and Xiamen. It is, of course, even more difficult for most freshmen to speak English themselves. So they say they feel nervous in class and vexed after class. Another problem is that freshmen cannot easily finish the long texts in the extensive reading books in the fixed time because of their low reading speed. Thus, "a lot of college students complain that they spend too much time studying English and they consider it a heavy burden to them" (Huang 1993, 13).

It is obvious that students with high marks in the CEE remain weak in speaking, listening, and reading. So college teachers cannot teach English by the expected method; in other words, they have great difficulty in teaching

---

4. One of the leading cities of Liaoning, a province in northeastern China. (Ed.)

English by using it. As a result, we can say two contradictions exist. The first is between the requirement of the syllabus for secondary-school English and the real outcome of secondary-school English teaching. The second is between the expected learning and teaching situation and the present-day teaching practice in Chinese universities and colleges. My study is intended to find the reasons for the two contradictions.

Methods

To find out how secondary-school teaching and learning affect university teaching and learning, I decided to compare secondary-school English lessons and university lessons. I focused on how senior-secondary-school students learned English, how their teachers dealt with English lessons in the classroom, and how examinees got their scores. The senior-secondary-school classroom observations I made will help us to see why college students remain weak in using English.

My observations were based on one class each of Senior Two and Senior Three in a key senior-secondary school and also one class of non-English-major freshmen in a college in Anshan. Senior Two was chosen for the secondary school in addition to Senior Three, because it is the last year in which new material is presented. Senior Three is devoted entirely to review.

I did my observations on March 27 and 28, 1995.[5] The secondary-school students I observed were those who had passed the examination to key senior-secondary school. They were only nine percent of the junior-secondary-school students in Anshan, and their aim in studying in a key senior-secondary school was to go to college. They had five English lessons per week.

The college students were freshmen who came from several areas of China. Many of them came from rural areas, and their English was consequently poor. All the students were required to pass the College English Test Band Four.[6]

I kept notes from the beginning till the end of each lesson. These notes formed the basis for the following analysis.

Findings—Observation of Senior Two in Secondary School

The Senior Two class that I observed consisted of sixty students and an experienced teacher. The materials were a test paper and the English textbook for Senior Two. The lesson, lasting forty-five minutes, was divided into three parts.

---

5. Gu had had to go back to Anshan from Nanjing, although it was the middle of term, in order to take a promotion exam. She took the opportunity to collect data in institutions that she knew. (Ed.)
6. The college English course throughout China is divided into four compulsory stages, or "Bands," each of which is covered in one semester; the culmination of the course for most students is the taking of the College English Test at the end of Band Four. Following this test there are two optional Bands, with a further, more advanced, test at the end of Band Six. Thus, most college students study English for two years, while the more able, or more ambitious, study it for three (see Cortazzi and Jin 1996, 65). (Ed.)

Part I   A three-hundred-word passage with multiple-choice questions was selected from a test paper. Three students were asked to read sections of the passage in turn and to translate difficult sentences. While the students were working, the teacher corrected the translation and helped to find proper Chinese words for it. The following is the last paragraph of the passage:

> Business meetings are tedious and interminable. I've only been to half a dozen business meetings in my life, but I've got tired of them. If weddings and funerals could be cut in half, the average business meeting could be cut by seventy-five percent. There are very few meetings that should take more than fifteen minutes. After that, it's repetitious hot air.

The third student read, ". . . If weddings and funerals could be cut in half, the average business meeting could be cut by seventy-five percent." Then the teacher told him to translate it into Chinese, because it seemed more difficult to understand than other sentences, so the student translated,

> *Rú guǒ hūn lǐ hé zàng lǐ néng gòu bèi suō duǎn yí bàn, nà me shāng wù huì yì yīng bèi qiē duǎn 75%.*

The teacher was not satisfied with some words of the student's translation, so she corrected them:

> cut in half—*jiǎn qù yí bàn.*

> cut by seventy-five percent—*jiǎn qù bǎi fēn zhī qī shí wǔ.*

After the whole passage had been read, another student was told to find the best answers to the four multiple-choice questions. The following example is the last question:

> The author's attitude towards the question of different kinds of meeting can be expressed like this:
>
> (a) he is not opposed to attending funerals or weddings, but only twice or three times a year.
>
> (b) business meetings should be held not more than six times a year.
>
> (c) 75 percent of the meetings should be held within 15 minutes.
>
> (d) repetition and waste of time should be eliminated from all kinds of meetings.

The student's reply was "fill (d)" (in Chinese). It seemed all the answers were right, so the teacher only said, in Chinese, "All the answers are right," without elaborating on them.

Part II   The students and teachers spent fifteen minutes learning new words in Lesson Twelve in the textbook.

Step 1. Students read the new words aloud by imitating the teacher.

Step 2. Students read new words aloud together.

Step 3. The teacher corrected the pronunciation of some words that were difficult to pronounce.

Step 4. A few students stood up to read new words one by one.

Step 5. Students tried to memorize the words by reading them mechanically again and again individually.

Step 6. The teacher dictated the words learned to the class. Two of the students were called to go to the blackboard to write down a couple of words according to the teacher's dictation while the others did it in their seats.

Step 7. After that, the teacher asked the students to correct the mistakes on the blackboard together.

Part III   The students were given twenty minutes to understand the text of Lesson Twelve. The text told about what the Soviet astronaut, Leonov, and his companion, Beliaiev, did before their historic journey to outer space, what they did on the journey, and what they saw there.

Step 1. The teacher asked the students to spend ten minutes reading the text on their own. During reading, a few of the students read aloud. Two of the students talked about something with each other. The teacher walked around without saying anything. No one asked any questions.

Step 2. The teacher asked some questions on the text. All the questions could be answered by reading directly from the text or by changing it a little; for example:

T: Who was the first man to walk in outer space?

S: Leonov.

T: What did Leonov and his companion do after their flight began?

S: They began making preparation for the historic walk shortly after their flight began.

We can see from my description that the teacher tried his best to use English in the class and it seemed that he and his students did use it. But if we examine the process, we will find most of the English the students uttered was by reading aloud and reciting the sentences in the text. They learned to speak English by mimicry and memorization. The way the teacher organized the lesson was similar to the popular saying about foreign-language learning in China—language should be learned first and put to use afterwards.

Findings—Observation of Senior Three in Secondary School

Senior Three is the top class in secondary school. The students in this class will take the CEE in about three months, July 7 every year. So the teacher and the students are occupied with preparation for the decisive test.

The Senior Three class that I observed consisted of sixty-two students and an experienced teacher. The lesson lasted forty-five minutes. Forty multiple-choice questions from a simulated test paper were used. The students had finished them before the class, and the teacher only wanted to check and correct the answers.

The first five multiple-choice items were about phonetics. The first student was told to read aloud each word in this item and then choose the one that is similar in pronunciation to the one given. For example:

1.   glad

(a) late   (b) name   (c) fat   (d) save

The student gave the answer (c).

Another five items were about spelling. A second student was called to stand up to read the words aloud and give the best choice for each one. For example:

s__v__ge

(a) a, e   (b) o, a   (c) o, e   (d) a, a

The student said in Chinese that (d) should be the correct answer.

The other thirty questions were about grammar and vocabulary. Each student who was called read aloud three of them and then gave the answers. If some sentences were not easy to understand, the teacher would ask students to translate them into Chinese. During this period, the students were often interrupted by the teacher's asking for the reason for their selections. Sometimes the teacher herself analyzed the difficult sentences grammatically. For example:

It is for the people _____ we all study harder and harder.

(a) which   (b) who   (c) that   (d) whom

S: (c) is right.

T: Why?

S: This sentence is an emphasizing sentence pattern, it is . . . that + clause, so we are not allowed to—fill the others, especially "who."

All of this conversation was in Chinese.

This was a class based on language form, like most English classes in Senior Three. The teacher explained the rules of the language carefully in theory as if she were teaching physics or chemistry. She hoped that the students could receive the language knowledge and grasp it by being able to explain the rules as she did, and this is why the students were always asked by the teacher to give reasons for their answers. It is obvious that both the teacher and the students were interested in getting knowledge about language rather than developing competence in using it.

Findings—Observation of a Class in College

The college class I observed was hardly more communicative. The class consisted of twenty-nine first-year non-English-major students. The lesson lasted fifty minutes and focused on reading-comprehension exercises. Three passages were selected from a test paper, each of which had five multiple-choice questions, and the students had prepared the answers before the lesson. The teacher read the whole passage by translating some sentences. The following is a sentence of the first passage:

> For example, they buy old books to use the old aged papers of the title page, and they can treat paper and ink with chemicals.

The teacher translated:

> *Tā men mǎi lái yì xiē jiù shū, yào lì yòng nà xiē dài biāo tí de chén nián jiù zhǐ, zài duì zhǐ hé mò shuǐ zuò huà xué chù lǐ.*

The teacher paraphrased a noun phrase in this sentence: "'Aged paper' means paper produced many years ago." Then the teacher translated the paraphrase into Chinese:

> *Hěn duō nián yǐ qián shēng chǎn chū de zhǐ.*

She also paraphrased the word *treat* as *deal with*. Sometimes she explained how she decided on the best answers, as in the case of the following question:

> According to the passage, forgeries are usually sold to _____.
>
> (a) sharp-eyed experts   (b) persons who are not experts
> (c) book dealers   (d) owners of old books

The teacher explained the sentence relating to this question in English,

> A forger can't approach a respectable buyer but must deal with people who don't have much knowledge in the field.

and then paraphrased it:

> A forger can't sell his forgeries to a buyer who is good at collecting this kind of things. They must sell his forgeries to the persons who know a little about that.

Then the teacher translated the paraphrase into Chinese and said in Chinese, "So I decided that the best choice for the twenty-ninth question was (b)."

This procedure suggests that the teacher wanted to teach the lesson in English and make the students understand the text also in English, but she seemed to know that few of the students could follow her, so she translated her paraphrases into Chinese. Her purpose was to help students to surmount the obstacles in listening and speaking, and to help them form the habits and foster the ability of using English little by little. The intention of the teacher was good, but the result might be the opposite, because her translation would make students go on relying on Chinese. As for speaking in English, in this class there was little time for the students to talk at all.

Conclusion

Evidently, secondary-school teaching does not really lay a solid foundation in English. Teachers put undue emphasis on commonly used vocabulary, essential grammar rules, and mimicry-memorization, but totally neglect the training of their students' communicative abilities (Hu 1990). As a result, some students can hardly speak a sentence in English outside the text after six years' study, let alone communicate with others. Thus, great obstacles lie before college English teaching.

But we cannot lay the blame for the difficulties solely on the secondary schools. There are problems within tertiary educational institutions as well. First, the Chinese traditional view of teaching for thousands of years was that "Teachers talk and students listen," and college teachers still maintain this view. Second, teachers' habits and abilities are not adapted to communicative methods, because they themselves were taught English in secondary school and college in the same way as their students are now, and in their working experience they have had little opportunity to learn and try new teaching methods. Third, college students are required to pass the college-graded English tests. In many colleges, the scores on the examination determine whether a student will get a degree and what kind of job a student will get upon graduation. Therefore, for most students, the primary goal is to pass the examination, which, as Campbell and Zhao assert,

> . . . consists mostly of multiple-choice questions devoid of meaningful context and . . . mainly measures the students' ability to memorize and recognize grammatical structures and patterns. (1993, 4)

Thus, students who cannot communicate can pass the exam and even get high scores.

Hence, the improvement of English teaching at the college level should not only rely on or wait for success in improving English teaching in secondary school. College English teachers should, through their teaching, help students to recognize that English should be used and not only memorized. The communicative-language teaching method is feasible, provided that English is actually used in class. It will require the teachers to do different work from before and harder work than before, but it will enable them to resolve the contradiction between their practice and what is expected of them in modern China.

5. Traditional and Communicative Approaches in China's College English Teaching

He Yue

In recent years, English teachers in various parts of the world have found a new excitement and confidence in adopting a communicative approach in language teaching. However, in China, this approach has not yet been widely accepted. Most teaching methods in China's college English classrooms remain traditional, drawing on grammar-translation, direct, and audio-lingual methods; the text-analysis method also has found its way into teaching. So there has appeared a problem of how to adopt communicative-language teaching because this approach seems to be successful in many classrooms in other countries. We are quite clear that the traditional language-teaching method has been challenged by the new communicative approach, so teaching reform is necessary.

Then what is the present situation in Chinese college English classrooms? What are our teachers' and students' attitudes toward English-language teaching? I have done six classroom observations at Nanjing Auditing Institute and interviewed some teachers and students to find out the answers.

Classroom Observations

The classes I first observed were three Band Two reading classes. There were about fifty students in each class, and the students were average in level except for those in Class Two; the students in this class were majoring in foreign trade, which demands high-level English, and so they were particularly strong. The class tasks all dealt with Unit Three, "Lessons from Jefferson." The text passage was adapted from *Progressive Reading Series Book Eight,* compiled by Dr. Virginia French Allen. It told about Jefferson's attitudes toward social life: "Go and see; You can learn from everyone; Judge for yourself; Do what you believe is right; Trust the future, trust the young."

In Class One, the teacher, who was thirty-two, explained the vocabulary and the text for almost the whole lesson. Only seven students were called to answer questions about the text, such as "Who was Thomas Jefferson?", "What is he famous for?", and "What was his opinion about young people?" The teacher's method of explanation was to translate every new word into the native language and to give several examples to illustrate the usage of certain words (e.g., *appoint, reject, prefer,* and *hesitate*). Then the teacher explained the text itself by first paraphrasing each paragraph and then translating some sentences. For example, he said:

The paragraph "Go and see" tells us that book is not enough for us. We have to obtain knowledge in nature by self-observations. In Paragraph Four, the sentence "By birth and by education, Jefferson belonged to the highest social class" means: Judging by his family and educational background, Jefferson was a member of the group with top social status. In Chinese, it means: *Àn chū shēng jí qí suǒ shòu de jiào yù, Jefferson shǔ yú zuì gāo de shè huì jiē céng.*

The students simply listened, which made the classroom extremely quiet.

Class Two turned out to be somewhat different. The teacher was an old man. He put forward ten questions about Jefferson and the text for ten students to answer, like "What are Jefferson's extraordinary characteristics?", "What was Jefferson's opinion about freedom?", and "In which fields was Jefferson an expert?" Then he went on to explain the text sentence by sentence, but unlike the teacher of Class One, this old professor spoke the target language ninety-eight percent of the time. The students could understand their teacher very well without his translating.

As to Class Three, the activities were done in connection with the exercises of Unit Three. The first activity was to check the answers to the exercises done by the students themselves; for example, Exercise V: Fill in the blanks with the adjectives given (*alike, alive, alone, asleep, astir,* and *awake*), and Exercise VI: Fill in the blanks with the words or expressions given (*act on, owe to, go out of one's way, in existence, except*). The other activity was directed by the teacher, which was to ask the students to offer their answers to certain exercises. The teacher, a woman of about forty, used the target language seventy-five percent of the time.

For the three Band Four classes, the situation was almost the same as in Band Two. The text they were dealing with was Unit Five of Book Four, " To Lie or Not to Lie—The Doctor's Dilemma." The author of this article, Sissela Bok, takes an unusual view on this subject. She gives several reasons to show why patients, especially those who are dying, should be told the truth.[7] She also discusses the harm doctors' lies do, not only to their patients, but also to the doctors themselves and to the entire medical profession. The teachers of the Band Four classes, like those of Band Two, began by presenting new words with Chinese translations. Then they explained the texts sentence by sentence, and finally they led the students through the required exercises. The three Band Four classrooms were also mostly teacher-centered, except for Class Six, in which the students discussed the exercises for about an hour, just like Class Three in Band Two. The three Band Four teachers spoke the target language seventy percent of the time. For the other thirty percent, they either translated some words or sentences or phrases that were difficult for the

---

7. This opinion is more unusual in China than it is in the United States. Doctors and relatives often avoid telling patients that their illness may be fatal, for fear that it would distress them and so reduce still further their chances of recovery. (Ed.)

students to understand in English, or they explained some language points in Chinese. In each of the three Band Four classes, there were five to nineteen students who were asked to answer the questions or make up sentences with the phrases given. The students' activity in all the six classes was mostly listening with very little speaking.

Interviews with Teachers

The eighteen teachers I interviewed all claimed that the grammar-translation method was generally used in intensive-reading and extensive-reading classes, and they were quite familiar with it. Five teachers added that they were also familiar with the audio-lingual and direct methods, and they occasionally used a few communicative activities. Seven teachers who had been trained or were being trained in the Nanjing University/United Board Program claimed that after learning or having been trained communicatively, they really thought the communicative method was a good way to teach English, but it was difficult to adopt at present. Most of the teachers remarked that they had already developed quite a lot of excellent students with the traditional teaching method, so it was not necessary to adopt a new method, such as communicative-language teaching.

Interviews with Students

Students, too, expressed similar attitudes. I interviewed seventy-six students and, of these, fifty-nine said that traditional language teaching was acceptable and welcome. Only eight said that new methods should be used. Most of the students interviewed thought that communicative activities could warm the classroom atmosphere and would arouse their interest, but they would not form a systematic knowledge structure and would make it difficult for them to firmly master language knowledge. My own students also told me that they could not see how important the communicative activities were, and they complained that because they had not been trained communicatively before, it would cost time to achieve good results in this way.

Conclusion

Why do our teachers insist on the traditional language teaching and regard the communicative approach as difficult to adopt even though they have realized its importance and necessity? I think, for one thing, it requires not only highly professional training and teaching strategies, but also solid language knowledge. Since most teachers themselves were not trained communicatively when they were studying in college, it is not so easy for them to get used to the communicative-language teaching without being pretrained and practicing for some time. Thus, teacher training should be given special attention, and should be placed before everything else to accelerate English teaching in China. For another, present teaching materials used in college-English classrooms are not communicatively designed. If we produce or select materials ourselves, we will not fulfill our teaching curriculum, which is the basis for the exams in each semester and of the Band Four and Band Six tests. Furthermore, many students are understandably bound to official textbooks in all formal study. Thus, they need a new orientation. Our teachers must help them to see that, like their first language, English is a means of communication. They must dramatically experience the fact that a command of even a few elements of the foreign language can enable genuine interaction and bring minds together toward a satisfying end.

We should acknowledge, however, that the traditional teaching approach can get efficient results, especially the grammar-translation method, which should not be completely driven away. It has brought great success both in secondary school and in college for a long time, and we can easily see this from the achievement of Chinese students in TOEFL, GRE, and the other tests organized for students worldwide. The *Yangzi Evening Post* and some other newspapers have frequently reported that Chinese students have got much higher scores in those tests than students from any other country.

So, is it possible to combine the two approaches, traditional and communicative, in our English-teaching classrooms? I think it is as long as we make enough effort. In my opinion, the way to conduct the combination is to take advantage of the present traditional approach and adopt the new communicative approach appropriately, for neither of them can be applied extremely. For example, we can keep on teaching vocabulary before we start a text, but we have to do it in various ways, not just translating and paraphrasing. We can ask students to preview the new words with the help of dictionaries and can arrange some kinds of activities practicing the words learned (e.g., whole class work, small or big group work, pair work, and role play). However, the teacher's explanation of word usage is also helpful and necessary. It can be carried out either before or after students' activities in class. Similarly, in text teaching, it is necessary to use some native language to illustrate certain language points or expressions so as to make sure students, especially lower-ability students, fully understand them; translation exercises both from English into Chinese and from Chinese into English can help students comprehend English more precisely. But in addition to teacher-student interaction in text explanation, student-student interaction should be put to use.

I have tried from last semester to use communicative activities, especially in going over exercises. The effort has resulted in more success than I expected. Before each class, I do much more work than I did previously, preparing and creating activities and rearranging the exercises in the textbook. I have to be sure that the activities arranged should be not only meaningful, but also interesting so that my students will be greatly attracted. After each activity, I ask my students to summarize what they have learned in the activity and whether anything is still unclear for them. At last, the problem will be solved either by the students themselves or by the teacher. Then the students will get the idea that communicative activities are not just games, and they will begin to see language learning as a matter of applying information rather than simply obtaining it.

Although so many changes have to be carried out gradually, and we cannot predict whether the reform will be successful, the contradictions between the two approaches to teaching may eventually be solved, through the use of various methods and strategies. If communicative-language teaching can be combined with traditional methods in an efficient way, it will surely result in great success in Chinese college-English-teaching classrooms.

6. The College Entrance Exam and College English Test Band 4: Effects on English Teaching

Du Qunhua

Chinese present-day education has been greatly influenced by the ancient examination tradition,[8] though the forms and content of the exams may differ. The two most influential exams in China today are the CEE and the College English Test Band 4 (CET-4).

The CEE, which was restored in 1977 after having been abolished during the Cultural Revolution, is a major exam that is taken at the end of secondary school. It is offered in a number of subjects, but English is the key one, because colleges and universities will not admit students who fail in English, however well they do in other subjects. A failure in the English exam amounts to a failure to enter university or college, so students are extremely anxious to pass it.

The CET-4, first developed in 1987, is used to assess the English proficiency of university students. The exam, which is taken at the end of the second year after they have entered university, is the only unified exam that all students are required to take. Students, especially in key universities, will find it difficult to get their degrees or their graduation certificates without passing the CET-4.

Both of these exams are administered by the State Education Commission. CEE is administered once annually, CET-4 twice. Both include items dealing with reading comprehension, the knowledge of vocabulary and structure, cloze, and writing. The major differences between them are that the CET-4 includes listening comprehension and the CEE includes questions on pronunciation, spelling, and error correction.

The aims of language teaching are often defined with reference to the four language skills—listening, speaking, reading, and writing (Widdowson 1978, 57). In these terms, the exams sound reasonable because they test the students in a comprehensive way and, in addition, they promote teaching and learning. When I asked Chinese teachers of English, "What would happen if there were no exams?", all of them answered that the exams were necessary "because without [them], both the teachers and students would feel relaxed, and the students would not work as hard as they are doing now." So the exams have powerful effects on China's English-teaching practices and are usually regarded as the only criterion for evaluating the teaching.

8. See Su Xiaojun's essay in Chapter Two. (Ed.)

Given the importance of these two exams, I decided for my research to study both of them closely and to investigate teachers' attitudes towards them. I focused on the reading component because reading is thought to be the most important skill for Chinese students to have in English. My concern was to document the effects of the exams on the teaching of English in China.

The CEE and CET-4: Overview

The CEE, the total mark for which is 150 points, is divided into five sections: Section I (multiple choice) consists of phonetics, word spelling, vocabulary, and structure. Phonetics requires the test-takers to choose a word whose under-lined part has the same pronunciation as the given one; for example:

1. spe<u>c</u>ial

(a) <u>sh</u>allow   (b) offi<u>c</u>er   (c) <u>ch</u>oke   (d) trou<u>s</u>ers

For spelling, an incomplete word is given. What the test-takers have to do is select a suitable one from the four choices given:

6. s__v__ge

(a) a; e   (b) o; e   (c) o; a   (d) a; a

As to vocabulary and structure, the test-takers are required to choose a suitable one from the four choices given:

15. Tom ought not to _____ me your secret, but he meant no harm.

(a) have told   (b) tell   (c) be telling   (d) having told

Section II is also a set of multiple-choice questions, which is presented in the form of a passage. Some words are deleted from the passage on purpose. The test-takers are asked to choose from the four choices given:

Jenkins was a jeweller, who had made a large diamond ring worth $57,000 for the Silkstone Jeweller Shop. When it was ready, he made a copy of it which looked __41__ like the first one but was worth only $2,000. This he took to the shop, which __42__ it without a question.

41. (a) only   (b) surely   (c) nearly   (d) exactly
42. (a) accepted   (b) received   (c) refused   (d) rejected

Section III, reading, is very long. I will deal with it in detail in the latter part of my paper.

Section IV is presented in the form of a passage. The test-takers are required to find mistakes if there are any, mark the mistakes, and then write down the correct answers in the blanks:

When I have free time I go a long walk. Some   (a) _____

people read the books or watch television while   (b) _____

others have sports. Charles and Linda Mason do all (c) _____

of the things as well as climbed buildings.   (d) _____

Section V, writing, is a guided exercise. A situation and some details are given. What the students have to do is to organize them into a passage by adding several more sentences. Typical kinds of writing are letters, announcements, or stories to be told from pictures.

The CET-4, the highest mark for which is one hundred points, is also divided into five sections. The form of Sections II, III, and IV is the same as that of the CEE. Only the listening-comprehension section is different. It includes ten short dialogues and three short passages, with three to four multiple-choice questions attached to each passage.

Section V, writing, is also a guided exercise based on a situation that is provided. The composition should be no less than one hundred words. The students are usually required to write three paragraphs; namely, a topic paragraph, a developing paragraph, and a concluding paragraph. The topics are typically related to issues of social and economic development, such as pollution, electricity, or afforestation.

The sections of each exam and the marks allotted to each are summarized in Tables 5-1 and 5-2.

Table 5-1
The sections and the time distribution of the CEE

Section	Content	Number of Questions	Mark	Time (in min.)
I	Multiple choice (phonetics, vocabulary, and structure)	40	40	25
II	Filling in blanks	20	30	15
III	Reading comprehension	20	40	40
IV	Error correction	15	15	15
V	Writing	1	25	25
Total		96	150	120

Table 5-2

The sections and the time distribution of the CET-4

Section	Content	Number of Questions	Mark	Time (in min.)
I	Listening comprehension	20	20	20
II	Reading comprehension	20	40	35
III	Vocabulary and structure	30	15	20
IV	Cloze	20	10	15
V	Writing	1	15	30
Total		91	100	120

Method

To investigate what the teachers' responses are to the exams, I developed a questionnaire, including the following questions:

1. To what extent is your teaching governed by CEE (or CET-4)?
2. What would happen if there were no such exam?
3. How do you prepare your students for the exam?
4. Have you ever thought of changing your way of teaching?
5. Do you know anything about the teaching of English in universities? (for secondary schoolteachers)
6. Do you think your students are well prepared before they come to you as first-year students? (for college teachers)
7. What are your students' strongest points and weakest points in English?

The respondents were eighteen teachers of both levels from Guangdong, Hunan, Xi'an, and Wuhan. All of them had more than ten years' experience in teaching. I supplemented my study with the findings provided by my colleagues, who had done a class survey in both high school and university in Anshan.

In addition, I examined closely examination papers of the two kinds: CEE and CET-4. I especially studied the components intended to test reading comprehension. The two I chose are from the 1993 examination papers, respectively. In analyzing these papers, I used techniques suggested by Hill and Parry (1994a), Widdowson (1978), Carrell (1987), and Brown and Yule (1983), all of whom view written text as communicative interaction.

CEE and CET-4 Reading Components

The reading-comprehension section in both tests takes up a larger percentage of the total score than any other section. The questions are all presented in multiple-choice format, and fall into two major categories. The first category calls for a demonstration of what Widdowson (1978) calls the learner's comprehending skill and makes appeal to the test-takers' knowledge of usage. The second category calls for a demonstration of the test-takers' reading ability, to use Widdowson's term, and requires them to infer meanings from context. From Widdowson's point of view, comprehending skill only refers to one's ability to provide correct answers by noting how the signification of the sentence of the question relates to the signification of the sentence in the passage. Reading ability means more than that; it refers to the understanding of the deeper meaning of the passage, which requires the use of background knowledge and the ability to interpret the author's ideas.

Most of the questions in the CEE belong to the first category. I'd like to take the reading passage from the CEE 1993 for example:

> For thousands of years, man has enjoyed the taste of apples. Apples, which are about 85 percent water, grow almost everywhere in the world but the hottest and coldest areas. Among the leading countries in apple production are China, France and the United States.
>
> There are various kinds of apples, but a very few make up the majority of those grown for sale. The three most common kinds grown in the United States are Delicious, Golden Delicious, and McIntosh.
>
> Apples are different in colour, size, and taste. The colour of the skin may be red, green, or yellow. They have various sizes, with Delicious apples being among the largest. The taste may be sweet or tart. Generally, sweet apples are eaten fresh while tart apples are used to make applesauce.
>
> Apple trees may grow as tall as twelve metres. They do best in areas that have very cold winters. Although no fruit is *yielded* during the winter, this cold period is good for the tree.

This passage is probably an extract from a book on plants or, to be exact, from a particular section focused on the introduction of different fruits. Now it is adapted and has become part of a reading test. In this sense, it does not carry any sense of authenticity because the readers are required to deal with a passage in a way that does not correspond to their normal communicative activities at all. Consider the question:

71. Cold winter weather is good for _____ .

    (a) the growth of apple trees   (b) producing large apples

    (c) improving the taste of apples   (d) the increase of water in apples

The answer (a) can be drawn by referring to Sentence Two in the last paragraph, "They do best in areas that have very cold winters." The pronoun *they* is used to avoid the repetition of the noun *trees* in the previous sentence, and the verb *do* carries the same meaning as the verb in the previous sentence, *grow*.

The test-takers have simply to trace the structure in the passage that corresponds with one of the alternatives. All they are required to do is recognize that the following two sentences have the same signification:

A. They do best in areas that have very cold winters.

B. Cold winter weather is good for the growth of apple trees.

The following question rewards such matching techniques even more:

73. The word *yielded* in the last sentence means _____ .

   (a) improved   (b) increased   (c) produced   (d) sold

As the four choices are supposed to be from those listed in the syllabus, they are presumably not new to the test-takers. If they happen to know the word *yielded* in the question, the students only have to find a synonym to identify the answer. Even if they do not know the word *yielded,* they are very likely to choose the key (c) by leaving *yielded* blank and then substituting the alternatives offered to see which one fits best.

   This material illustrates a typical practice of testmakers: While constructing a passage, they usually "depend on no cues other than linguistic cues" (Hill and Parry 1994a, 15). The questions asked are very straightforward. All the test-takers have to do is scan the reading passage until they arrive at a sentence that is related in meaning to the questions given. Because these kinds of questions frequently appear in the exam, they have led both teachers and students to a bad habit in dealing with the reading passages. While explaining a reading passage to students, teachers do not focus on the global understanding of the text; instead, they ask students to read the passage word by word, translate it sentence by sentence, and then find equivalent answers from the text. It does not sound like reading comprehension at all, but rather translation. As Widdowson remarks, "The students' attention is very often directed to the signification of sentences as separate units of meaning: the rest of the passage might just as well not be there" (1978, 102).

   The form of the reading test has also led to the erroneous view that the difficulty of a reading test largely depends on the difficulty of the vocabulary and structure. So teachers usually take it for granted that if the students have a large vocabulary and are strong in grammar, they are likely to get high marks in the reading test. Those who get high marks are then usually regarded as having strong reading abilities. Thus, the teachers confuse the ideas of comprehending skill (as defined by Widdowson) and reading ability. The result is that when students graduate from high school, they still cannot read English with any fluency.

   However, there are many other factors that contribute to the difficulty of a text.

Everything in one's prior experience or one's background knowledge plays a potential role in the process of reading. Included in background knowledge are knowledge of subject matter, genre, sociocultural and general world knowledge, [as well as] linguistic knowledge of text code. (Carrell 1987, 25)

So sometimes even if we understand every single word, it is not necessarily the case that we understand the meaning of the whole passage.

As with the reading test in the CEE, most of the questions in the CET-4 still stay at the level of understanding the surface meaning. But there exist some other problems that should not be neglected by testmakers. I should like to take the reading passage from the 1993 CET-4 as an example:

If women are mercilessly exploited year after year, they have only themselves to blame. Because they tremble at the thought of being seen in public in clothes that are out of fashion, they are always taken advantage of by the designers and the big stores. Clothes which have been worn only a few times have to be put aside because of the change of fashion. When you come to think of it, only a woman is capable of standing in front of a wardrobe packed full of clothes and announcing sadly that she has nothing to wear.

Changing fashions are nothing more than the intentional creation of waste. Many women spend vast sums of money each year to replace clothes that have hardly been worn. Women who cannot afford to throw away clothing in this way, waste hours of their time altering the dresses they have. Skirts are lengthened or shortened; neck-lines are lowered or raised, and so on.

No one can claim that the fashion industry contributes anything really important to society. Fashion designers are rarely concerned with vital things like warmth, comfort and durability. They are only interested in outward appearance and they take advantage of the fact that women will put up with any amount of discomfort, as long as they look right. There can hardly be a man who hasn't at some time in his life smiled at the sight of a woman shaking in a thin dress on a winter day, or delicately picking her way through deep snow in high-heeled shoes.

When comparing men and women in the matter of fashion, the conclusions to be drawn are obvious. Do the constantly changing fashions of women's clothes, one wonders, reflect basic qualities of inconstancy and instability? Men are too clever to let themselves be cheated by fashion designers. So do their unchanging styles of dress reflect basic qualities of stability and reliability? That is for you to decide.

The point of view presented by the author of this passage may not be approved by all readers, especially women. When the author says "when comparing men and women, the conclusions to be drawn are obvious," the conclusions are, as a matter of fact, not obvious at all, because the author's point of view that women constantly change their clothes to pursue the fashion while men do not cannot be accepted by all readers. In this case, as Carrell said, "text may break down when the intentionality and acceptability are not upheld" (1987, 29). This problem is highlighted by Question 40:

By saying "the conclusions to be drawn are obvious" (Para. 4, Lines 1–2), the
   writer means that _____ .

   (a) women's inconstancy in their choice of clothing is often laughed at

   (b) women are better able to put up with discomfort

   (c) men are also exploited greatly by fashion designers

   (d) men are more reasonable in the matter of fashion

The test-takers, while doing Question 40, have to choose answer (d), however offensive the supposed obvious conclusion may be to them. In this situation, we can only view the reading as "a narrowly circumscribed activity in which personal knowledge must be continually suppressed for fear of making an inappropriate response" (Hill and Parry, 1994a, 33).

Provided that readers succeed in suppressing their personal knowledge, the questions in this passage, like those in the CEE, can all be answered by referring to particular sentences in the passage. For example, consider Question 39:

According to the passage, which of the following statements is true?

(a) New fashions in clothing are created for the commercial exploitation
     of women.

(b) The constant changes in women's clothing reflect their strength of
     character.

(c) The fashion industry makes an important contribution to society.

(d) Fashion designers should not be encouraged since they are only
     welcomed by women.

Initially, it seems as if this question tests the test-takers' global understanding of the text. However, if we study it carefully, we see that it still stays at the level of the literal meaning. If we compare the phrases italicized in the passage version with phrases italicized in the task version, we can see that the test-makers are actually playing a word game.

Passage version:

If *women are mercilessly exploited* year after year, they have only themselves to blame. Because they tremble at the thought of being seen in public *in clothes that are out of fashion*, they are always taken advantage of by the designers and the big stores.

Task version:

According to the passage, which of the following statements is true?

(a) *New fashions in clothing* are created for *the commercial exploitation of women.*

(b) The constant changes in women's clothing reflect their strength of character.

(c) The fashion industry makes an important contribution to society.

(d) Fashion designs should not be encouraged since they are only welcomed by women.

We can interpret the passage version and task version in this way: Since "they (women) tremble at the thought of being seen in public in clothes that are out of fashion," then designers and big stores create "new fashions in clothing" in order to meet the women's needs. The second half of the sentence in the task version, ". . . for the commercial exploitation of women," matches very closely in meaning with the conditional sentence in the passage version, "If women are mercilessly exploited year after year . . ." The answer (a), in fact, can be arrived at by referring only to the first two sentences in the first paragraph. So the skill that the testmakers test consists mainly of "perceiving the very words of the text and manipulating them so as to draw logical inferences from the propositions that they convey" (Hill and Parry 1994a, 19).

Thus, the problems presented here are similar to those discussed by Hill and Parry. I'd like to use their words to end my discussion of the reading tests:

> Any test is, inevitably, to some degree, artificial . . . and the tasks, however carefully designed, force students to engage in prescribed activities during a prescribed period of time, usually one that is so short that students have little opportunity to engage in critical thinking. (1994b, 263)

This is undoubtedly true of the CET-4.

Teachers' Responses to the Exams

As has been mentioned previously, both levels of the exams are designed in separate sections: seventy-eight percent of the questions in the CEE and fifty-four percent in the CET-4 are focused on words, phrases, and grammar, and these questions consist mostly of multiple-choice questions. For the section on vocabulary and structure, the questions are devoid of meaningful context and primarily measure the students' ability to memorize and recognize grammatical structures and patterns. Because of the proportion these items take up in the exam, both levels of teachers usually follow a rigid procedure in their teaching. This can be seen from the answers given by six of the eight respondents who are teaching in secondary schools. When I asked them how they prepared their students for the exam, their answers were very similar to each other. The following is typical:

We prepare our students by reviewing all the old textbooks we have covered, going over language points, word-building, grammatical items. Besides, we give them a lot of passages to read and teach them the skills in the exam.

While seven of the ten teachers from college answered in nearly the same sense, one of them said:

We prepare our students by means of much listening, reading, and writing, and give a series of sample tests and comments on these tests, so that they get familiar with different skills involved in the test.

It is obvious that the skills that are irrelevant to the exams are simply ignored. Such approaches only leave students with unbalanced linguistic skills.

For these reasons, all that the teachers require of students is the ability to receive and store up in their heads knowledge handed out to them. The students just wait to be filled with knowledge or to be trained in habits (Li 1990, 129). In this situation, the students seldom get a chance to speak in class. Even if they do have a chance to speak, they are only required to repeat some sentences or do some questions and answers mechanically. The English lessons are usually conducted in Chinese; this is especially obvious in secondary school. Students who are taught in this way may be able to identify a large number of words in isolation and explain their grammatical functions, but they are unable to assign appropriate meaning to these words with regard to how they are used in context. Thus, when asked about their students' strongest and weakest points in learning English, teachers of both levels gave almost the same answers: listening and speaking are the students' weakest points, while grammar, idioms, and reading are the strongest ones.

Given this exam system, it seems that there is no other way to teach the students. Just as one of the secondary schoolteachers said:

We have to face reality—to send students to university. So I would rather stick to the traditional way of teaching; otherwise, my students will feel strange if I change my way, thus influencing their results in the exam.

So if teachers wish to try different methods, they must first convince themselves that their method will adequately prepare students for the exams (Campbell and Zhao 1993); under such pressure, few are prepared to take the risk. No wonder when asked to what extent their teaching is governed by the exams, the teachers presented almost identical answers. As one of them put it, "It is just like a rope around the necks of teachers and students."

But this kind of teaching in secondary school has left a difficult job for college teachers. When asked, "Do you think your students are well prepared before they come to you as first-year students?", all the teachers gave a negative answer. They said the students, especially those from the remote areas, felt at a loss when the teacher spoke English in class, and they were used to being instructed rather than studying actively by themselves. When I asked secondary schoolteachers, "Do you know anything about the teaching of English in university?", most of them replied that they did not know. Some gave vague answers. It is obvious that secondary schoolteachers care how many students will be able to go to university, but they do not care much whether their students will be able to adapt themselves to study in college.

Conclusion

Through studying the examination papers and the questionnaire, we can see that although the intentions of the testmakers are good, the CEE and CET-4 have negative effects on China's present-day English teaching. First, the exams at both levels do not adequately test listening and speaking. This has discouraged the students from developing their oral English and has resulted in the teachers' failure to integrate the four skills in their teaching. Second, the students' reading is also influenced by the form of the exam. Whatever the questions are, they usually stay at the level of testing students' knowledge of structure and vocabulary and they seldom require the readers' active participation. As a result, students tend to process the texts in a bottom-up manner, and are not required to develop their reading abilities for practical use.

Although CEE and CET-4 have been responsible for this sort of English-language teaching and learning, the problem now is what we, as teachers, should do, given the present form of the exams. One question is how we can avoid separating students' learning into discrete skills; another is how we can improve the students' reading abilities beyond the skill of answering exam questions.

The experiments carried out by my colleagues and myself in the two-month teaching practicum in several institutions in Nanjing show that we can, to some extent, integrate the four skills in teaching (see Chapter Seven). The exercises in each unit of the textbooks, like the sections in the exams, are all presented as separate items, thus encouraging teachers to treat them separately; yet they can be changed into communicative activities. For example, while doing exercises concerned with words and phrases, we do not necessarily have to deal with them item by item. On the contrary, we may make a list of the words and phrases on the blackboard, and then ask the students to make up stories and report them to the class so that the students have a chance to practice their listening, speaking, reading, and writing at the same time. As the space here is limited, I will not list all the available examples, but I will simply sum up with the suggestion that if students do not know how to put what they have learned into use, then what they have learned is of little value.

As for students' reading, it is not necessary for teachers and students to follow a rigid process of doing only multiple-choice questions. In the course of teaching, we can develop students' global understanding of the text, for example, by asking them to write a summary or comments on the text so that they can be fully engaged. Alternatively, we may focus on the teaching of the background knowledge, and the understanding of the text itself may be left to the students without explaining every detail to them. Thus, it may promote a richer, more interactive approach to reading than do comprehension tests that focus mostly on details (Cohen 1994, 203), and students may be able to "learn techniques of reading by writing and techniques of writing by reading" (Widdowson 1978, 144).

Thus, teachers do not need to think that they are powerless to improve the situation. Even within the framework of the present exam, they can make their teaching more lively and communicative. However, the fact remains that the exams are in many ways counterproductive; there is an urgent need for the authorities to examine the tests critically and to consider how they can be improved.

6

Strategies for Reading
in English

As literacy, however defined, has become increasingly valued and necessary for living in the modern world, there has been a steady growth of research into the psycholinguistic processes involved in reading. These processes, being invisible, are not easy to study, but through a combination of experimental, observational, and introspective methods (see Clark and Clark 1977; Faerch and Kasper 1987; Goodman 1982; Smith 1982), researchers have developed, if not a complete model, at least one that is of considerable practical use in explaining reading problems and helping to solve them.

While there are differences of emphasis, most researchers seem now to agree that reading is a complex process involving interactions in at least two dimensions: between the reader and the text, on the one hand (or, to put it in more communicative terms, between the reader and the writer, as represented by the text), and between different levels of representation and interpretation on the other (Carrell, Devine, and Eskey 1988; Coady 1979; Grabe 1991; Rumelhart 1977). Thus, the reader perceives certain low-level cues—particular combinations of graphemes, for example—and ascribes meaning to them on the basis of linguistic knowledge; this perception of meaning then activates high-level concepts, or schemata, based on the reader's knowledge of the world and prior experience of text. These schemata in turn enable the reader to predict what will come next and to use this prediction to interpret further low-level cues; as these cues are perceived, the predictions are confirmed or revised (Goodman 1967; Smith 1982). Through the whole process, the reader builds up a representation of the text and develops some sort of relationship with the writer, whether that writer is perceived as a living human being or as a depersonalized authority (Hill and Parry 1992; Widdowson 1978).

At least that is the ideal, but the process is not always so smooth, especially when the reading is to be done in a second or foreign language. There will, for example, be obvious difficulties when low-level cues either are not recognized (as when they consist of new vocabulary items) or are misinterpreted (as when one graphemic combination is perceived as another).[1] Especially when reading is done in a second writing system as well as a second language, a disproportionate amount of energy may have to be spent on simply putting an oral representation on the graphemic display. Such problems in low-level, or "bottom-up," processing may in turn make "top-down" processing—the application of high-level schemata—difficult or impossible; thus, the reading process as a whole is, as Clarke (1980) has put it, short-circuited. On the other hand, problems can originate at the high level too: Many studies have shown that where readers are unfamiliar with the text structure or where they have no appropriate knowledge of the content, their interpretations can go badly awry (Carrell and Eisterhold 1983; Parry 1987, 1994; Reynolds et al. 1982; Steffenson et al. 1979). Difficulties may also arise from the fact that readers may feel alienated from the people or institutions that they perceive the text to represent, or if they misgauge the communicative intentions of the writer (Hill and Parry 1989).

The problems are not, of course, the same for all individuals, nor, when they are the same, are they dealt with in the same way. Hill and Anderson (1994), for example, document considerable variation in how readers handled a lacuna in a reading-comprehension test passage: some focused narrowly on low-level textual cues to solve the problem, while others drew massively on their extratextual knowledge to make sense of what is, as it stands, an inadequate text. My own work has shown similar diversity in how individuals cope with unfamiliar vocabulary: Of the two individuals whom I studied closely, one was clearly much more attentive to unfamiliar words than was the other and was much more concerned to put a precise and consistent representation on each lexical item (Parry 1991, 1996b).

Such variation is undoubtedly a function of individual personality, but since personality develops only in the context of culture, it probably reflects cultural differences too. In Hill and Anderson's and my own studies, differences definitely occurred across cultural lines, although there were other factors besides cultural membership that could be adduced as explanations. Other more quantitatively oriented studies lend support to the idea that cultural background is an important factor in determining reading strategies: Pritchard (1990), in particular, found that Americans and Palauans responded to passages of familiar and unfamiliar content in significantly different ways. Similarly Davis and Bistodeau (1993) found that French and English speakers used different strategies from each other, whether they were reading in their first language or in their second (the relationship between first- and second-language reading strategies was also different for the two groups). It was precisely such findings that inspired the work that is represented here. The

---

1. This latter phenomenon is characterized by Huckin and Bloch (1993) as "mistaken ID," a clear example from my own research being the reading of "peasant" as "pheasant." For a discussion of this and other kinds of lexical misinterpretation, see Parry (1991).

question was whether the participants in the Nanjing program would be able to establish any connection between their own cultural background, specifically with regard to Chinese literacy and their relationship to the English language, and their own and/or their students' strategies for reading in English (Parry 1993a, 1996a).

At the end of the first term, then, having completed their essays on "Literacy at Home," "Literacy in School," and "Approaching English," the participants were asked to write essays on "Making Sense of English Text." Many chose to write about their own reading strategies and about how those strategies had changed through the assignments they had done for the course. This chapter includes three essays of this type, together with two research papers written during the second term, when Wang Kui and Wang Jian followed their work on their own reading by examining the reading habits and strategies of their students.

A striking point about the participants' own English reading before they came to the program was their deliberate use of bottom-up rather than top-down strategies when they encountered difficulties. Bao Jingying, for example, asserts in "Learning a New Way of Reading" that the very concept of top-down as opposed to bottom-up processes was a revelation for her. She describes the strategies that she brought to the first reading assignment as closely corresponding to the methods used in a college English intensive-reading class: reading the text word by word and finding Chinese equivalents for all the new vocabulary. Given the length and complexity of the article assigned, this method proved unproductive; she was unable to relate to the content because of the frustration of not knowing individual words. This experience was common to many of the participants (see Parry 1995), but frustrating as it was, it did not cause her or the others to give up. On the contrary, by applying the concepts described in the article and in subsequent readings, she developed a strategy by which she focused on top-down processes, first of all, and postponed the conscious use of bottom-up ones until the second reading; she also modified her methods of learning new vocabulary. The changes were considerable and the results, apparently, gratifying.

Du Qunhua's account of the same experience, "Getting to Know a New Genre: Academic Articles" is less upbeat, but it is evident that her reading, too, developed considerably in the three months between reading the first article and writing the present essay. She describes in some detail the difficulties she encountered and discusses the strategies that she found most helpful in dealing with them. A particularly interesting feature of this account is the role that she ascribes to the requirement that she write a response to each reading. The responses were free in form and communicative in intention, and—as in the cases reported by Zamel (1992)—they had the effect of helping Du to integrate the text and to engage fully with the argument. Discussion with classmates, another communicative activity, was also helpful, she says. Despite the diffidence that she expresses in her conclusion, her research paper, which is printed in Chapter Five (see pp. 178–181), shows that she was indeed attaining proficiency in reading professional materials in English, as well as a sophisticated understanding of the processes involved.

When Zhu Xiaowen started the course, she was rather more confident about her English than the other two, but in "Reading Two Articles: A Comparison," she describes a similar progression. The first of the two articles of her title is the one referred to by Bao (Parry 1993a; as the first of the readings that I assigned them, it made a strong impression on them all), while the second (Hill and Parry 1992) is one assigned two months later (it has some stylistic affinity with the first since I was involved in the writing of each). Drawing on the responses that she wrote at the time of each assignment, Zhu gives a richly detailed account of the difficulties that she encountered in reading each article and of the strategies she used to deal with them. Like the other participants, she reports that the first assignment was difficult and that she consciously used a bottom-up process to build up a representation of the text from the interpretation of each and every sentence. It is interesting that she explicitly relates her strategies to her training in classical Chinese, as well as in English intensive reading.

The second assignment was an even longer and more difficult article, yet Zhu's approach to it was very different. She describes herself as coping far more "actively" with the text, by skimming the examples, for example, rather than working them out in detail, and using instances from her own experience to illustrate the ideas described. She was enabled to do this, she maintains, by the experience built up through the term of reading many articles of the same genre and about the same range of topics, so that the style of presentation, the issues raised, and much of the vocabulary had become familiar to her. She did not, however, abandon analytical strategies entirely, and she gives a fascinating description of how she used her analytical skills to deal with complex sentences, the syntax of which was radically different from what it would have been in Chinese.

These three are a small minority of the introspective essays that were written for this assignment, but they illustrate themes that were common to them all. In describing their own reading, the participants demonstrated that their analytical skills were strong, but that their integrative skills, especially for long texts, were relatively weak. This pattern of strength and weakness seems directly related to the experiences described in previous essays of learning to read in Chinese first and then English. The participants were also virtually unanimous in recognizing their integrative weakness as a problem, for it effectively prevented them from using their English to engage in professional discourse, and they were gratifyingly enthusiastic about the ways in which the course had helped and was helping them to address the problem. They identified a number of factors as contributing to this success:

First was the sheer volume of reading to be done—if they were to get any sleep at all, they simply had to learn to read faster.

Second was the coherence of the subject matter—I did not use the term with them, but in choosing the assignments I had deliberately followed the method recommended by Krashen (1981) of "narrow reading."

Third was the guidance given in class toward interpreting the text structure—I had, for example, given them a set of questions for reading research reports, and several of them commented on how useful these were.

Fourth were the interactive activities associated with the reading—writing response papers on the one hand and discussing their reading with each other (both in and out of class) on the other.

I should say, however, that an important factor that the participants did not identify (because they took it for granted) was the diligence and sheer tenacity that they brought to the task of learning new strategies; this too can be seen as an effect, perhaps the most important one, of their early training.

The linguistic experiences that the participants brought to the course and the ways in which they responded to it seem to have been fairly uniform—remarkably so, given the geographical distances between their homes, the range of their ages, and their obvious differences in personality. But can the same be said of their students? Unfortunately, only a couple of the participants decided to focus on reading strategies for their research. But those two, Wang Kui and Wang Jian, produced studies that fill out the picture, both of the common tendency to focus on analytical, bottom-up strategies, and the ability and desire of some individuals to transcend this tendency to achieve, through reading, fuller communication in English.

Wang Kui's paper, "Extensive Reading in College English: Attitudes, Strategies, and Problems," focuses on a neglected aspect of the college English curriculum, namely, reading for speed and fluency. Materials are provided for this purpose and the syllabus states that it is important, but the students that Wang surveyed reported that little or no time was spent on these materials in class. The teachers made no attempt to encourage students to work with them on their own, and the students, accordingly, did little such reading. Yet the students reported that they thought that extensive reading was important, they would like to do more of it, and they would like to have a wider range of materials with which to work. Here, as Wang points out, is a paradox, and the findings on the reading habits and strategies of four individual students are more paradoxical still, for it appears that of the four, those with the best reading habits (as seen from a Western perspective) were the least successful, in Chinese as well as in English. The measure of success is, of course, an exam (the CEE in this case) and, as one of Wang's informants pointed out, the short passages used for testing reading comprehension do not measure students' ability to work with longer texts and do not, therefore, reward those who learn to do so (cf. Du Qunhua's discussion in Chapter Five).

Besides the exam, there are other inhibiting factors too. Like children in primary and secondary school (see Chapter Two), the undergraduates that

Wang was working with complained that they had too little time for extensive reading, whether in Chinese or English and, as regards English, they also had insufficient materials. The overall picture that emerges is one of people who are unable to develop any substantial communicative use of English because of largely institutional constraints. Yet, as Wang points out, the potential for development is there, for the students reported a strong wish to do more extensive reading, and they also reported a greater tendency to use holistic reading strategies than one might have expected from their training.

Wang Jian, in "Chinese Students' Reading Strategies: A Study in Contrasts," reports think-aloud protocols made by two of her students while reading an English text, supplemented by what they told her in interviews after the reading. The students, while not specializing in languages, belonged to an exceptionally strong group, so she deliberately chose a text that they would find difficult—Lewis Thomas' essay, "The Lives of a Cell" (1993), which includes a great deal of technical vocabulary, though a precise understanding of it is not necessary for following the argument. When confronted with this text, the two students responded in dramatically different ways. One, Liu Wanli, was markedly holistic in his approach, consciously looking for the "main idea" and deliberately ignoring unfamiliar words that did not seem to be essential. He did, however, notice and make use of low-level rhetorical cues, such as a "but" at the beginning of a paragraph in which the idea set forth in the previous paragraph is refuted and the author's thesis is presented by way of contrast. Wang's account shows that Liu did not interpret everything in the text correctly, but it is clear that, despite the large numbers of unfamiliar words, he did establish real communication with the author, a point on which he commented explicitly himself. The other student, Lin Yanqing, had a less happy experience. He began with an attempt to be holistic but soon got bogged down with the unknown vocabulary, while he apparently missed important rhetorical cues. His response, once he realized he was in difficulties, was to start by looking up the new words in the dictionary and then to attempt to translate each paragraph. This is not to say that his approach was entirely bottom-up. Wang presents evidence that he did refer to his world knowledge while reading, but the schema in question seems to have been activated by an isolated lexical item without any relation to the broader configuration of concepts represented in the text. Thus, despite the large amount of time that he spent on the task, Lin never succeeded in integrating the text as a whole, and confessed at the end that he could not see what the author was getting at.

Wang Kui's and Wang Jian's studies are too small-scale to be used as a basis for generalizations, but taken together with the participants' own experience, they do suggest that, while Chinese students are likely to have strong analytical tendencies in their reading, they are certainly capable of a more holistic approach and would probably welcome it if encouraged by their teachers. The papers in this chapter suggest a number of ways in which this might be achieved, even within the context of the present exam-dominated system. Of first importance is the provision of more English reading materials; but for those materials to be maximally effective, they need to be systematically presented so as to be mutually reinforcing. Students also need explicit instruction in using rhetorical cues and inferring the meanings of new words from context, and they need assignments and class activities that will encourage them to respond to the texts actively and holistically. In these ways, the already considerable achievements of those Chinese students who do well enough in English to enter college can be built upon constructively so as to promote a fuller interaction—not only between levels of the text, but also between Chinese readers and foreign writers. It is through such an interaction, I believe, that Chinese reading of English can be transformed from what can be a somewhat sterile exercise in translation into one of potentially enriching intercultural communication.

1. Learning a New Way of Reading

Bao Jingying

It has been three months since I became a student in the United Board class at Nanjing University. What I appreciate most is my development of language-learning skills and strategies for reading original English texts. Now I have come to know that both top-down and bottom-up processes are best for reading in a communicative way. Before, I never heard anything about it.

At the beginning of my time here, what I usually did in reading was as follows: I read the English text only once, but I always read very carefully and attentively word by word, trying to decode the words for exact Chinese equivalence and trying to translate them into standard Chinese sentences. When I came across new words, I would stop at once to look them up in a dictionary and to select an appropriate meaning that would fit the text in which the word occurred. Then I would write the new words down in the margin of the text or in my notebook, including their pronunciation, parts of speech, and Chinese meanings. So I used a dictionary many times in reading a text. It always took me quite a long time to finish reading an English text, and I found it especially slow and tedious to read a long or difficult academic essay.

For example, the first article assigned this term was the first academic essay I had read. After I finished reading, I had not got the main idea. A lot of new words made me feel crazy and the unfamiliar content made me feel tired and want to give up. Though I have learned English for many years, my English was not so good—I did not know why. I used to ascribe this to my intelligence, but here I came to know that it was because of my learning strategies. I just tried to remember each individual word; I did not relate it to my own lexicon or put it into practice immediately. As a result, the new words went into my left ear and come out of my right ear at once. Thus, in order to write a response, I had to read again and again. Obviously, my learning strategies should be improved right away.

Gradually, with the development of my vocabulary and knowing something about the background knowledge of what we were reading, and especially the questions we were given to guide us, I felt my reading ability becoming better. The fact that we were always required to write a response to our reading reinforced my growing skills and competence.

Now when I read an English text, first I use top-down strategies; that is, I read the whole text very quickly—I have stopped reading word by word. Once I encounter a new word, I infer its meaning from its formation or from the context in which it occurs. For example, in the article, "The Social Construction of

Reading Strategies," the word *strenuous* appears in the sentence, "Similarly, strenuous efforts were put into measuring and grading individuals in terms of their ability to read, following basic principles that Thorndike laid down" (Parry 1993a, 149). I guessed from the context and the formation that it is an adjective, because of the suffix "-ous," and it means "great" efforts or "all of one's" efforts. Thus, I got the word's meaning. If I can't guess the meaning of a new word, I give it up and just outline it. Then I go on with my reading.

We have been taught before that an author usually uses one of two ways to present an argument, either an upright triangle (i.e., from general statement to particular examples) or a falling triangle (i.e., from particular examples to general statement). So I pay special attention to the first and last paragraphs of the text, in order to get a clear clue to what it is about. The topic sentence often appears either at the beginning of a paragraph or at the end, and sometimes in the middle. When I am reading, I focus on finding out the topic sentence. Thus, through the first reading, I can get a general idea of the text.

For the second reading, I use bottom-up strategies. I focus on some details and try to see how the author gives his or her argument, and I also try to fill in the gaps that I did not get from the first reading. As for those outlined new words, I look up the ones that I am interested in. If I find the word particularly interesting or think it is frequently used, I will copy the example sentences from the dictionary, paying attention to the new word's synonyms or antonyms and to its formal similarity to other words that are different in meaning. For example, the word *desert* has two different pronunciations and different parts of speech: When it is used as a noun, it is pronounced ['dez ə:t] and means a large piece of sandy land; but when it is used as a verb, it is pronounced [di 'zə:t] and means to leave completely, as in, "When he had to speak to her, his courage suddenly deserted him." I also try as much as possible to use the new words within my lexicon right now. For example, I made up a sentence with "desert" by myself: "All my friends deserted me when I needed them most."

Finally, I skim over the whole text again so as to make sure I understand it and go over the useful expressions. For each English text, I choose only five new words that I think are most important to learn by heart. I also outline the topic sentences and scan them one more time. Sometimes I make notes in the margin to help me remember the structure of the text as a whole. For example, I might write "introduction," "prose topic," "positive concept," "by contrast," "good evidence," and so on.

In short, those are my strategies for making sense of English text. I have not practiced this method for very long, but it has helped me a lot in developing my reading speed and comprehension. At the same time, writing responses to the reading materials has also reinforced my reading ability. In a word, I think it is really worthwhile for me to study here.

2. Getting to Know a New Genre: Academic Articles

Du Qunhua

I seldom read academic articles in English before I came to this teacher-training class, so the first time I took up an assigned article ("The Social Construction of Reading Strategies," Parry 1993a), I really felt frustrated. I felt the article was so abstract that I did not even get a rough idea of what it was saying. The first time I used a top-down strategy, but it came to nothing. I felt puzzled as to how to write the response. My mind seemed totally empty. I was especially confused by the arguments held by different researchers; I could not tell which was which.

When the top-down strategy failed me, I had to use a bottom-up one, consulting the dictionary when particular words baffled my understanding. Besides, I made some notes while reading, jotting down some ideas presented by different researchers so that I could make some comparisons in my response later. As a result, I felt my way of reading was not worthwhile, because my chain of thought was interrupted every now and then by looking up the unknown words in the dictionary; it also took me a long time, which I felt I could not afford, for I had a lot of other reading to do. Having finished the second time, I had to go over the article once again. This time I got much more idea of what the author was saying, and it was not until then that I began writing my response.

What on earth are the obstacles that have prevented me from making sense of the articles so far? I summarize them as follows: First, I have not had enough practice in reading academic articles, which usually appear very abstract and include a lot of special terms that make understanding difficult. For example, the term "the social construction of reading strategies" puzzled me when I first began reading this article; I really did not know why the word *social* was used. I did not understand it until I had read the article through twice. It means that one's reading strategies can be influenced by one's surrounding circumstances, by the environment in which one grows up, by the education one receives when young, and by personal preferences.

Second, academic articles usually involve a lot of ideas and arguments. The articles we have read so far are of two major types: review articles and research articles. I find the former type is more difficult, for this kind of article consists of comments on somebody else's point of view. For example, in Gee's article, "Orality and Literacy: From *The Savage Mind* to *Ways with Words*" (1986), so many researchers' points of view were presented that I got confused. Another important reason is that I had not read their original articles, so

Gee's discussion appeared very abstract and difficult for me to grasp. On the other hand, the latter type seems easier to follow because there are usually concrete subjects, materials, and ways in which the researchers are making experiments or doing surveys. When reading this kind of article, I find it helpful to keep in mind the questions we were given in class:

1. What did the researchers want to know?
2. How did they look for information?
3. What did they find?
4. How did they explain their findings?

I find these four questions extremely useful, because they will help me develop my understanding in a systematic way. If I neglect these questions, I usually get a mess in my mind.

Third, I often feel it difficult to understand an article thoroughly because I lack the appropriate background knowledge. For example, when we were asked to read Hatano's "How Do Japanese Children Learn to Read?" (1986), it really took me a long time. For much of the article, the author describes the two orthographies used for Japanese: Standard Japanese Orthography and Children's Japanese Orthography. The two orthographies are presented differently and are acquired at different stages, which sounded totally new to me. The special terms *hiragana* and *katakana* alone took me a long time to distinguish. If I had learned Japanese, I would not have found it so difficult.

Some of my reading habits can also slow me down, but I find them difficult to get rid of. Whatever the material I am reading and regardless of whether it is easy or difficult, I tend to think aloud, which I think will force me to concentrate. This will no doubt cause me to read more slowly, but I sometimes find it works if I read sentence by sentence, especially when the sentence I am reading is the key point of a paragraph. I find it worthwhile to read or reread it because it will help me digest what the author wants to say. Another habit is my way of dealing with new words. Before I came here and at the early stage after I came here, I used to consult the dictionary, write down the Chinese equivalent and usage of the word I had looked up, and then copy it down on a piece of paper. I thought I could enlarge my vocabulary in this way, but now I have found it no easy job to memorize those words out of context, especially those special terms that are seldom used in our daily life. What is more, this exercise will not be applicable when we are only required to write a response to what we read instead of memorizing new words.

Three months have gone by. We have read a lot of articles, some of which are easy, some more difficult. No matter what they are, I try to stick to the top-down strategy, because I am sure it will improve my efficiency in reading sooner or later. When confronted with words I do not know or sentences I cannot understand, I do not turn to the dictionary for help immediately, but try to find hints elsewhere in the article that will help my understanding. For example, while reading Gee's article, I encountered this sentence: "Writing is integrated and detached, while speech is fragmented and involved" (1986, 726). I did not know the word *detached,* but I can guess the meaning from the sentence structure. The word *while* here introduces a clause whose meaning is contrary to the meaning of the main clause. *Fragmented* and *integrated* are antonyms; so are *detached* and *involved.* Because I know the word *involved,* I can guess the meaning of *detached.* If the article is a long one, I am now used to making some notes along the margin, writing a few words here and there, such as "the author's idea," "controversial problem," "key point," "three stages," and "contrast," all of which will remind me of what I have read and make it easier for me to write the response.

Subtitles help me a lot to trace the main ideas of an article, especially when it is a long and difficult one. For example, in "Participant Structures and Communicative Competence: Warm Springs Children in Community and Classroom," Philips (1972) presents her ideas by giving subtitles such as "Introduction," "Cultural and Educational Background of the Warm Springs Indians," "Conditions for Speech Use in School Classrooms," "Conditions for Speech in the Warm Springs Indian Communities," and "Conclusion." Skimming the subtitles, we get a rough idea of what the author is going to dwell on: that what affects the Warm Springs children's communicative competence has a lot to do with their educational background, and with the conditions in both schools and their own communities.

Throughout this semester, we have been required to write responses to the academic articles that we read. The responses may include our reactions to the ideas that we have encountered, and we are free to present our own ideas on whether we agree with the ideas in the article, whether the material is relevant to our concerns, or whether we can see any flaws in the argument. We can also express the difficulties that we have in doing the reading or our strategies for dealing with the difficulties. If I am not required to write a response, I will find it difficult to concentrate my mind on what I am reading. Then I will fail to follow the author's intention in writing the article; what I have got may be only fragments instead of a coherent picture of the whole. But things will be quite different if I begin reading with the intention of writing a response afterwards. It compels me to think and ask myself frequently why and how the author has come to a conclusion.

Sometimes I can benefit a lot from discussing some points in the article with my classmates. I find their way of thinking and the way of understanding the article are worth learning. I once talked with Zhu Xiaowen about Gee's article. I was puzzled by the author's intention because his article involves several researchers' ideas. I failed to understand the significance of the title, "From *The Savage Mind* to *Ways with Words.*" She said the word *savage* here did not have the usual meaning we ascribe to it. Before the invention of written language, people could convey their thoughts and ideas orally. That was limited, for it restricted the spread of people's thoughts. With the development of society, people found it necessary to invent some means by which they could write down what they were thinking. With written language, people read at a high level. . . . So talking with somebody else has helped me a lot in making sense of a text.

In a word, my reading ability, especially my ability in reading academic articles, has improved to some extent, but I still remain poor in some respects; for example, my reading speed is still very slow. Sometimes I fail to understand thoroughly the author's intention or get confused by the author's ideas. Such things, which happen when time is limited, show a need for further improvement; it is only by constant reading that I can make progress.

3. Reading Two Articles: A Comparison

Zhu Xiaowen

Parry (1993a) suggests that one's reading strategies are formed by the process of literacy education and through the ways of socialization, and thus they are closely related to one's particular social and cultural background. It follows that these strategies will probably change and develop in accordance with one's educational improvement, intellectual advancement, and changing sociocultural experience. By studying two cases of my own reading experiences, I have discovered development, as well as continuity, in my own reading strategies.

The first case was at the beginning of our teacher-training program at Nanjing University in September 1994. The reading assignment was an academic paper by Parry (1993a), "The Social Construction of Reading Strategies: New Directions for Research." Because I had rarely read any academic papers by English-speaking researchers before I participated in this program, I was bogged down in my very first reading assignment.

To understand the paper, I spent at least four hours reading the five-thousand-word article four times. In my response to the paper, I complained that I had great difficulty in comprehension after reading the opening lines, which were the abstract of the paper (for it was quite different from the kind of summary of a story that I was familiar with). So I decided that I was not going to read a story but do a piece of work! Being anxious to know just how difficult this work was going to be, I quickly went through the whole paper, making as many assumptions as possible. Even this rough reading took me more than one hour. As I completed the first reading, I knew no more than that the author had a new theory, a sociocultural theory of reading.

The second time when I began to read the article, I found it was even more difficult, for I suddenly realized there were not only lots of words and terms I did not know, but also many theories and researchers I had never come across. So I had to slow down, repeatedly looking back and forth, figuring out the meanings, translating English into Chinese occasionally, and looking up words in dictionaries. I tried hard to make sure I could read every sentence and make out its structure with subject and predicate, though not necessarily understanding every word. However, when I finished the second reading, I was still not sure how the author formed her theory. I did not realize until I finished the third reading that it was because I was concentrating too much on the small details of lexis and syntax to pay attention to the paper's rhetorical structure and organization.

While I was reading for the third time, I gradually felt that there was something lightening my brain, as I put it in my response. Everything became brighter and brighter. I could see how the author drew on the other researchers' theories and studies, from early psycholinguistic work to later and up-to-date achievements in the research field of reading strategies, and how she presented her own argument—a couple of case studies that aroused my own interest, for one of the two types of reading was so familiar to me and somewhat a reflection of my own reading.[2] At this stage, I began to agree with the author occasionally, trying to search for similar examples in my memory. As the author was comparing people from different countries, ethnic groups, and communities, I was thinking of my own students who come from different backgrounds—rural or urban, educated or illiterate.

I read the article a fourth time because I wanted to make sure I was not making too many presumptions and improper relations that would easily result in misunderstandings. The third and fourth reading took me one and a half hours.

I concluded my response saying that this process of reading was like finding a way out of a dark forest single-handedly. However, I enjoyed doing that very much, partly because of the pleasure and satisfaction that followed the hardship, and partly because I had a great deal of similar experience and enjoyment in learning and studying texts in old Chinese (文言文 , *wén yán wén,* which is different both in characters and syntax from modern Chinese)[3] in my secondary-school years and in studying English in my college-English intensive-reading courses. Our textbook for the third year in college was *Advanced English* compiled by Zhang Hanxi. Some of the texts in this book were very difficult, and we were completely at a loss when we began to read them. To do the work, our teacher usually explained them sentence by sentence and paragraph by paragraph, analyzing syntax and paragraph development and pointing out rhetorical devices, topics, and themes. Because I was an attentive student and was always following the teachers' instructions, I could use these procedures in my own reading as well.

After two months' studying, at the end of October, my reading strategies seem to have changed a bit because I have been reading a large amount of materials, mainly academic papers, as well as books on linguistics, grammar, and semantics. My vocabulary concerning language, grammar, pedagogy, and psycholinguistics has enlarged, and I have been familiarized with the development and new achievements in the linguistic and pedagogical fields. As to the academic articles, not only have I gained much knowledge in the vocabulary, syntax, and organization of research papers, but also about

2. Zhu is referring here to the case of Ae Young, a Korean student who appeared to have highly analytical reading strategies. Her behavior was in marked contrast to the more holistic approach manifested by Dimitri, a Greek Cypriot. See Parry (1996b). (Ed.)
3. See Wu Lili's essay in Chapter Three. (Ed.)

the work and theories of certain well-known researchers, linguists, educators, and authors. In addition to these improvements, I have also realized some differences between Chinese and English that have influenced our thinking models. Thus, I have become less passive and am no longer dragged by the text, but am rather actively coping with it, paying different attention to different parts of it.

Here is a description of my reading at the end of October. The particular reading assignment was "The Test at the Gate: Models of Literacy in Reading Assessment" by Hill and Parry (1992), the latter being the same author who wrote the first assignment, while the former had been introduced to us a couple of times before my reading.

This paper was not easy reading; for one thing, it was rather long (about nine thousand words), and for another, it was written in unfamiliar language, using close-fit syntax and academic vocabulary, and introducing specialized terms such as "autonomous model of literacy," "reading assessment," "pragmatic model of literacy," "metalinguistics," "ascribed" versus "assumed identity," and "external" versus "internal reciprocity." The sentences were comparatively long and varying in structure, with many inversions; parentheses; structures in the passive voice; and long complex noun, prepositional, and verbal phrases. The unfamiliar words like *paramount, indigenous,* and *elucidated* also made the reading more difficult.

However, I could arrange my own reading process for this particular text with the help of my past experience and strategies. I made up my mind to read as fast as possible, for I knew the faster I read, the less translation I would do—too much translation not only slows down your reading speed, but also hinders your comprehension from context.

While reading through the paper, I found the ideas were easier for me to catch than the vocabulary and sentence structures. The test examples (one is British and the other American) were even more familiar to me; so I immediately called on my knowledge of our own testing systems and test contents, quickly labeling them as reflecting the autonomous model of literacy. I went through the whole article with a circling process of four stages:

1. Looking for ideas while making guesses.

2. Skimming the examples and thinking of examples from my own experience.

3. Understanding the ideas and checking the guesses.

4. Skipping the examples and complex syntax; only looking for key words and simple sentences to form ideas in my mind.

I know well that my reading is often stopped by the English passive voice and inversions. Because Chinese seldom uses such structures and often has different orders of words, my thinking tends to go just the opposite way of the thoughts that are flowing on the paper I am reading. For this reason, I paused and spent some time on these sentences on purpose. For example, I read the following long sentence twice and thought about it for one minute before going on: "The relationship between literacy and the development of philosophical and scientific thinking parallels the relationship between understanding rotary motion and the development of wheeled transport." My Chinese thinking mode immediately occupied my brain, and I considered the subject was terribly long and had an inversion; in Chinese, we seldom have such a long subject and the equivalent of "the relationship" usually comes at the end. Also the Chinese word for *parallel* here could not be a transitive verb, and thus it could not stand in the middle of the sentence. So I was trying to adjust my thinking to the sequence of the English sentence:

A. Relationship between (1) literacy and (2) the development of philosophical and scientific thinking.

B. Relationship between (3) understanding rotary motion and (4) the development of wheeled transport.

C. A parallels B.

D. $(1) \rightarrow (2)$ parallels $(3) \rightarrow (4)$.

When I am studying my mental analysis now, I can understand that what I was doing then was reorganizing my thinking sequence from the original author's thinking mode (if I put the sentence in Chinese, its sequence should be {(1) + (2) + relationship} + {(3) + (4) + relationship} + parallel).

In Chinese, a comparative degree is rarely expected to occur in noun phrases, especially when two things are compared. So I also took a few moments to make sense of the following sentence:

> According to Olson, not only is a wider range of vocabulary typically used in text than in speech, but words are used in more precise ways; similarly, the syntactic resources of the language are exploited more fully for the purpose of rhetorical emphasis, especially given the substantial loss of paralinguistic cues in writing. (Hill and Parry 1992, 455)

Again, I looked for "in text" and "in speech" because they should come out first in my thought sequence, and I thought over the phrase "given . . . in writing" because it should also come before the main clause. However, I was just hesitating for a little while, not actually making the inversions.

I also took precautions to cope with long subordinate clauses; but they did not bother me a lot, for I could easily understand them in a coordinate way (as Chinese has only coordination). Despite the Chinese-thinking interruptions, I could read the whole article fluently without stopping for translation into Chinese.

Although this paper was much longer than the reading assignment at the beginning of the program and in spite of occasional stops, my first reading was completed, albeit roughly and inconsistently, within one and a half hours. The second time I read the article, I followed similar procedures to those of the first reading; however, I dwelt upon every example carefully, as well as on all the complex syntactic structures and vocabulary, and the relationships between sentences and paragraphs. This time I gained a much better understanding, for I could comprehend the special terms by making inferences from the context, especially from the examples cited to support the ideas. I did look up several new words, but I did not do that for the technical terms because the dictionaries did not help, while the context could explain them quite well.

To understand the text, I read for ideas while making guesses. Also, I read quickly or just skipped some examples, while drawing on my own experiences of reading at different times or for different purposes. Through the examples of other people and my own experience, I could understand those ideas I had read and thus check my assumptions. Once I got the authors' ideas, I again skipped the examples, trying to relate the ideas to my own store of knowledge. For instance, when I read about the interaction between a reader and a writer, I immediately thought about my reading novels and how I often felt myself drifting into the setting; the nearer to the setting, the better and more enjoyable. Thus, I understood the notion of ascribed and assumed identity.

When comparing my second case of reading with the first one, I find that my interaction with the text takes place at an earlier stage in the second case, and my reading speed has improved a lot. I spent three hours reading nine thousand words for the second paper, compared to four hours reading five thousand words for the first one. I could solve lexis and syntax problems after having a general understanding of the second paper. However, at the beginning, I simply could not understand anything without making out the words and sentence structures. Now I even more believe that my reading strategies will surely improve further if I can keep on my academic reading.

4. Extensive Reading in College English: Attitudes, Strategies, and Problems

Wang Kui

At advanced proficiency levels in a second language, the ability to read the written language at a reasonable rate and with good comprehension has long been recognized to be as important as oral skills, if not more so (Eskey 1970). *College English* is a series of textbooks in nationwide use for teaching English to nonmajor college students in China under the authority of the State Education Commission. It gives great emphasis to learners' reading abilities and provides reading materials under three categories: *Intensive Reading, Extensive Reading,* and *Fast Reading. Intensive Reading* aims mainly at developing learners' vocabulary, grammar, and some basic reading skills through teachers' careful and detailed explanation of short texts. *Extensive Reading* and *Fast Reading,* although named separately, have the same aim: to develop learners' reading fluency and accuracy through contact with large quantities of reading materials of different styles and contents.

While intensive and extensive reading are complementary, and both are necessary to language acquisition, extensive reading is in one sense the kind of reading that really counts. The best way to learn to read is, after all, by reading (Goodman 1993). People read because they want to get something from the writing: facts, ideas, enjoyment, and so on. They are interested in the content of the writing rather than in the particular grammatical and lexical items used. But extensive reading is also an effective means of extending the command of the language (Nuttall 1982). As Parry suggests in her study about vocabulary:

> The process of ascribing a precise set of semantic features to a particular word is necessarily a gradual one and will usually require several encounters in informative contexts. (Parry 1993b, 109)

It is quite obvious that reading widely—that is, extensive reading—can enable learners both to get the meaning of the writings and to learn the language.

Based on these language-learning and -teaching theories, *College English* supplies the learners with extensive-reading materials that are three times the amount of the intensive-reading materials so that learners can have opportunities to gradually master the reading skills through a large amount of practice. However, in the actual teaching and learning process, extensive reading has long been neglected. Both teachers and learners of college English pay much more attention to intensive reading than they do to extensive reading. The result is that learners have insufficient opportunity to be exposed to extensive reading, despite its importance in the improvement of reading skills.

Why does that happen? What are learners' attitudes toward extensive reading? What reading strategies do they usually employ in dealing with extensive-reading materials? What can college English teachers do to improve the situation? This paper reports an initial attempt to examine these questions.

Method

Subjects   The study reported here was based on a class of thirty-two first-year English learners majoring in chemistry at Nanjing Institute of Chemical Technology. The class consisted of five girls and twenty-seven boys. They came from twelve provinces of China and their average age was twenty-one. Their average Chinese and English scores in the CEE were 93 and 109, respectively, with 150 as the full mark. By the time the study took place, these learners had had six years' experience of English study in secondary school plus one year of English-learning experience at college. They were studying Band II of *College English,* and they had four hours per week of English classes for intensive reading, extensive reading, and fast reading, and two hours every other week of English-listening classes.

Instruments   A questionnaire and an interview schedule were designed to investigate the subjects' attitudes toward and experiences of reading. The questionnaire consisted of three parts entitled, respectively, "Some Personal Reference," "Reasons for Studying English," and "Reading Attitudes and Strategies." Under these titles, nineteen items were given, most of which were in the form of multiple choice, but blanks were supplied for subjects to make free comments.

The interview schedule was an expansion of the questionnaire. It consisted of thirty-eight items, most of which were open-ended questions, and these items fell into four parts entitled "Background," "Chinese Reading," "English Reading," and "Chinese and English Reading."

Procedures   The study was completed in two steps. First, the questionnaire was administered to the subjects in class. When all the subjects had handed in their questionnaires, I analyzed the results by making a table, which enabled me to see the general tendency of the subjects' answers. After that, I chose four subjects according to their Chinese and English scores in CEE: one with the highest scores in both Chinese and English, one with the lowest scores in both, one with a high Chinese score and a low English score, and one with a low Chinese score and a high English score.

Then I interviewed these four subjects using the interview schedule. The interviews were carried out in Chinese. In the interviews, the students were encouraged to give free and detailed descriptions and comments. The interviews were recorded with the students' permission and then transcribed and translated for descriptive analysis.

Findings

Students' Responses to the Questionnaire   The results of the survey were analyzed and the final figures constituted a group portrait of the students' reading experiences in Chinese and English and of their attitudes and strategies in dealing with extensive reading in English.

On the question of Chinese reading, twenty-three of thirty-two subjects claimed they often read newspapers and magazines, and nine claimed they sometimes read these materials. Twenty-two said they sometimes read novels, and only nine often read novels. As to reference books, fifteen reported they never read anything outside class, and eleven said they read some. It was obvious that newspapers and magazines were the subjects' first choices of Chinese reading materials outside class and novels were supplementary.

Then the subjects reported their Chinese reading strategies. Of the thirty-two subjects, fourteen claimed the practice of a main-idea-to-detail strategy and fifteen a detail-to-main-idea strategy. Yet when dealing with difficult words and sentences, only two subjects admitted the use of dictionaries, while fourteen said they tried to guess from the context and fifteen said they ignored the difficulties and went on with their reading.

When asked about English reading, fourteen subjects said they had not read any materials outside class before college and fourteen said they had read a few. After coming to college, thirteen subjects read a few, eleven read some, and only one said she read a lot. The figures here indicated the fact that this group of subjects did not have much English reading experience outside class.

With regard to the *Extensive Reading* and *Fast Reading* materials included in their *College English* series, the subjects reported that they were usually expected to read these materials by themselves as homework, and no instruction or help was given by their teacher. Twenty-four subjects regarded these materials as useful to the improvement of their reading skills, seventeen thought them important for the acquisition of general knowledge, and five considered them beneficial to their vocabulary study. Twenty-six subjects claimed they spent less than two hours per week on these materials, four spent two to four hours, and only two spent more than four hours. However, all of them wished that they could get some instruction from their teacher about the reading, and twenty-four subjects said they felt the reading materials included in *College English* were far from enough for them to develop their reading abilities if they had time. What is more, thirteen subjects said that they would like to read newspapers and magazines, and twelve would prefer novels if they were free to choose the reading materials.

The subjects also gave a brief report about their English reading strategies. Of the thirty-two subjects, nineteen claimed the practice of a main-idea-to-detail strategy and eleven a detail-to-main-idea one. The result was quite similar to that of their Chinese reading. Similarly, only three subjects admitted the use of dictionaries. But the number of people saying they tried to guess the difficult words and sentences from the context, in contrast to fourteen in Chinese reading, rose to twenty-one; the number saying they just neglected the difficulties went from fifteen in Chinese reading to six. This can be explained by the fact that twenty-one subjects found vocabulary was the biggest obstacle in their reading.

Results of the Interviews   The personal backgrounds of the four interviewees were as follows:

1. Zhou Xiaobin was a twenty-year-old male student from a rural area in Fengxiang County, Baoji City in Shaanxi Province. He got 115 out of 150 in Chinese and 130 out of 150 in English in CEE, the highest scores in the group.

2. Wang Shuang was a twenty-year-old male student from the suburb of Nancong City in Sichuan Province. He got 78 in Chinese and 91 in English in CEE, the lowest scores among the group.

3. Chen Qianjin was a twenty-year-old male student from a small town in Feng County, Xuzhou City in Jiangsu Province. His Chinese score was 107 and English 91, the former quite high in this group and the latter the lowest.

4. Qian Hong was a twenty-year-old female student from the urban area of Suzhou City in Jiangsu Province. Her Chinese score was 93 and English 127, the former just at the average level of the group and the latter the second highest.

Starting from such a variety of personal backgrounds, I expected to see a wide range of reading experiences and strategies in the interviewees, both in Chinese and in English, and thus to illuminate the way they dealt with English extensive reading.

Chinese Reading. Though born and brought up in different environments, the four interviewees showed some common experiences of Chinese reading. They all began their outside class reading from the second year of their primary schools with picture books designed for children. Differences could only be noticed in their later stages of reading. Living in peasants' families and having limited access to reading materials, Zhou and Chen did not do much reading before college. When they read the storybooks and magazines available from other people, they just read for fun. When they came across difficult characters or sentences during the main-plot-oriented reading, they skipped them or asked for others' help instead of consulting dictionaries.

In Qian's case, access to reading materials was not a problem. Her father, an engineer, and mother, a worker, read a lot themselves, and they sent her many novels. She also could borrow books from school libraries. Her Chinese teachers asked her to read books outside class and to hand in short reflections on the reading. She developed the habit of reading Chinese character by character without skipping any detail, even if the details were boring ones, because she wanted complete understanding of the materials. In college she spent about six to eight hours every week reading magazines, essays, and novels by famous Chinese writers because of "the relaxation I found in the reading, the elegant, fluent language used, and the strong, deep emotions conveyed in the materials."

The most striking experiences of Chinese reading were reported by Wang. Although born in a poor peasant's family, Wang was lucky because he had some kind teachers and neighbors. They lent or gave books to him, stimulated his interest in reading extensively, and helped develop his habit of making reflections after reading. He adopted a somewhat holistic strategy, as he said:

> Usually I read for main plots of the articles or books. For the difficult characters and structures, I ignore them in my first reading. Then, if I feel the theme or message implied attracts me greatly, I will do the second or even the third reading, in which I try to guess the meaning of the difficult parts.

Even in college, he stuck to the habit of spending ten to fifteen hours every week reading newspapers, novels, and biographies of famous people, because, he said:

> I want to enrich my knowledge, to feel the beauty of the writings, and to see through the reading how other people speak and behave so I can cultivate my own moral ideas, develop my own image, and set up my own identity in the society.

English Reading. The four interviewees claimed that before college, their main source of reading besides textbooks was the model tests for CEE, and they read these materials only for the purpose of finishing the exercises after them. To deal with such materials, they usually read them through without paying attention to isolated difficult words and sentences. When they had trouble getting answers to the exercises, they would read the materials again and try to guess the meaning of the puzzling parts, then turn to dictionaries if necessary.

Despite the similarities of the interviewees' reading experiences before college, Wang reported something special. Having much Chinese reading experience, Wang had had a strong desire to read some English materials in junior-secondary school because he thought that reading extensively would help him approach English language as it did for his Chinese. However, having no access to any English materials outside class, he could only begin his reading in his last year of senior-secondary school when he got his first English novel, *The Adventures of Tom Sawyer*. He remembered that at the beginning of his reading, he tried to understand every detail. But soon he found it time-consuming to look up every unfamiliar word, so he began to guess words from the context. To his surprise, he understood the material quite clearly even without knowing the exact meaning of every word.

When Wang finished his novel, he felt his improvement in reading speed and comprehension. He also felt it urgent to enlarge his vocabulary. So he recited all the words listed in English textbooks. In addition, he summarized the words that he got from the second reading of the novel and tried to memorize them.

After coming to college, there were no more model tests, and the English teachers only concentrated on *Intensive Reading* textbooks in class, leaving *Extensive Reading* and *Fast Reading* to the learners themselves. The four interviewees developed quite different attitudes toward reading outside class. Zhou said he did not even have time to prepare for intensive-reading class. Chen claimed he spent at most two hours every week on *Extensive Reading* and *Fast Reading* materials just to finish the exercises, never bothering to consider particular difficulties in the reading. Qian and Wang, the only two claiming that they spent more than four hours every week on reading English in their responses to the questionnaire, actually spent eight to ten hours and thirteen to fifteen hours, respectively, every week. In addition to the *Extensive Reading* and *Fast Reading* materials, Qian had been reading *Gulliver's Travels* and Wang *The Three Musketeers*. Both of them reported that unfamiliar words were their biggest obstacle in reading, and to deal with these words, they guessed a lot. Wang added that in order to grasp more words, he usually consulted dictionaries and purposefully put the words into different categories to memorize. He thought this worked well for his vocabulary.

With all the differences in the time and effort they put into English reading, all the interviewees expressed the view that reading extensively was a good way of studying English and the *Extensive Reading* and *Fast Reading* materials were far from enough if they wanted to achieve English reading proficiency. If they had time, they claimed, they would like to read some famous English novels, newspapers, and magazines under the guidance of their English teachers. They believed that such reading might help them improve their English and acquire some background knowledge about English language and culture. "What's more," added Wang and Qian, "such reading enables us to taste the flavor of real English."

When asked about the reading strategies they would possibly employ in such reading, the four interviewees listed reading roughly for main plots, main idea, and framework as the most important, and only in the second reading, as Wang put it, "Will I read in some detail with the help of a dictionary."

Finally, the interviewees gave some comments about Chinese and English reading. In their opinion, the purpose of doing extensive reading in Chinese was mainly to get knowledge and entertainment, while the reading in English mainly aimed at learning the language. However, there was some relationship between Chinese and English reading. Wang summed it up in this way,

Both for Chinese and English, reading extensively and persistently is the best way to improve reading abilities. These abilities can't be achieved by reading one or two books. And Chinese proficiency can facilitate English reading comprehension and reading speed.

Discussion

The preceding analysis suggests some characteristics and problems of the English reading practices of the group.The students did not seem to have much opportunity to read English extensively both before and in college. The reasons were various. In the first place, they did not have enough time. Before coming to college, they had to prepare for the CEE, and the limited English reading they had done was test-centered and thus exercise-centered. In college, they were busy with their studies in their major and the *Intensive Reading* books alone took a lot of their time and effort. In the second place, the students did not seem to have a high motivation for reading extensively. In their opinion, Chinese reading provided them with information and entertainment. Although English reading might achieve the same purposes, it was mainly a means of language study. Such factors as vocabulary, grammar, writing style, and cultural background knowledge constituted great difficulties in their reading and made them feel it fruitless to spend a lot of time on the work. Besides, because the various kinds of English tests they had experienced and would take did not reflect actual reading proficiency, they did not see why they should assign time and effort to reading extensively.

Take Wang's case, for example. From his report of his reading experiences, we can see that he was strongly conscious of the importance of reading extensively and he seemed to have good reading habits—a successful combination of the holistic and analytical methods. Yet he did not get much reward in the tests. He said:

> I only got seventy-eight out of 150 points in the CEE on English. The reading section took forty points of the paper and I don't think the short passages and the few multiple-choice questions in the section could measure the reading proficiency of the test-takers.

It seems that the present examination system does not reward the communicative-reading approach—a point that Du's research demonstrates in detail (see Chapter Five, pp. 157–168).

The last reason for the students' lack of English extensive-reading experiences was their lack of access to proper reading materials and instruction in reading. Compared with the chances of their getting Chinese reading materials and instruction from people around, their chances of approaching English materials were few. Most students had not read anything outside class before college. Even in reading the few materials available, they focused on nothing but the exercises set on them. In college, their English teachers never made any suggestions as to what materials they should choose to read after class or what strategies they should employ in dealing with *Extensive Reading* and *Fast Reading* books in order to improve their reading abilities.

Despite the problems existing in practice, the reading experiences of the group show some promising features. Most important of all, the students showed awareness of the significance of reading extensively and said they would like to read more if possible. They thought the materials included in *College English* were insufficient if they wanted to improve their reading skills, acquire knowledge, and enlarge their vocabulary. They would like to read some English newspapers, magazines, and novels if they were left the freedom to choose more materials.

Another striking finding about the group was that these students employed a much more holistic method than might be expected in both Chinese and English reading. This tendency might be observed in more detail from the four interviewees' reports about the reading strategies they would like to use in future reading, and these strategies seemed to be quite different from the traditional ones used by Chinese students in their intensive-reading classes.

Conclusion

This paper presents a group portrait, though incomplete, of how college English students deal with extensive reading. The findings may not be considered universal to all college English learners, but they do present to us an interesting and paradoxical situation: students perceive the significance of extensive reading, but they have actually done little of it. The blame cannot be put solely on students. The educational system, the design of tests, the teachers' application of the teaching materials, and the allocation of class time all play an important part in the fact that extensive reading, though important, has long been ignored in college English learning and teaching. The exploratory research reported here shows that immediate attention should be given to extensive reading and there is urgent need for further research in this field.

5. Chinese Students' Reading Strategies: A Study in Contrasts

Wang Jian

China, with a population of 1.2 billion or so, may claim to have more EFL learners than any other country: nearly all secondary-school children are required to study English for six years and many adults take English courses for various purposes.[4] However, China is far behind other countries in the field of EFL research. Little is known in China about developments and discussions in EFL research in Western countries, and little is known, in particular, about research in reading of English as a foreign language. The teaching of reading in China continues to follow the traditional pattern. Most Chinese teachers use a bottom-up approach, and many people believe that mastery of English can be achieved only through command of vocabulary and grammar at the sentence level. Consequently, many university students regard their English class merely as a continued study of vocabulary and complicated structures.

Such an approach not only ruins their interest in English study, but also causes problems when they are required to read a lot of specialized texts in English within limited time. So it becomes increasingly important to help students develop reading strategies for their future study. Such efforts have been made in some Chinese universities by setting up two English reading courses: intensive reading and extensive reading. A recently published college English textbook series for intensive reading teaches reading strategies in each unit. But are these efforts effective? Do students actually use the reading strategies they have learned? What really happens when students approach reading in English?

Method

This paper reports case studies of two EFL learners at Nanjing University, China. As one of the most competitive universities to get into, Nanjing University has specific requirements in English, in addition to general entrance requirements, for all applicants for admission. At the beginning of their first year, all entering freshmen students are asked to take an English-proficiency test. Then they are assigned to English classes of different proficiency levels by their test scores. Most of them begin from Band 1 and reach

---

4. Dong Li makes a similar claim: "China is not only the country with the largest population in the world, but also has the greatest number of students who learn English in the world" (1995, 53). (Ed.)

Band 4 at the end of their second year (all students are required to study English for at least two years at the university). Some students who do well on the test are allowed to start from a higher proficiency level than Band 1.

The two students who participated in my study were second-year students in the university's Department of Electronics. Both of them did fairly well in the university's English-proficiency entrance test and began their English study from Band 2. Compared to average students of their age, they were regarded as successful learners of English. At the time of my study, I had worked with them for six months or so. From my observation and experience of working with them, I found that one of them, Liu Wanli, seemed to do better in English than the other, Lin Yanqing. That point is important because the different strategies Liu and Lin employed might explain what made Liu a more successful learner than Lin, although they shared similar experience in secondary school and had started at the same proficiency level at college.

Both subjects were given the same essay to read: "The Lives of a Cell," by Lewis Thomas (1993). Before they began their reading tasks, they listened to a tape-recording of one of my colleagues doing a think-aloud so that they would know how to do it. Then they were given the reading passage and were told to read the essay in the way they usually approached English reading. They were asked to think aloud while they read and were told that their thinking aloud would be recorded. An interview was conducted immediately after each subject finished reading so as to obtain information not covered in the think-aloud process. Liu and Lin were told to feel free to use either Chinese or English in the think-aloud and the interview. Liu chose to use English while Lin preferred Chinese.

The think-aloud and interview recordings were then transcribed and studied carefully, with a focus on the differences between Liu's and Lin's approaches to the text. Such differences were assigned to three categories for analysis: overall strategies, use of rhetorical signals and morphological cues, and approaches to individual words.

Findings

Liu Wanli   Careful study of Liu's think-aloud protocol suggests that he was quite experienced in reading in English. His reading seemed to follow what Rumelhart (1977) describes as the interactive model of reading, in which processing takes place at different levels ranging from recognition of individual graphemes to the application of high-level schemata representing world knowledge, there being a constant interaction between these levels (Huckin and Bloch 1993). Liu employed a variety of reading skills, all aimed at a global interpretation of the text. As he put it, "I skim it and choose the cream of it." Therefore, despite the many new words in the text, he would go on reading once he thought he had got the topic sentence or the main idea of a paragraph. He then brought together his understanding of all the paragraphs to form his text representation.

When Liu began the reading task, he first read the title carefully, thought over it, and then commented that the text was "about biology." He reported in the think-aloud protocol that "the title can tell me something." He seemed to believe that there was a significant relation between the title and the content of the text, and thus he showed some knowledge of the role of the title in framing a discourse (see Brown and Yule 1983).

The first paragraph of the text reads as follows:

> We are told that the trouble with Modern Man is that he has been try-
> ing to detach himself from nature. He sits in the topmost tiers of poly-
> mer, glass, and steel, dangling his pulsing legs, surveying at a
> distance the writhing life of the planet. In this scenario, Man comes
> on as a stupendous lethal force, and the earth is pictured as something
> delicate, like rising bubbles at the surface of a country pond, or flights
> of fragile birds. (p. 373)

When Liu finished this paragraph, he decided to read it again because his "reading was interrupted several times" by the many new words in it. The fact that he did not look these words up in the dictionary at this point does not mean that he was ignoring them, but that he was trying to get the main idea or, in his own words, "the author's thinking" in the paragraph. We can see this intention of his from his use of the dictionary for the definition of a new word after re-reading the paragraph. He made a considered decision: of the many new words he had encountered so far, he would look up only *detach* because, as he said, "this word determines the way of the author's thinking." Once he had located the word in his English-Chinese dictionary, he translated its defini-tion back from Chinese into English and noted down "separate" alongside the word *detach* in his vocabulary list. Now he seemed to feel that he had under-stood "the author's thinking" in the first paragraph and went on reading. His approach to the word *detach,* as well as other vocabulary items, seemed to indicate a general principle: Attention was given to a new word only if it affected understanding of the text as a whole.

In his reading of the second paragraph, Liu demonstrated use of rhetorical signals in adjusting and developing his text representation. The paragraph begins with the following:

> But it is illusion to think that there is anything fragile about the life of
> the earth; surely, this is the toughest membrane imaginable in the uni-
> verse, opaque to probability, impermeable to death. (p. 373)

Liu recognized the cohesive relationship between "to think that there is any-thing fragile about the life of the earth" and the last sentence in Paragraph 1, "the earth is pictured as something delicate, like . . . flights of fragile birds." He also recognized the use of "But" to indicate that Paragraph 2 refuted the idea in Paragraph 1. Then he realized that the introduction of the text consisted of the first two paragraphs instead of Paragraph 1 only. Soon he concluded that

"Man is embedded in nature," the last sentence in Paragraph 2, was the topic sentence.

After he finished the whole article, he decided to re-read only the first two paragraphs, the introduction. Then he came up with a good understanding of the whole text in terms of its organization and the author's message. When asked to divide the text into parts, he divided it into three: the first two paragraphs as the beginning, the last paragraph as the end, and the paragraphs in between as the body. He first summarized the main idea of the text in his own words in English: "Human beings are not isolated in nature, but part of this world." Then he identified what seemed to him the thesis statement in Paragraph 2: "Man is embedded in nature."

Liu's goal of achieving a global text interpretation in reading was most evident in his solution of his puzzle over the title, which he seemed to have stored in what Huckin and Bloch (1993) refer to as the "buffer" until he finished reading. Here is an excerpt from the transcript of his protocol; the speech was in English, and square brackets indicate notes added to help readers understand his speech clearly:

> I read it [the title] and produced a problem. I think [now after reading the whole text] I get something about the key to my problem. "The Lives of a Cell." Why does a cell have lives? I can't [could not] get it. A cell, a single cell has several lives. I also think here *cell* refers to many things. It can be a cell, a physical cell, a human being, or even the earth.

Apparently, his interpretation of cell as "a human being" was based on the thesis statement, and his interpretation of cell as "the earth" on the author's conclusion, "it [the earth] is most like a single cell." It can be seen that in working out his puzzle over why a single cell should have plural lives, Liu stepped over the many new words (forty-nine in his list) in the text and skillfully integrated the title, the thesis, and the concluding paragraph of the text.[5] He seems to be one of those globally oriented readers Hill and Anderson (1994) describe who work off a "situation model"—that is, a holistic view of the situation described—rather than "the text base"—that is, an analytical interpretation of the words used.

Apart from his top-down, globally oriented overall strategies in reading, another characteristic that marked Liu's reading process was his approach to new vocabulary. It is not known how many new words there were in the text for him, for while he recorded forty-nine of them in his list, it is possible there were others that he did not recognize while reading. Throughout his reading, Liu seemed to be working on the principle that understanding of the text as a

5. On the other hand, Liu shows here a sensitivity to a grammatical distinction—that between singular and plural—which is marked at the low level (by the suffix -s). This distinction is often missed by Chinese users of English since in Chinese it is not grammatically indicated. (Ed.)

whole should be given priority and that reading should not be interrupted by vocabulary items, unless they made it impossible to get a general understanding of the text or "the essential opinion of the author," as he put it. So he would skip a new word if he thought that he had got the main idea of a paragraph. For example, when he came to the sentence:

> We live in a dancing matrix of viruses; they dart, rather like bees, from organism to organism, from plant to insect to mammal to me and back again, and into the sea, tugging along pieces of this genome, strings of genes from that, transplanting grafts of DNA, passing around heredity as though at a great party. (p. 375)

Liu reported that *dart* was a new word to him but he simply skipped it because "it doesn't mean any difficulty for me to understand the whole idea."

However, his focus on the text as a whole does not mean total neglect of new words. Often he would make guesses based on the context in which a word appeared, its spelling, or his own background knowledge. Take, for example, his interpretation of the word *chloroplast*. The written context in which it appears is as follows:

> I am consoled, somewhat, by the thought that the green plants are in the same fix. They could not be plants, or green, without their chloroplasts, which run the photosynthetic enterprise and generate oxygen for the rest of us. (p. 374)

In the think-aloud protocol, Liu read the sentences and then offered a correct Chinese translation of *chloroplast*. He reported that he guessed the word by using his background knowledge:

> Here the author uses the structure "They could not be plants, or green, without their chloroplasts," which means chloroplasts make them green.

Liu must have learned the word in Chinese from his biology teacher in secondary school, but this was the first time he had encountered the word in English. So here in working out the meaning of *chloroplast,* he was relying on the context and his knowledge of biology.

Liu's strategy of contextualizing vocabulary interpretation is not only evident in his guesses at new words but also in his awareness of potential new meanings of learned, familiar words in the context. After Liu figured out what *chloroplast* meant, he discovered that:

> *Fix* may have a special meaning here. I think, eh, fix means structure. Structure, exactly.

The definitions of *fix* within his knowledge obviously did not fit in the context. In interpreting its meaning, he again integrated his knowledge of cohesion in writing into his approach to vocabulary. To provide a better picture of what Liu did, it would be necessary to give the immediate context in which the word *fix* appeared:

> My cells are no longer the pure line entities I was raised with; they are ecosystems more complex than Jamaica Bay.
>
> I like to think that they work in my interest, that each breath they draw for me, but perhaps it is they who walk through the local park in the early morning, sensing my senses, listening to my music, thinking my thoughts.
>
> I am consoled, somewhat, by the thought that the green plants are in the same fix . . . (p. 374)

Here, the anaphoric function of the three *theys* referring to *my cells* and the cohesive relationship between the last paragraph in the quotation and the previous writing, which was indicated by *same,* played a crucial part in Liu's interpretation of *fix.* That can be observed in his protocol when he tried to complete the elliptical sentence by saying, "Same fix as my, as, as the speaker, 'I.' He must have thought that green plants also had cells which carry out many jobs." Then he concluded that "the plants are in the same fix as I am made up of many kinds of cells." And from there he got his interpretation that plants and the "I" in the text were "in the same fix"—that is, the same structure—"made up of many kinds of cells."

Besides contextualization of interpretation, another striking characteristic of Liu's approach to vocabulary is his tolerance of ambiguity in guessing. Of the forty-nine words in his list, he looked up only two in the dictionary. For the rest of them, he either made an effort to guess them or just skipped them. In making guesses, he said, he only wanted "the outline of its meaning." When he met many biology terms, he said that he would only "determine which is a noun and which is an adjective. That's enough for me." It is possible that his intentional reluctance to try to get a clear well-defined meaning was only another piece of evidence that he wanted to focus on the global interpretation of the text rather than being distracted by new words.

Lin Yanqing   Lin's overall reading strategy was strikingly different from Liu's. In his first reading, he glanced at the title and then simply ignored it. He did not think about it or make any prediction about the text. Neither did he get any hint or suggestion from the title to help or guide his understanding. He did not believe that there would be any connection between the title and the text:

> What the title means is not important. The point is that you understand what is written in the text. I have read a lot of books. Some books are given strange titles. For example, people's names are often used for titles of many books.

Brown and Yule point out that the title of a piece of discourse should not be confused with the topic. That title is "a particularly powerful thematisation device . . . a starting point around which what follows in discourse is constructed, and which constrains our interpretation of what follows" (1983, 139). Lin seems to have fallen into the pitfall Brown and Yule warn us against: he seems to have confused title with topic, or rather with topic entity (Brown and Yule 1983, 137), and failed to see that the title was important as a guide to his reading.

Lin showed a reasonably good understanding of the first paragraph when he reported that it meant "man tries to detach himself from nature as much as possible." Here the word *detach,* which was crucial in Liu's interpretation of the first paragraph, was not new to Lin. He made no use of the dictionary at this stage although he recorded all the new words in his list.

He seemed to have some difficulty with the second paragraph and decided to read it again. However, after the re-reading, he reported that "the meaning of this paragraph is still very vague" to him. Nevertheless, he decided to continue reading. Unfortunately, he also had difficulty understanding the third and fourth paragraphs. He seemed frustrated and decided to give up. He glanced through the rest of the article (Paragraphs 5–11) in less than three minutes, whereas the first four paragraphs took him ten minutes, and he stopped recording any new words in his list. When he finished, he said that he had no idea what the article was about. So his first attempt to read the text was abandoned halfway through the reading. It produced nothing but a word list.

Lin decided to start all over again. But this time the reading was a painful experience. In fact, he read nearly every paragraph twice. First he would read through a paragraph and decide which words to look up in the dictionary. He would record the definitions in Chinese alongside the new words in his list. Then he would read that paragraph again, translating almost every single sentence into Chinese. He could not have been more bottom-up or more locally focused in reading than he was then.

Take, for example, Lin's reading of the first paragraph. Although he had understood the main idea of the paragraph in his first attempt to read the article, he still used the dictionary for definitions of new words, trying to be accurate in reading. When he finished the first sentence, he paused when he was reading the second one:

> He sits in the topmost tiers of polymer, glass, and steel, dangling his pulsing legs, surveying at a distance the writhing life of the planet. (p. 373)

He asked himself, "Writhe, writhe, what does it mean?" He located the word in the dictionary and recorded in his list its definition in Chinese, which I translated back into English as "feeling uneasy, troubled." Then he worked on the next sentence. He read "In this scenario" and put it into Chinese (meaning "under such circumstance" if translated back into English). Then he read, "Man comes on as a stupendous lethal force," and put it into Chinese again (meaning "man has a kind of power superior to the power of nature"). He went on reading the rest of the paragraph like this, reading and translating, using the dictionary if he met a new word.

When asked about the meaning of the first two paragraphs after he finished them, Lin answered in Chinese:

> The first two paragraphs mean that the trouble with modern men is that they detach themselves from nature. This is what the first paragraph says. The second paragraph tells us that we are the fragile part. People are always trying to create a millennium, but in the past five years such efforts have been unsuccessful.

Here, he obviously missed the marked rhetorical signal given by the very first word of the second paragraph, *But,* a coordinator indicating two contrasting sentences. So he failed to see that from the very beginning, Paragraph 2 rejects the picture of modern man drawn in the first paragraph.

Lin's misrepresentation of the text developed as he continued reading, and he missed another important rhetorical signal at the beginning of Paragraph 3. The sentence reads, "The biological science of recent years has been making this a more urgent fact of life" (p. 373). Here, Lin failed to see that the word *this* refers to the last sentence in Paragraph 2, "Man is embedded in nature," and that it functions as a cohesive device to link the second and third paragraphs. When asked what *this* refers to, he reported that he had not thought about it.

Lin was so immersed in his attempt to understand all the individual sentences in the text that his attention was divided. He failed to treat the essay as a whole and made no attempt to look for the topic sentence or main idea of a paragraph to guide his reading. When asked about the main idea of the essay after he finished the whole text, Lin seemed unable to summarize or point out what the main idea was. Below is a translation of part of his think-aloud protocol in Chinese. Sentences are numbered for easy reference.

> (1) It is about the weakness(es) of modern people. (2) Then it says that our planet is actually very fragile in the universe, just like a cell. (3) Then it talks about cells, genes inside cells, and so on. (4) In the end, the author writes that he first regarded the earth as a living thing, then he thought it would be better, more suitable, to look on the earth as a cell.

It is not difficult to see that Sentence (1) was what Paragraph 1 describes about Modern Man, that Sentence (2) came from the second paragraph, and that Sentence (3) from Paragraphs 3–10, and Sentence (4) from the last paragraph. Lin failed to come up with a satisfactory understanding of the article. In fact, he seriously misunderstood some important points. He said that the author believed the earth was like a cell because:

> On the earth there is not enough communication. And we are surrounded by viruses. Eh, that is to say, our planet is too fragile and there are all kinds of evil things on the earth, like viruses.

When asked what message the author was trying to convey in this article, Lin responded:

> I am puzzled. I think the author first thought of the earth as an organism, then he thought it was most like a cell. Cells, the author writes, the genes derived from ancient times and have passed on to us today. Genes come from all kinds of sources in nature. Then the article says that the normal (healthy) genes of people are surrounded by viruses and the genes of these viruses are changing all the time. So human beings' fight against viruses is a task that will last a long, long time. So I wonder if the author is comparing the earth to a cell for the purpose that he is in fact comparing all kinds of evil things on the earth to viruses. And our fight against these viruses, these evil things, will last a long, long time, perhaps forever.

From these two quotations, we can see two major characteristics in Lin's reading process. On the one hand, he was what Hill and Anderson (1994, 122) describe as a locally oriented reader. He adjusted the focus of his camera to so many individual sentences in the text, taking pictures of all of them, that he could not get a picture of the whole. On the other hand, his reading was interfered with by his personal experience. Like the inexperienced test-taker Hill and Anderson describe, who "draws massively on personal experience in responding to the passage" (1994, 138), Liu relied on his knowledge of the word *virus* in Chinese in his text representation. Because *virus* does not conjure up pleasant images in people's minds, Lin seemed to think that here viruses must mean something bad, and he depended on this extratextual inference in his reading.

Another aspect in which Lin was different from Liu was his approach to vocabulary. As to new words, he would note them down in his list when he read through a paragraph. Then he would look up all the new words in the dictionary, making no attempt to guess, and write down the definitions in Chinese alongside the words. The pitfall in so doing would be that he might take a definition from the dictionary that was inappropriate in the context where the word appeared. A good case in point was his treatment of *millennia*. The immediate context in which this word appeared is:

> Nor is it a new thing for man to invent an existence that he imagines to be above the rest of life; this has been his most consistent intellectual exertion down the millennia. (p. 373)

Lin noted down in his list the third definition of *millennia* given in an English-Chinese dictionary, which means a period of peace, prosperity, and happiness, instead of the first definition, which is one thousand years. It was self-evident that his mistake was due to isolation of words from the context. No wonder he would misrepresent the text when he re-read the paragraphs after use of the dictionary, referring to the inappropriate definitions he had recorded.

Such absence of context was evident not just in Lin's approach to new words, but also in his treatment of familiar words. Take, for example, his interpretation of *delicate* in the following context:

> In this scenario, Man comes on as a stupendous lethal force, and the earth is pictured as something delicate, like rising bubbles at the surface of a country pond, or flights of fragile birds. (p. 373)

In this case, Lin's translation of the target word into Chinese, which I back-translated, was *delicate* in the sense of fine workmanship. This definition certainly did not fit in the context. So it seems that absence of context marked Lin's approach to individual words, whether they were new vocabulary items or they were within his learned vocabulary.

Summary

The two students' reading strategies can be summed up in terms of a metaphor. Lin, a bricklayer, translated every sentence into Chinese but, unfortunately, failed to achieve satisfactory comprehension of the text. Liu, a carpenter, used his interpretation of the title, the thesis, the conclusion, and the main ideas of paragraphs to construct a framework for his understanding while ignoring the many new words. To many Chinese learners of English who believe that understanding vocabulary will necessarily lead to understanding sentences, paragraphs, and eventually the whole text, it must be an interesting puzzle how Liu acquired a good understanding of the text while Lin did not. A brief review of the most important differences between Lin's and Liu's reading processes will explain why the bricklayer who worked so diligently on every brick could not see what the house looked like, and why the carpenter who built up a frame had a clear idea of what he was working on.

Liu demonstrated a clear focus on global interpretation of the text and his reading was guided. He contextualized his vocabulary interpretation, whether it was a new word or a familiar one. He did not commit himself to precise understanding of new words, but kept potential ambiguity in mind when he made guesses. He also made use of rhetorical signals in making sense of the text. Liu seemed experienced in reading texts in English in that he not only showed a variety of skills in reading, but also integrated these skills, knowing when to use what.

Lin appeared to be locally oriented in his text representation, and his reading was guided by his understanding of a few sentences in the text, with occasional extratextual interference. In his approach to individual words, whether they were new or familiar to him, there was no reference to context; vocabulary was learned in isolation. He aimed at precision, "the exact meaning," in his vocabulary interpretation, and he gave no indication of successful use of rhetorical signals in reading.

Conclusion

There are many issues concerning students' reading that are not discussed in this paper. For example, how did Liu develop his holistic approach to reading although he had similar learning experience to Lin's? Further research needs to be done on elements that affect how models of reading develop before teachers can fully understand the challenges students face in reading English and are able to help them. I have the impression, however, that there are more locally oriented readers like Lin than globally oriented readers like Liu in Chinese colleges and universities. After all, this is the way Chinese students are taught to read, especially in English.

The format of the intensive-reading textbook in the *College English* textbook series is almost exactly the same as that of a typical secondary-school English textbook: reading text, vocabulary list, and exercises designed to review the structures and vocabulary items in a lesson. The only difference between them is that in the *College English* textbook, there is a brief discussion of some reading skill at the end of each lesson. But it is hardly considered important or relevant to teaching or learning. In a college English classroom, usually the teacher leads the students to go through the vocabulary list first (or they are expected to have studied the list before class). Then the teacher explains the text sentence by sentence, making no use of the reading skills discussed in the book. The teacher paraphrases all the sentences in English, translating some complicated ones into Chinese so that students can understand, and analyzing their structures. It is a very analytical approach to the text. Reading skills are treated only as a theory and are not put into practice. Such teaching only makes students more dependent on the analytical approach to reading in English by dissipating their energy in trying to get the exact meaning of individual words or sentences. It also develops a sense of insecurity in students when they encounter new words in reading. In Lin's first attempt to read the whole article, he tried to read through it and get a general idea of the text. But soon he was intimidated by the many new words he met and gave up. Then he turned to the bottom-up model of reading, in which he looked up all the new words and translated every sentence into Chinese.

How can students like Lin be helped in their study? What can be done to help them build up reading skills and become better at making sense of English texts? Here I would like to make some suggestions.

First, changes can be made in the format of the *College English* textbook. Vocabulary lists should be cut out so that students will not be tempted to refer to them when they meet new words in reading, and each lesson should begin with the discussion of reading skills to alert students to use them when they read the text. Second, teachers should change their approach to reading skills. Instead of being discussed only, these skills should be practiced whenever students read in English. To help students move confidently from the analytical approach to the holistic approach, teachers can use articles that do not contain so many new words as to discourage students from applying the reading strategies they have learned. They can also provide questions to lead students to the main idea of a paragraph or the text. Finally, teachers need to think about how they themselves read, for how the teacher approaches reading in English usually plays a crucial part in the development of the students' approach. After all, how a teacher teaches reading is determined by what he or she believes reading should be, just as how a student approaches reading shows what he or she thinks reading should be.

In the interview after the think-aloud and over the lunch the two students and I had afterwards, Liu, the more successful reader, suggested what might be a more productive conceptualization of reading. He said that he had found the task "a very helpful experience":

> This kind of article, before, I would read two or three times. After the two or three times, I will find it. I will never find so many things like this. Before, as usual, I only want to take some facts, some numbers, some knowledge and, at most, the author's opinion. But I did not touch the structure, the way the author writes and calls his opinion to me. Next time I meet this kind of article, I will get deeper. I think this kind of article is no longer a report for scientists, but it comes to be a talking between the author and me. It tells me something. And I have found something important in his talking. And I have the feeling that I thank him. Before I never had this kind of feeling. This kind of article is no longer abstract. It is from a man's mind, not from a computer. It makes me feel close to it.

It is true: Reading should be a talking between the writer and the reader, a two-way communication. And only when students stop being just on the receiving end and begin their talking with the writer of their reading texts will they find reading a pleasant and delightful experience.

7

New Directions in Teaching

In Western teacher education, it is now generally assumed that if learning is to take place, students must be actively involved in the process, and because such involvement cannot be taken for granted, it is the responsibility of teachers to stimulate it. Accordingly, the pedagogical literature emphasizes techniques that will do this: activities that will encourage students to discover information rather than being given it (e.g., Duckworth 1987); the use of group work as well as class discussion to promote interaction among students (e.g., Johnson, Johnson, and Holubec 1986; Slavin 1983); and the investigation of students' interests, preferences, and learning styles so that individuals can discover and work from their own strengths (e.g., Dunn and Dunn 1972). This emphasis on student initiative and autonomy has become particularly marked in discussions of language teaching (e.g., Stevick 1976). Recognition of the social and affective aspects of language learning has combined with more general educational theory to discredit what Freire has called "the banking concept of education" (1970, 58): Students' minds are no longer seen as accounts for depositing information, but rather as organic entities which, if properly nurtured, can be expected to grow on the basis of their own potential rather than of what is put in them.[1]

Such ideas are not, however, the received professional wisdom in China. Paine, for example, found that in Chinese teacher-training universities, "Even the psychology and education faculty . . . shared the view that discipline-based knowledge is the cornerstone of good teaching" and that "associated with and reinforcing this message . . . is another prevalent conception . . . : the view of teaching as performance rather than interaction" (1992, 189). This view prevails in the teaching of English as it does in any other subject: In her discussion of teacher-training courses in China, Sunderland (1990) points out that most participants (and Chinese faculty

1. In the past couple of decades, however, there has been a strong current of opinion against this conception of the relationship between teacher and student. Writers such as E. D. Hirsch (1987, 1996) and Allan Bloom (1987), in particular, have argued that the emphasis on student involvement has so watered down the content of education as to render it useless. Their criticisms have been hailed with enthusiasm by many parents, whose concerns have been expressed publicly under the slogan of "back to basics."

members too) expected and wanted to improve their own knowledge of the language, while they considered work on methods of teaching it to be irrelevant; and Bao Jingying's account of a model lesson in a key secondary school (Chapter Five) illustrates well the value put on performance on the part of a language teacher rather than on interaction with and among the students.

As Chapter Five shows, the participants in the Nanjing program were increasingly questioning these values by the end of the first semester's work. At the same time, they were acutely conscious, as those surveyed by Burnaby and Sun (1989) were, of the constraints under which they had to work: They had to satisfy their superiors; they had to teach to a prescribed schedule and use prescribed material; and, above all, they had to get their students through the exams. Consequently, they tended to think, like the teachers described by He Yue and Du Qunhua (see Chapter Five), that they had no choice but to follow the traditional pattern. One of the major aims of the program, therefore, was to suggest that they did have some choice, that they could spend more class time on student-centered activities and still convey the information necessary for doing well in exams. For the participants to believe this, however, they had to try it out for themselves, and that was what the teaching practice was designed to help them do.[2]

In previous years, teaching practice had proved difficult to organize, so in 1994–95 we devised a new method which, for that year at least, worked well. Of the twenty five participants, nine worked in colleges sufficiently nearby for them to be able to continue teaching while taking courses in the program. These nine were asked toward the end of the autumn term to request permission to bring in one or more of their classmates to teach with them, as a team, for six weeks during the spring. Permission having been obtained, the nine acted as team leaders to whom the other participants attached themselves, on the basis of already established friendships, so as to form groups of two to four people. The team members then took turns to teach, and when not teaching, they attended class to observe their colleagues; they also collaborated in the development of lesson plans. Thus, in addition to being observed and assessed by the program staff—Sarah Towle, Wang Xueli, and me—the participants got ample support and feedback from their peers.

This arrangement proved ideal for doing "action research"—that is, trying out new methods and documenting how they worked—because the team members could help each other in collecting data. I encouraged them, indeed, to do team projects, as Chang Qian, Sheng Ping, and Xu Ju did: one member of this team taught while the others recorded what was happening; by this means, they were able to collect particularly rich data.[3] In the other teams, too, the

2. Our interpretation of teaching practice as a time for the participants to develop and apply new teaching methods was in marked contrast to the established Chinese view of it as a time to learn how to perform from "master teachers," with occasional opportunities to perform themselves. See Paine (1992).
3. The team also cooperated impressively in writing the paper: Xu Ju drafted it, Sheng Ping rewrote it, and Chang Qian typed up the final draft.

participants readily helped each other with data collection, even though it was not for their own projects, and this was how Zhang Weinian and Li Xiaozhong were able to keep track of the students' group work that they describe.

This chapter includes three papers that came out of this teaching practice: Zhang Weinian's, Li Xiaozhong's, and Chang Qian et al.'s. The chapter begins, however, with one written by a participant from the 1992–93 group: "Improvement in Classroom Teaching of English," by Zhang Jianying. It is a personal essay describing the impression the College English Teacher Training Program made on her and how it has affected her teaching two years later; it thus gives some indication of what the long-term effects of the program may be. Zhang describes how our discussions of classroom interaction and the demonstration lessons she observed have led her to modify her own approach to intensive reading. Although she has retained the traditional three-part approach to a passage (i.e., teaching vocabulary, explaining the text, and using exercises to reinforce the language points learned), within each she has developed techniques to encourage greater participation by the students and to draw more fully and explicitly on their existing knowledge. She is sanguine about the results: Not only do her students evaluate her highly, but, perhaps still more important, she is enjoying her teaching more. What makes this report particularly encouraging is that she is working in that same institution where He Yue (Chapter Five) found such skepticism about adopting new methods.

Li Xiaozhong in "Vocabulary Teaching or Vocabulary Learning?" considers the first aspect of intensive reading, the teaching of vocabulary, in more detail. Encouraged by my own work (Parry 1991, 1993b), Li chose to replace the traditional explanation of new words by an activity in which her students worked systematically on identifying them for themselves and guessing their meanings. The guessing was done first as an individual and then as a group activity, and Li presents interesting findings on how the students in group discussion worked out the meanings and explained them to each other (cf. Faerch et al. 1984, 97–98 and 100–101). Not all the words were correctly defined, but a high proportion of them were, demonstrating that these students, at least, could do much more for themselves than teachers in China commonly assume. Moreover, the students were deeply involved in the activity, so their chances of remembering the words were probably quite good. Li's study would be worth replicating, especially if a control study could be done in which the words were presented in the usual way; then the hypothesis that the experimental group would remember the words better could be tested.

Zhang Weinian, the writer of "Toward a Reader-centered Approach in Intensive Reading," was on the same team as Li and, therefore, teaching the same group of students.[4] She, too, decided to experiment with a new way of presenting an intensive-reading passage. She had been much impressed by our

---

4. It was Wang Jian's class at Nanjing University and so included the two students described in Wang Jian's paper in Chapter Six.

discussions of top-down as opposed to bottom-up strategies in reading (see Chapter Six), and also by the work we were doing at the same time as the teaching practice in our course on discourse analysis[5] so she developed an exercise that would encourage the students to adopt a more holistic approach to the passage than they customarily did. Like Li, she used group work (in addition to other activities) and, with her teammates' help, was able to ascertain that all the students were fully engaged and that they were able to form a coherent picture of the text as a whole without attending to each word individually first.

Chang Qian, Sheng Ping, and Xu Ju went further, perhaps, than any of the participants in restructuring their teaching. They set out from the start to teach intensive reading in such a way as to address the problem universally lamented by teachers of English in China—the reluctance of students to speak in English. Their class (despite the program's terms of reference; see Introduction) consisted of students who were specializing in English, and Chang Qian had deliberately arranged to take it over from the regular teacher in order that they might work on intensive reading (she normally taught a conversation class). In fact, though, the course, as defined by their textbook, did not involve reading so much as practice of language forms that were presented in texts in dialogue form. Essentially, then, it was a structure course, and the team concentrated its efforts on teaching the structures they were required to cover in ways that would induce all the students to do a great deal of talking. They used a variety of methods to document the changes they made and their degree of success. While the class activities may not always seem, to a Western observer, to be as "authentic" and "communicative" as the writers claim, all of us who observed the class were impressed with the liveliness of the lessons and the involvement of the students—as, indeed, were Chang Qian's superiors in the college.

To Western teachers of English, the ideas discussed in this chapter will not seem so very new (imperfectly though they may be realized in many Western classrooms), and students in Western institutions might not find the activities described extraordinarily exciting. To Chinese teachers and students, however, the methods described here represent a radically new departure, for they posit a restructuring of classroom relationships, both between teachers and students and between readers and (English) texts. Such restructuring is, in turn, based on a conception of the purpose of education that is essentially Western and, indeed, American.[6] When Thomas Jefferson advocated the education of the people, he did not have in mind the Confucian notion of inculcating a common ideology to maintain an already established social and political order (see

5. This course, for which we used Brown and Yule (1983) as a text, emphasized not only the linguistic signals of macrostructure, but also the role of context and schemata in the interpretation of text.

6. I use the word *American* in two senses, both as referring to the United States of America and as referring to the "New World" (in contrast to the "Old" one), in which immigrant communities and individuals have felt a freedom from the past that can hardly be attained in Europe—and still less in China.

Chapter Two), but rather the training of independent individuals to know their rights and make their own decisions as to who should represent them in the development of the new republic (Cremin 1980).[7] In this view, education—specifically education in literacy—supports the political process by promoting individual autonomy (cf. Goody and Watt 1968), and it is clear that the classroom activities described in this chapter are intended to do precisely that. In recognizing this fact, we encounter (again) a contradiction in the Chinese enterprise of teaching English: It is mandated by the authorities and conducted within an authoritarian educational system; yet, if done by what these writers have come to believe are the most effective means, it promotes attitudes and behavior that are essentially inimical to authoritarianism.[8]

Students in the classroom, however, are hardly concerned with such issues. They want, first of all, to pass their exams, but as this chapter makes clear, they also would like to enjoy their studies if they can. Chinese teachers generally are wary of such enjoyment, for it makes education look like fun and games when it should be hard work. However, the participants in this program demonstrated, triumphantly, that enjoyment and hard work are not mutually exclusive—that students can, in China as elsewhere, work extremely hard, learn an enormous amount, and have a good time in the process. Moreover, the participants discovered that they, as teachers, could have a good time too. The six weeks of the teaching practice (which, for most of them, were also weeks of data collection) called for an immense input of energy, but the experience was, at the same time, profoundly stimulating, and they emerged from it with a greatly enhanced sense of professionalism. If they can, as Zhang Jianying has, sustain the effort now that they are back in the routines of their home institutions, they may help to make English in China not only a tool for economic advancement, but a means of nourishing their own and their students' creativity, independence, and problem-solving abilities.

---

7. This representation is, however, an idealization: Cremin's view of Jefferson has been criticized by Graff (1987), and Cremin himself acknowledges that there was a considerable gap between Jefferson's declared principles and his actual practice.
8. This contradiction is one aspect of the broader dilemma of modernization in China. See Hayhoe (1992).

1. Improvement in Classroom Teaching of English

Zhang Jianying

After ten years of teaching at Nanjing Auditing Institute, I was getting tired of it and felt it was more and more difficult to continue. Neither the knowledge I had learned nor the teaching method I was using could meet the needs of my students, so I much appreciated the chance to gain refreshment that the United Board and Nanjing University supplied in the College English Teacher Training Program.

English teachers in China seldom have an opportunity to be taught by experienced foreign teachers. I was fortunate, then, since in 1992–93, when I participated in the program, the United Board sent three excellent foreign teachers, and they taught us many advanced courses such as linguistics, teaching methodology, the history of English,[9] advanced reading and writing, and intercultural communication.[10] These courses are all helpful in teaching, but the most important effect of the program was the teaching practice activity, which was supervised by foreign and Chinese teachers together. During this time we discussed our teaching methods among ourselves and observed each other teaching. I really learned a lot from this activity. I also got the chance to observe intensive- and extensive-reading lessons given for the main courses of college English by Kate Parry and John Ingulsrud.[11] I was deeply impressed by their way of teaching. Instead of giving lessons by themselves as teachers (as I always used to do), they gave students more chance to speak in class and tried to raise the students' communicative abilities by giving them more background knowledge, and leading them to understand the implied meaning of a passage rather than just the language points and grammar. Kate Parry once told me that language teaching is a kind of two-way operation: teachers must try their best to help students get involved in class activity by making their lessons as vivid as possible and by letting students speak and think more so that they can develop their skill of communication and master the language more naturally.

All this affected me greatly and gave me quite different ideas about my own teaching. Now when I look back on what I used to do in class, I think it was less than satisfactory. Like most teachers in China, I had been busy with

9. This course was offered only in the first year of the program and was then discontinued as being of less practical use than other courses that we could offer. (Ed.)

10. This course, again, was offered only in the first year, it being a specialty of Eva Fizette, who taught in the program in the spring semester of 1993. (Ed.)

11. John Ingulsrud and I taught a Band 3 demonstration class together in the autumn semester of 1992. In the autumn of 1994, a similar demonstration class was taught by Sarah Towle in collaboration with Wang Haixiao. (Ed.)

teaching all the time, working like a machine that pours out knowledge from the beginning to the end of a lesson, without taking any time for refreshment. In this kind of situation, students become very passive and expect to be mere recipients, mechanical notetakers who bring only their ears to class. Certainly, both my students and I felt very dull in class time. Now, after coming back from the program, I have tried to improve my teaching, and I have had some success, particularly in the following three respects.

Teaching New Words

Each unit in the *College English* intensive-reading book has many new words that students are required to master and remember. I used to explain all these new words to the students one by one, while the students just sat and took notes. I would be tired out after giving the new words, but when I gave a dictation on them the next day, few students could write them correctly. Now I have changed my method of teaching new words by asking students themselves to give them to the class. I ask four or five students to prepare the words beforehand, and then have them come up to the blackboard to explain them to their classmates. I myself pretend to be a student and ask questions when I feel confused or think their explanation is not so clear. If the student teacher is not sure about a question, I have all the class discuss it. The student teachers really prepare the work very carefully and most of them do excellently. Some of them have even brought a big dictionary or other reference book with them and given many suitable examples of the key words. The new words can thus be understood more clearly, and the dull and difficult task of remembering them is made much easier.

Explaining the Text

After learning the new words, most students find it easy to understand the text except for some sentences that have complicated structures. So during this stage of the lesson, I used to find that many students did not concentrate on what I was saying; they only wrote down some important language points. But mastering a text is not only a matter of understanding the language points or grammatical structures; it is also one of perceiving the implied meaning, and the latter is more important. It is imperative, then, that teachers give some kind of introduction to the text, including background information about the author or the subject matter, so that the students can see the text as a whole. So now, while teaching a text, I purposely tell them something about the background and ask them more questions instead of just explaining the language points. Most of the texts chosen for the intensive-reading book are interesting and instructive, and provide ample opportunity for students to respond and develop their own ideas.

For example, when my class was studying the passage "Lessons from Jefferson," I first told the students a story about Thomas Jefferson, introducing his biography without telling them at first who he was but asking them to guess. Then I asked them to give me more information about this great man. The text altogether quoted six suggestions for living that Jefferson made, all of them very helpful for modern youth. The students had a heated discussion about which piece of advice was the most practical and useful for them. Thus, they not only learned some new words from the lesson, but also some information about Thomas Jefferson in particular and American history in general. Later, I asked the students to write a kind of biography introducing some famous person that they knew. Many of them went to the library to find some information for their essays. Some of them wrote about great people from China, such as Mao Zedong or Zhou Enlai; others wrote about American leaders, such as George Washington or Abraham Lincoln; while others wrote about famous writers such as Mark Twain, Charles Dickens, or Lu Xun.

Another example I should give was a lesson I gave recently. The title of the passage we were studying is "My First Job"; it is a short and easy story about a young man who went to an interview for a job advertised in the newspaper. The young man was waiting to enter university and needed money badly, but the working conditions proved far from his expectations. The worst thing was that he would have to work under a woman. The clever writer did not give a clear indication as to whether the young man accepted the job or not. Before we went over the text, I gave all the boys in the class a question: "If you were that young man, would you accept the job? Why or why not?" Then I asked the girls in the class to argue with those who said "No." One of the girls quoted a sentence we had learned from the Jefferson passage, which said that all men are created equal; this got a warm clap from the other girls.

Checking the Work Through Exercises

After the students have gained a clear understanding of the text and the language points, they need to do a number of well-chosen exercises. When they do these, the teacher had better take the part of a director or conductor while the students play the important roles of actors or actresses so as to make the whole teaching process more energetic and lively. In the course of doing the exercises, the students can quickly raise their language-proficiency level. It is natural for students to make mistakes while doing oral practice, so teachers must not expect perfection but be generous with their praise. We cannot stop a student numerous times to correct errors in his or her speech, because if we do so, we run the risk of silencing the student forever—although, of course, this is not to say that errors should never be corrected.

Take the students in my class, for example. Some of them are from a part of the country where students' pronunciation and listening ability are very poor in spite of their high marks in English exams. When I invite these students to do some oral exercises, they are afraid of making mistakes and being made objects of laughter, so I seldom stop them except when the most obvious violations appear—the other minor mistakes are corrected during the break time when I can speak to them alone. In class time, I try my best to compliment them and encourage them by finding one or two good points in their work. So all the students feel lighthearted in my class and like my lessons better. The scores they give me when evaluating their teachers' work keep increasing year after year, which shows clearly their attitude towards this kind of teaching.

Conclusion

Through years of practice, I think the new way of teaching is beneficial for both teachers and students. In the past, I paid attention only to students with high scores, but now I pay equal attention to all students and help develop their communication skills. Not only do I enjoy my teaching more now, but I also feel more confident that I am doing a good job.

2. Vocabulary Teaching or Vocabulary Learning?

Li Xiaozhong

No matter how well the student learns grammar, no matter how successfully the sounds of L2 are mastered, without words to express a
wide range of meanings, communication in an L2 just cannot happen
in any meaningful way. (McCarthy, 1990, p. viii)

That is, without vocabulary nothing can be conveyed.

In China, although much attention has been given to vocabulary teaching,
students still have a great deal of trouble remembering words. This is mainly
due to the traditional way of language teaching, which is totally teacher-
centered. In the *College English* textbooks, there are some instructions for students to use various methods to learn vocabulary (e.g., guessing the meaning
of a word from context or from the formation of the word itself), but the
students are usually left to themselves to use the recommended methods out of
class. Obviously, it is not so efficient, for as Gu points out:

Ask any foreign-language learner about his headaches in learning the
language and one thing you will surely get is the difficulty in remembering words. (1994, 2)

Most students usually feel at a loss and we can often hear the students complain about the difficulty of learning vocabulary.

To solve this problem, first we must look at the present trend in language
teaching, namely, the adoption of more communicative methods. Gairns and
Redman assert:

There has been a trend in recent years to develop more self-access
materials and in the classroom a desire to shift the focus away from
the teacher and concentrate on more student-centered activities. This
not only makes the student more responsible for his own learning, but
also permits greater attention to individual needs. (1986, 76)

H. Douglas Brown also emphasizes student-centered activities. He discusses,
in particular, the advantages of group work. He says:

Group work generates interactive language, offers an embracing
affective climate, promotes learner responsibilities and autonomy,
and [it] is a step toward individualizing instruction. (1994, 173–4)

Again, from Bruner's "Learning the Mother Tongue," we learn that:

> Language acquisition should be looked at not as a solo flight by the child in search of rules, but as a transaction involving an active language learner and an equally active language teacher. (1993, 66)

Taking all these arguments into account, this study presents an attempt to use group work to teach students vocabulary, which means learning vocabulary through meaningful context embedded in social interaction. Such an approach will bring second-language learning more into line with first-language learning.

Methods

Subjects   I tried this approach with 18 students, whom I had a chance to teach in my teaching practicum. These students were non-English-major students, who had all had six years' experience of learning English as a course in their secondary schools around China, plus one and a half years' English learning experience at Nanjing University, one of the key universities in China. These students skipped learning *College English Book One* and started from *Book Two* because they had achieved good marks in the English test taken after entering the university. So they were now learning *Book Five*. Thus, we can see that the English proficiency of these students was better than that of most others.

Instruments   For this study, I chose a reading passage from the book *Readers' Choice*, which is similar to *College English Book Five* in terms of difficulty. The passage I used is called "The Talking Flowers" (Durrell 1978). It is about eighteen hundred words long.

Procedures   First, I distributed the reading passage to the students, together with paper and carbon paper, and asked them to read it on their own and write down the words that caused them difficulty. They were also asked to write down what they guessed these words to mean, either from the context or from the words themselves. If they found it difficult to express their guessed meanings precisely in English, they could use Chinese. Having finished reading, they were asked to hand in one copy of their word list and keep one copy for themselves.

Then I asked the students to form groups and discuss the words on their list. They were to write down the words that caused the whole group difficulty, together with their guessed meanings. Then they were asked to hand in their groups' word lists. During the group discussion, I or one of my colleagues observed each group and kept notes of what the students said.

After collecting the groups' word lists, I asked the students to come back as a whole and discuss these words. Then we got the whole class's word list. With these words, they were encouraged to make one last effort to figure out the meanings. If they found it difficult, the meanings were not given directly, but rather some hints were given until I was sure that they understood the words completely. This class discussion was all recorded on audio-tape and transcribed for analysis. As for the word lists, I assessed the students' glosses according to the criteria suggested by Parry:

> A correct guess is one which I characterized as a good translation of the word in question; or when the guess was given in English, it is one which I judged to be either a synonym or a good definition of the word. An incorrect guess is one which, when decontextualized and compared with the original word, seems to bear no relation to it—beyond one of a most general kind such as their both being abstract nouns; antonyms were also included in this category. A partly correct guess always does bear some relationship to the original, such as one of superordination, or belonging to the same superordinate category, or sharing one or more semantic features; the gloss and the original word therefore overlap but do not coincide in meaning. (1991, 638–9)

Findings

The information given in the students' word lists is summarized in Table 7-1.

Table 7-1
Average numbers of words identified and classification of assessment

	Words Identified	Correct	Partly Correct	Incorrect	No Attempt
Individual	35	10.6	12.3	9.1	3
Group	24	9.7	8.4	5.9	

It indicates that the average number of difficult words is reduced a lot after group work. This tells us that students can teach each other without the teacher's help. Another important point is that more students get involved in the process of learning. For example, in their group discussion, students were free to speak out their guesses, while in traditional class, they either are not given the chance or dare not speak in public.

Now I want to discuss in detail the students' group discussions. I will deal with them according to Table 7-1.

Correct Guesses   During the group discussion, the students were very involved in trying to figure out the meanings of the words. From the table, we can see that their success in guessing the meanings of the words is about 42 percent of the words identified as difficult. This shows that we can trust the students to solve many problems among themselves. On examining my records and those of my colleagues, I find that the students' ways of arriving at the correct meanings fell into the following categories:

1. Some words were new or only partly known to some students, while they were already known to the others. Thus, those who knew the answers told the others. Actually, this way of learning is beneficial to both kinds of students. For those who know the answers, this is a good way to review the words, for it gives them a chance to teach the others. To those who do not know the words, it is also good, for they learn the words from their classmates. What is more, because it leads them to say the words aloud, the visual presentation of each is reinforced by oral presentation. Such words in this study were *lavatory, queer, petal, gloom,* and *mushroom.*

2. Sometimes the students used neither Chinese nor English to define the words. Instead, they demonstrated these words to show what they meant. A good example is *strand* and *twist* in the sentence, "Mrs. Kralefsky smiled at me, and lifted a strand of it in her fingers, twisting it gently so that it sparkled." A girl student in the group I observed lifted a strand of her hair and twisted it. Her demonstration showed exactly what the sentence is intended to express. The other girls laughed and nodded. It is good to use demonstration to learn vocabulary because it is vivid and can easily make a deep impression on the learners. In this study, words like *pat, droop,* and *pluck* fell into this category.

3. There were also a few cases when some students confused the word in question with another similar one. Huckin and Bloch (1993, 160) characterize this case as "mistaken ID." During the group discussion, it was the students' classmates who pointed out to them their mistakes. Take *bud,* for example. "And he was not a bud when he came. No, no, he was fully open." One student said it meant "泥巴, *ní bā* ," "earth," but another student said that was "mud." Here, according to the context, *he* refers to a flower. *Bud* refers to the stage before it is in blossom. Thus, it was easy for the students to define it as "花苞, *huā bāo*" or "花蕾, *huā lěi*," which means "bud" in Chinese. In the other two cases of this kind, students mistook *courteous* for *courageous* and *harried* for *hurried.*

4. With several words, the students tried to figure out the meaning from the context. Among them, some were correct guesses. Let's take *auburn,* for example. The whole sentence is:

    > It [the old lady's hair] was the richest and most beautiful auburn color imaginable, shining as though on fire, making me think of autumn leaves and the brilliant winter coat of a fox.

    From the context, the students reached an agreement that *auburn* meant "yellowish brown," "red," or "brownish red." They also guessed *garnet* in this way. There is another example that is very interesting. In the phrase, "a ravaged old queen, lying in state, surrounded by her whispering court of flowers," one group did not know the word *court.* A girl student associated the scene with ancient China. She said the author was describing the old woman as the queen and all the flowers in the room as her attendants and officials. So *court* means "attendants and officials."

Partly Correct Guesses   Among each group's glosses, there are some that are partly correct. This means that even when the words and their glosses are decontextualized, there is a clear semantic relationship between them, although the gloss does not constitute a good translation. First, there are cases when their glosses are one of superordination, like *daisy* in the following sentence:

> You have no idea how cruel the daisy family is, on the whole. They are very rough-and-ready sort of flowers, very down to earth, and, of course, to put such an aristocrat as a rose amongst them is just asking for trouble.

From the context, the students could easily guess that *daisy* is a kind of flower, but could not tell exactly what kind of flower it is. Another word is *oyster* in the following sentence:

> All the old people I know have had their minds locked up like grey, scaly oysters since they were in their teens.

One group wrote that "It belongs to shellfish," for two students in this group had a vague idea of this word, but could not remember exactly what it was. Others wrote "something that locks itself up." Of course, they got this interpretation from the context. They also used their background knowledge and thought it meant "antique." In China, we usually call a person *lǎo gǔ dǒng* (an old antique) if he refuses to accept new ideas. It is quite reasonable to interpret the word in this way, but to an English speaker this may seem quite off the track. Words like this are *vanity, bob,* and *aristocrat.*

Incorrect Guesses   There is a significant point about the students' incorrect guesses, which is that a lot of them make perfectly good sense in the context. They seem to have something in common with those of Ae Young, a student described by Parry (1991). Take *tawny* in the following sentence, for example:

> The minute figure on the bed lifted thin, pale lids and looked at me with great tawny eyes that were as bright and intelligent as a bird's.

One group and several other individuals glossed this as "bright, clever, or intelligent." It was not surprising that the students got the answer from the structure "as . . . as."

There is also something particular about the word *belligerent* in the following sentence:

> I was dozing here when they started, particularly, it seemed to me, the yellow ones, who always seem so belligerent.

Some students glossed this as "active," while others guessed "beautiful, bright." Here we can see that they were badly off track with the original word. However, looking at the word's immediate context, we find that their glosses are not unreasonable, because in China, we usually describe the person who starts doing something as "active." As to "beautiful," it is because of the phrase "the yellow ones." Usually, yellow flowers make people think of something beautiful. Another case of this kind is *husky* in the following sentence:

> "I am so very flattered that you asked to see me," she said in a soft, husky voice.

One group thought it meant "pleasant" because the word before *husky* is "soft" and a soft voice is pleasant to the ear.

Disagreement   There are also some words that students within each group could not agree on. The reason for this is that all their guessed meanings seem to fit into the context very well; for example, the word *finicky* in the following sentence:

> Since Kralefsky was so finicky about the subject of lavatories, I decided that I would have to phrase my request politely, so I thought it best to adopt his own curious term.

In China, people also feel uncomfortable talking about the toilet in public, so some students thought it meant "shy, embarrassed." Some thought it meant "sensitive" or "careful," because in China, people describe a subject that is unsuitable for public mention as something sensitive. Another word is *eccentric* in the following sentence:

> I thought it was carrying politeness to an extreme to talk about the lavatory as if it were a human being, but, since Kralefsky was obviously a bit eccentric on the subject, I felt I had better humor him.

In one group, the students stuck to their own meaning. Some thought it meant "sensitive," some thought it was "fussy," and some thought it was "embarrassed." Their guesses for this word were based on the same kind of reasoning as those for *finicky* were.

Conclusion

I have spent a large space talking about group discussion. In the findings, we can see that the students can be trusted to solve some of the words in question and we do not need to spend the time teaching what they can solve among themselves. Of course, there were some words the students guessed wrongly, so group discussion alone is not enough. It should be supplemented by whole-class discussion. Another point is that in this paper, I mainly focus on how the students acquire receptive knowledge of the words. We still do not know if they can use them productively.

However, from group discussion, they certainly can remember the words better. This way of teaching vocabulary can develop the students' inferencing skills and habit of checking for mistaken IDs without mediation of the teacher. From the classroom observation, I can say that the students definitely enjoyed the group discussion. Of course, I do not mean to suggest that this should be the only way of teaching vocabulary, but I do suggest that it is a viable and, indeed, attractive alternative. As teachers, we all know that different students have different learning habits. This approach can meet the needs of those who are interested in interactive learning. Thus, students can acquire vocabulary in a communicative way, not only by interacting with the author through the text, but also by interacting with each other.

3. Towards a Reader-Centered Approach in Intensive Reading

Zhang Weinian

In China, intensive reading is not actually a reading course, but a course in explaining grammar, analyzing sentence structures, paraphrasing sentences, asking questions, practicing patterns, translating sentences, and retelling. According to Li Xiaoju (1990), a class in such a course cannot be called student-centered, even if the students "speak" and "practice" one hundred percent of class time, because full rein has never been given to their initiative and they never become actively involved in communicative activities requiring speaking, listening, writing, or reading—or, indeed, thinking. The way intensive reading is commonly taught in China not only fails to improve the students' reading skills, it may in fact limit their reading styles so that they never learn to read English efficiently.

A communicative approach requires that students take the central role in learning, and use language creatively and actively, not just receiving and storing up in their heads knowledge their teachers hand out to them.

> Communicative competence does not mean the ability just to utter words or sentences. It involves the ability to react mentally as well as verbally in communication situations, [and so] the communicative teacher's role is neither to give lectures nor to supply correct answers. The teacher's job is only to provide the conditions for the process of learning, set it going, observe it, try to understand it, give guidance, help it along, analyze and evaluate it. (Li 1990, 117)

Li also points out that intensive reading does not mean a focus on the individual words and sentences. It means getting at the relationship between the parts of the discourse and between the discourse and its context, and eventually also getting at a fuller meaning of the discourse as a whole. According to this, I would like to introduce a reader-centered approach to the intensive-reading class to see whether Chinese students accept it or not.

A reader-centered approach includes two types of activities on the readers' part: (a) using their background knowledge, and (b) following writers' instructions as given in signal words (e.g., *furthermore, then,* and *on the contrary*), which contribute to the cohesive ties that bind a text together. This approach is based on a top-down view of reading; that is, that it must start with the possession and application of schemata and the expectation of coherence (Brown and Yule 1983). The top-down approach suggests that the reader, rather than the text, is at the heart of the reading process, and it emphasizes the reconstruction of meaning rather than the decoding of form. The interaction of the reader and the text is central to the process, and readers bring to this interaction their knowledge of the subject at hand, knowledge of and expectations about how language works, motivation, and interest in and attitudes toward the content of the text (Carrell 1987).

With this theory in mind, I designed a study using action research to explore a reader-centered approach in my own intensive-reading class to see if such an approach is practical and if it has any good results for Chinese learners.

Methods

Learners   The eighteen students in the class are second-year electronics majors at Nanjing University. It is a high-level university, and the Electronics Department demands particularly high marks in the CEE. The students also got high marks in the university's own English Entrance Examination. They went directly into the Band Two class of college English, instead of beginning from Band One. Now they are in Band Five.

Material   The material I used for the learners' intensive reading is the last lesson from their textbook: *College English Book Five.* It is the famous speech "I Have a Dream" by Martin Luther King. I chose it for my research because the speech is based on a situation about which Chinese students would surely know something, since they had studied the course "History of the World" in secondary school.[12] Also, Dr. King organized his speech so well that the students could follow his thoughts easily.

I designed an exercise for the students to do in the class. It is based on the speech but includes only the signal words and some sentences as hints for the students to follow Dr. King's thoughts. The task was to fill in the blanks to complete the speech. Thus, the beginning of the exercise was as follows:

> Five score years ago, a great American, in whose symbolic shadow we stand, signed the Emancipation Proclamation. This momentous decree came as a great beacon light of hope to millions of Negro slaves who had been seared in the flames of withering injustice. It came as a joyous daybreak to end the long night of captivity.
>
> But one hundred years later, _____

---

12. As will be seen from the conversation reported in the "Results" section of this paper, this course is fairly uniform in content across China and reflects official attitudes towards Western societies. (Ed.)

_____ . One hundred years later, _____

_____

_____ . One hundred

years later, _____

_____

_____ . So we have come here today to _____

_____ .

The rest of the text was also presented in this fashion.

Procedures   Before teaching, I did not tell the students anything about the speech, so they would not know what would go on in the class and would not, as they usually did, have any preparation for the lesson.

In the class, first, I asked the students to do a warm-up activity: a guessing game. The game required one student to be a guesser, another to be a recorder, and the others to be knowers. The guesser had to stand in front of the classroom with his back towards the blackboard. Then I wrote "Abraham Lincoln" on the board. The knowers provided the guesser with information about the person until the guesser successfully guessed who the person was. Meanwhile, the recorder noted down the information on the board. The same procedures were used in guessing the name "Martin Luther King."

Second, after the guessing game, I asked the students to put forward more information about President Lincoln and Dr. King. When they did not remember any more, I raised some questions to activate their knowledge of black people's conditions in the past and the civil rights movement in the United States.

Third, I added some important information that they had not mentioned, such as the Emancipation Proclamation and the Amendments to the Constitution of the United States. Then I went on to review the five types of signal words together with the whole class, which they had studied in Band Three. The five types are as follows:

1.   Words that signal more of the same, as *and, moreover.*
2.   Words that change the direction of thought, as *although, however.*
3.   Words that signal order or sequence, as *first, afterwards.*
4.   Words that signal a summary, as *in short, consequently.*
5.   Words that signal cause and effect, as *because, therefore.*

Fourth, I formed the eighteen students into four groups to discuss the exercise. Each group was assigned to fill in different sections. The sections were approximately equal in length, so each group needed about the same time to complete their assignment. The exercise was done in twenty-five minutes.

All these activities were finished in one hundred minutes. Then I asked the students to listen to a tape-recording of the speech "I Have a Dream" and to follow it in their textbooks. Finally, I asked the groups to compare what they had filled in the exercise with the actual content of the speech and to report their discussion later before the whole class.

Results

For guessing "Abraham Lincoln," the students provided the following information:

> It's a person's name.
>
> He is a president.
>
> He is the leader of the Civil War.

For guessing "Martin Luther King," they provided:

> He had a very good education.
>
> He was a black leader.
>
> He won a Nobel Peace Award.
>
> He made the speech "I Have a Dream."

For the second activity, the following dialogue gives a detailed illustration of how it went (*Ss* stands for the students and *T* for me):

Ss: He was the sixteenth president of the United States.
     He abolished slavery.

T: (Wrote *slavery* on the blackboard.) Would you like to say something about slavery?

Ss: (Silent.)

T: (Guessed they might not know where to start.) Was it a person?

Ss: (Laughed.) No, it's a system.

T: What kind of system is it?

Ss: Slaves worked hard for slaveowners in the South.
     They were born to be slaves.
     They had no freedom.

T: What kind of freedom did they not have?

Ss: (No response.)

T: Could the slaves live in the same house as whites?

Ss: No, they couldn't. They were very poor.

T: Could they go to school and learn to read and write? Could they vote?

Ss: No, they had no freedom to do so.

T: (Put *social rights, education rights, political rights* on the board and explained them.)

Ss: They were beaten or killed by the slaveowners at will. The whites are landowners, so the slaves had to work on lands for them.
The slaves were black people from Africa.

T: Did they volunteer to go out to the U.S.?

Ss: No. They were kidnapped and forced to leave from Africa.
They were chained and marked because the slaveowners were afraid of their escape.
They were traded in the market.
Lincoln led the civil war to abolish the slavery in the South.
Yankees won.

T: Who were Yankees?

Ss: The North side.

  (When the students spoke, I was noting down on the board what they put forward.)

T: Did the blacks have freedom after the civil war?

Ss: Yes.

T: Could the blacks sit in the same restaurant with the whites? Could black children go to the same school with white ones? Could they really vote?

Ss: No, they couldn't.
They hadn't equal rights with the whites.

T: What did they do then?

Ss: They demonstrated.
They held the movement.
Martin Luther King led the movement.

T: All right. Let's turn to King first. What else do you know about him?

Ss: He made the speech in front of the Lincoln Memorial.
He led the March on Washington.
He was the leader of the nonviolence movement.

T: Can you explain nonviolence?

Ss: Nonviolence means fighting peacefully.
No use of weapons.

T: (Asked them to add more about Dr. King.)

Ss: He was assassinated.
A man killed him. He was sent by slaveowners in the South.
He was active in protecting blacks.

T: (Asked them to talk about the movement.) What caused the movement?

Ss: (Talked about the Rosa Parks incident in detail.)

T: (Added the time, the place of the incident, and what the blacks then did.)

Did the blacks fight against all the white brothers?

Ss: No.

T: In fact, Dr. King called on the white brothers to fight together with them.

In the exercise, the students did very well. Take one part, for example; the original text by Dr. King reads:

> But there is something I must say to my people who stand on the warm threshold which leads into the palace of justice. In the process of gaining our rightful place, we must not be guilty of wrongful deeds. Let us not seek to satisfy our thirst for freedom by drinking from the cup of bitterness and hatred. We must forever conduct our struggle on the high plane of dignity and discipline. We must not allow our creative protest to degenerate into physical violence. Again and again, we must rise to the majestic heights of meeting physical force with soul force. The marvelous new militancy which has engulfed the Negro community must not lead us to a distrust of all white people, for many of our white brothers, as evidenced by their presence here today, have come to realize that their destiny is tied up with our destiny and their freedom is inextricably bound to our freedom. We cannot walk alone.

The students' version reads as follows (the parts they wrote are underlined):

> But there is something I must say to my people who stand on the warm threshold which leads into the palace of justice. In the process of gaining our rightful place, we must not cause conflicts in society. Let us not seek to satisfy our thirst for freedom by using violence. We must carry out our task in a peace way. We must not lose the peace of mind. Again and again, we must remind ourselves that we should not use violence. The marvelous new militancy which has engulfed the Negro community must not lead us to a distrust of all white people, for many of our white brothers, as evidenced by their presence here today, have come to realize that their destiny is tied up with our destiny and their freedom is inextricably bound to our freedom. We cannot reject the support from the white brothers.

The students who wrote this version made the following comments on their work after they had compared it with the actual speech:

> What we filled has the same meaning, but not in the same words and the same structures. Some words of the speech, we think, came from the Bible. So we couldn't think of this kind of words. But the meaning is almost the same. Before we discussed we felt that the speech was very difficult because there were so many new words and difficult grammar. But now we found we have got the main idea of the speech.

Conclusion

After teaching through the reader-centered approach, I have found it much easier to teach a difficult text. The students were not only interested and active in the class, but were also involved in speaking out what they remembered about the background knowledge and doing the exercise. Their group reports indicate that the exercise, by requiring them to predict so much of the speech, gave them a new way to deal with new vocabulary, difficult grammar, and the overall structure of a text.

Being taught in this approach, the students will become more conscious of their background knowledge and of the cohesive relationships in a text, so that they can grasp the thread of thought more quickly. The process of learning is generally communicative. The students communicate not only verbally with each other and their teacher, but also mentally with the writer. The reader-centered approach is really a useful and helpful way of teaching intensive reading.

4. Let Them Speak: A New Approach to Intensive Reading

Xu Ju, Sheng Ping, and Chang Qian

It is generally agreed that communicative competence, oral or written, is the ultimate goal of EFL teaching and learning and that it can only be obtained in the process of communicating. We can draw some inferences from the process through which a child acquires his native language. Children are considerably exposed to their native language in situations where they are involved in communicating with an adult, usually a parent. Similarly, EFL learners must be provided with sufficient exposure to the target language. This is a principle that nobody will object to theoretically.

However, there is no natural environment to be provided for EFL learners who live far from English-speaking countries and so cannot subconsciously or naturally acquire that target language as a native-speaking child does. Most of the time, they must consciously learn the second language in the classroom. The partners to communicate with basically are their fellow students, as well as their language teachers, who are frequently of the same linguistic background. Therefore, there must be someone who deliberately creates scenes for them similar to the authentic environment and makes the language classroom resemble the situations in which the native child grows up. This responsibility naturally falls on the shoulders of EFL teachers, who may partly achieve this goal through communicative activities. Allwright gives a brilliant description of such an approach:

> If the language teacher's management activities are directed exclusively at involving the learners in solving communication problems in the target language, then language learning will take care of itself. (1977, 5)

The language teacher here is more like a parent than a teacher. The teacher is a partner of his/her students, or a participant in their communicative activities.

These ideas have had some influence on English teaching in China. In our national syllabus for college English majors, the ability to speak fluently and appropriately is described as one of the final ends of language teaching. After four years of training, our graduates who major in English should know what to say and how to say it to the right person at the right time without causing misunderstanding. However, establishing an aim is one thing, having it realized is quite another. In fact, there is little language teaching in China that can be called communicative. Our teaching puts more emphasis on accuracy of usage than on actual use of language, and Chinese EFL students are particularly reluctant to speak in English class.

In this study, we focus on the intensive-reading classroom because intensive reading is the predominant course in English teaching in Chinese universities. In our teaching-practice class of intensive reading, we designed a variety of activities, ranging from semi-manipulative to communicative ones, to stimulate classroom communication. Simultaneously, we observed the students' responses to each activity in an attempt to find the best way to get students to speak.

Method

Action Research   The research that the three of us did can be characterized, according to Nunan (1992), as action research. Our aims were through our own teaching to explore a solution to the pressing problem that students are poorly motivated to speak in the target language. Before class, we discussed and wrote lesson plans together, while in class we took turns to teach, trying a variety of teaching techniques to involve more students in speaking. While one of us was teaching, the other two observed and collected data regarding the classroom interaction.

Subjects   The subjects of our research were twenty-six first-year students, all of them female because they belonged to Jinling Women's College of Nanjing Normal University. They were majoring in applied English, which means that, no matter what they would do in the future (being a translator, an interpreter, a receptionist, or a tour guide), their jobs would have something to do with English. Development of communicative competence was vitally important to them. All of the twenty-six students came from a comparatively well-developed region, Jiangsu Province, where there is much contact with foreign countries. So their ultimate goals in learning English were explicit and concrete. They had extrinsic motivation to study well.

Besides the CEE, these students had been required to pass a special oral exam for English majors before they were enrolled in the college, and their original oral competence, at least in regard to accuracy of pronunciation, was generally higher than that of the non-English majors. However, at the time we began teaching them, their English courses had always been taught by either the traditional translation approach or the audio-lingual approach, both in secondary school and in college. They had not experienced any activities that could be called classroom communication. Instead, the oral activities they were used to were question-answer dialogues between teacher and students, text imitation, recitation, and memorization. Such activities did not have much appeal for them, for when we asked them whether they were interested in English, they answered definitely, "It is boring. We do not like it." As a result, their intrinsic motivation was rather low.

The two individual students that we chose as our special research targets at the beginning were two students of different abilities, according to the opinion of the regular teacher, as well as our own observation of his two lessons before we began our own teaching. We will call them Li and Wu. Li was chosen as the monitor in charge of study because of her outstanding performance in the CEE, as well as in classroom oral contributions. Wu, on the other hand, was quite mediocre in both items and, besides, she was a silent student. She said nothing except when her name was called by the teacher.

Teaching and Research Materials   Our teaching materials were predetermined by the college authorities: *A New English Course* (Li Guanyi 1986), Volume 1 (Units 17–18) and Volume 2 (Units 1–5). The books are arranged according to grammatical order and each unit focuses on one particular grammatical point. All units follow the same arrangement: (1) language-structure practice, with cues given in tables together with examples; (2) two dialogues, the first for basic structure application and the second for practice in special phrases and expressions; and (3) two reading passages on related topics for comprehension and further practice of the basic structure.

Procedure

1. Teaching Methods:

Before teaching, we designed a range of teaching techniques, based on the content of the texts to be studied, which varied from semi-controlled to free and from meaningful to communicative categories (see Brown 1994). In these activities, students were expected to engage in classroom interactions in pairs, in groups, or with the whole class. They were encouraged to combine the presented material with their own experiences and the things that interested them.

However, limited by the teaching materials and syllabus, sometimes we were really unable to make our activities as communicative as we would wish. We were not permitted to throw away the textbook in order to serve the communicative purpose.

2. Recordkeeping:

Preceding our formal engagement in teaching practice, we attended two lessons by the regular teacher and collected preliminary data to document the class's situation in the initial stage of our research. We recorded the types of teaching techniques, the time of teacher's talk and students' talk, the number of students engaged in talk in each activity, and the way of prompting students to talk. This data collection laid a good foundation for the subsequent similar acts while we ourselves were teaching.

During our own teaching process, every time one of us taught, the other two did research. If it was the teacher's or students' monologues or students' performances—either in pairs or in groups—the two researchers just sat in their own seats on the front-left side, observing and recording who was speaking and for how long. But if it was an activity that required the students to simultaneously practice dialogues or talk in pairs or in groups, the two observers would leave their seats and walk to the two groups where our two individual study subjects were involved. They would pay particular attention to the performances of these two students without the students themselves being aware that they were being observed. The two observers collected data on how frequently and how long the two subjects participated in the group interaction and what roughly their contribution was.

After the third, sixth, and seventh weeks of our teaching practicum, we surveyed the students to elicit their opinions on our various activities. Each time, we distributed a form to each of them, listing the activities they had just tried out, giving them four choices for evaluating each (i.e., "I like it very much," "I like it moderately," "I do not like it much," "I do not like it at all"), and requesting the reasons for their choices.

At the end of our teaching practicum, we did a further survey. We handed out a questionnaire to all the students that was intended to elicit their overall evaluation of our teaching techniques.

Analysis

When the teaching practicum was over, we summed up and rearranged our data and described them in several different ways. We chose four lessons to analyze and compare: the original lesson given by the regular teacher and three lessons given, respectively, in the third, sixth, and seventh weeks of our teaching practicum period and by each of the three of us. These four lessons, when put together, could roughly reflect the classroom situations in the early, middle, and final stages of our study.

We then went on to analyze the students' evaluations of our activities. For convenience of analysis, we converted the qualitative judgments (i.e., high, moderately high, moderately low, low opinions) into scores: 4, 3, 2, and 1 point, respectively. Then for each activity, we added up the total score and divided it by the number of students responding to get a mean score.

The data concerning the two individuals were analyzed separately.

Findings

Teaching Techniques

The Regular Teacher's Lesson

The teaching techniques adopted by the regular teacher in the original class (Lesson 1) were as follows:

1. Question-answer between teacher and students, using the target structure verb + -ing form.

2. Tape-playing for drills presentation.

3. Pairs of students' performances of drill repetition.

4. Cued drills substitution practice.

5. Question-answer between teacher and students about the language point in the drills.

6. Sentence-making with given phrases and presentation of the sentences by all the students in turn.

7. English-Chinese translation by student volunteers of verbal phrases and differentiation of present-participle/gerund phrases.

8. Chinese-English sentences translation using the target structures.

9. Tape-playing for presentation of Dialogue 1: "What cassette recorder to buy."

10. Teacher's analysis of language points in Dialogue 1.

11. Story-making by individual students, in writing using cued words, and one student reporting on her story.

12. Reading Dialogue 1 in chorus.

Evidently, this was a lesson based on a combination of audio-lingual and grammar-translation approaches. The teacher used a tape-recorder to present the texts, both drills and dialogues; he had the students repeatedly practice the drills in a mechanical way; he solved the grammatical problems by giving many instructions; and he enhanced students' comprehension of language points by providing them with translation practice. He also gave students chances to apply the vocabulary and grammatical structures in their own use of language, of which "sentence-making" and "story-making" were examples. However, he did not direct the potentially communicative activity of "story-making" in a communicative way. He asked the whole class to write individually and had only one student report on her story. This led to almost no classroom communication, in speech or in writing.

Among the regular teacher's techniques, only the first one involved some interaction between the teacher and students. Even in this one, the students' speech was limited by the teacher's "yes-no" questions. What students were expected to do was to give affirmative or negative answers in full or shortened forms.

So we can say this was a teacher-centered, grammar-based, and product-oriented lesson. It was typical of traditional English lessons in China.

Three Lessons During the Teaching Practicum

The following are lists of teaching techniques of three lessons given, respectively, in the third, sixth, and seventh week of our teaching practicum (Lessons 2–4):

Lesson 2

1. Warm-up activities.
   a. Transmission of two messages (group work).
   b. Students' asking ten "yes-no" questions of the teacher.

2. Discussion on differences between four pairs of sentences that illustrated verb tenses and reporting on the results (pair work).

3. Group development of a story by using the target structures, followed by reporters' presentation.

4. Presentation of Dialogue 1 on tape: "Professor Jia Recalling the Past."

5. Exchange of background information related to the content of Dialogue 1 between the teacher and students.

6. Broad questions to get students' reflections on ideas suggested in Dialogue 1.

7. Practicing using three set expressions in dialogue form (pair work).

Lesson 3

1. Warm-up: problem-solving (group work).

2. Word-guessing game.

3. Conversations from given prompts that consisted of unfinished sentences containing the target structure, modal auxiliary + perfect infinitive (the students were arranged in two concentric circles facing each other; the inner circle remained stationary while the outer circle moved so that the students regularly changed conversation partners).

4. Students' reporting on responses to Activity 3: sentence-making using the target structure.

5. Dialogue presentation through role-play demonstration by two students.

6. Role-play performances according to the given situations related to content of Dialogue 1: " Pollution Problems."

7. Discussion on the topic related to content of Dialogue 2: "Environment and Me."

Lesson 4

1. Warm-up: *yes* and *no* are forbidden words in the responses to "yes/no" questions (between individual student and the rest of the class).

2. Giving and reporting utterances for practicing indirect speech (pair work).

3. Giving and reporting utterances (whole class working in a chain).

4. Preparation for the next activity through negotiation of meanings in Dialogue 1: "The First Telephone Call Cao Made in London" (pair work).

5. Conversation: talking about the telephone service in China (group work).

6. Role-play: making a phone call to . . . (pair work).

The preceding lists show there were some common features in the teaching techniques used in Lessons 2, 3, and 4, which can be approximately categorized as follows:

a. Warm-up Activities

All three lessons started with warm-up activities. Instead of getting straight to the lesson itself, we had these activities for establishing a relaxed, lively atmosphere and drawing students' attention to the task at the beginning of a new lesson. They were appetizers before the formal meal.

In the warm-up activity of Lesson 4, the student who stood in the front gave responses to "yes-no" questions from the rest of the class while not being permitted to use the words *yes* and *no*. Thus, on the one hand, the voluntary questioners racked their brains to raise easily misleading questions to lure the questioned to say "yes" or "no" in her responses. The questioned, on the other hand, cracked one "hard nut" after another, smartly avoiding the "traps" devised for her. This activity resulted in the production of much unpredicted language and a lot of fun.

b. Approaching Grammar

Being limited by the teaching materials, some of our teaching techniques had to be designed around the understanding, practice, and application of the basic sentence structures. But unlike the regular teacher, we tried to make the use of these structures more communicative by introducing authentic situations or having the students use them in role play. We replaced the traditional teacher's instruction of grammatical rules by the students' own discovery of the rules in the process of discussion and application, such as in teaching Techniques 2 and 3 of Lesson 2.

Teaching Technique 3 of Lesson 2, for example, was story-making, also used by the regular teacher in Lesson 1, but, in contrast to that in the original lesson, here it resulted in many interactions between group members on how to develop the stories. So the stories made here were the products of collective efforts, and the process of making them was considered as important as the product itself. Besides, the reporter of every group got a chance to present her group's story, which made the activity still more communicative.

Teaching Techniques 2 and 3 of Lesson 4, "Giving and Reporting Utterances" in pairs and in a chain, were both designed for application of indirect speech. They differed only in the participants' organization. The former activity happened between two neighbors. Each time, one gave an utterance and the other reported it, using indirect speech. Then the two partners changed roles. The latter activity was more challenging. Each student was both reporter and utterer at the same time, reporting her predecessor's utterance and also giving an utterance for the next student to report. Uttering, reporting, uttering . . . , proceeding successively, connected the whole class like a chain. The originally boring grammar learning here became something vivid and appealing.

c. Approaching Vocabulary

In two of our lessons, we also adopted activities that were directed at the understanding and use of vocabulary. One was the "Word-guessing Game" in Lesson 3, in which one student was called to the front of the class, facing the others, and the others tried to give their own interpretations of a word written on the board by the teacher in an attempt to enable the student in the front to guess what the word was.

Another vocabulary-application activity was "Practice in Using Three Set Expressions," which were taken from Dialogue 1 of Lesson 2. One of the expressions was "for no reason at all." To begin with, the teacher demonstrated the kind of situation in which the expression might be used by telling a short story. Then, she had the students make up dialogues that included the expression. Nearly every pair could use it appropriately in their particular situation. Here, we present one of the dialogues made up by them:

A: I fell in love with my boyfriend at the first sight of him.
B: Why is he so attractive to you?
A: I don't know. I just love him for no reason at all.

d. Approaching the Text Content
We also employed a variety of activities to help our learners become familiar with the contents of Dialogue 1 in Lessons 2–4 and provided them with opportunities to have conversations and discussions on authentic topics. Teaching Techniques 5 and 6 of Lesson 2, Techniques 6 and 7 of Lesson 3, and Techniques 4, 5, and 6 of Lesson 4 are examples of this kind of activity.

Like the regular teacher in his original class, we used a tape-recorder in our lessons to help us present texts. While the tape was playing, the students were in a passive role as listeners, but each tape lasted only a few minutes and the listening served only as a preparatory activity.

In summary, Lessons 2–4 employed an alternative approach to grammar and vocabulary, in which students could discover the rules for themselves through oral interactions and negotiations. Our teaching techniques put more emphasis on the learning process than on the product. In addition, we directed students' attention to the content of the texts, which was not done by the regular teacher. We provided authentic topics or situations for our students to discuss or enact in role-plays. In these activities, the students were given considerable freedom to say what they wanted to say. Lessons 2–4, then, can be roughly claimed to have been communicative, student-centered, meaning-based, and process-oriented lessons.

Students' Participation in Class

Time Distribution
Table 7-2 shows the time distribution in Lessons 1–4.

Table 7-2
Time distribution in Lessons 1–4 (percent)
(total time for each lesson: one hundred minutes)

	Teacher's Talk	Students' Talk	Tape-playing	Students' Writing
Lesson 1	31	45	9	15
Lesson 2	17	79	4	0
Lesson 3	14	86	0	0
Lesson 4	12	88	0	0

It shows that from Lesson 2, progressively more time was devoted to students' talk, while the teacher's talk time was progressively reduced. By the last lesson, the teacher only talked for twelve minutes in all—to assign tasks, to give directions, to offer help, and to give some comments and encouragement. There was no time-consuming analysis of language points. Students, for their part, were engaged in classroom interactions through questions and responses among themselves, the giving and reporting of utterances, and role-plays and conversations on assigned topics.

Number of Students Participating

Table 7-3 shows two types of data for Lesson 1 and Lessons 2–4 about the numbers of activities in which given numbers of students were involved in talking.

Table 7-3

Numbers of activities involving given numbers of students in talking

	Number of Students Talking				
	0–5	**6–10**	**11–15**	**16–20**	**21–26**
Lesson 1	4	3	3	0	2
Lesson 2	2	1	0	0	4
Lesson 3	1	0	0	1	5
Lesson 4	0	0	0	1	5

Total number of students present: 26 in Lessons 1 and 4
25 in Lessons 2 and 3

In Lesson 1, there were as many as four activities that involved only one person or nobody at all in talking. They were the tape-playing time for text presentation, the teacher's monologue in analyzing language points, and a single person's reporting on her story.

In Lesson 2, there was also one time of tape-playing in which nobody talked. There was another activity, "Background Information Exchange," in which only four students spoke and the "Six Broad Questions About Dialogue 1" led to only six students giving responses. However, in four of the seven activities, the whole class was involved in speaking simultaneously or in turn.

In both Lessons 3 and 4, there were as many as five activities in which the whole class was involved in speaking. Over the two lessons, there were seven of the ten activities in which all the students were speaking almost at the same time. Therefore, we can say the teaching techniques from Lessons 2–4 involved increasingly more students in talking and this meant that the class time was more efficiently utilized.

Ways of Prompting Students' Speech

In Lesson 1, except for one time when the twenty-six students took turns to present the sentences they made and another time when twelve students volunteered to give Chinese translations for sixteen English verbal phrases, the students spoke only after their names were called by the regular teacher. In Lessons 2–4, the teachers still called students by name to prompt them to talk; for example, three of four speakers were called to give information about the Olympic Games in Lesson 2 and two students were called to present Dialogue 1 in Lesson 3 by reading the roles. However, as the practicum progressed, the students increasingly volunteered to talk, and many activities also involved the students' private conversations.

From the data collected from the classroom observation, we may infer that students were more willing to speak in the activities employed in Lessons 2–4 than in Lesson 1.

Students' Evaluations   Table 7-4 shows the students' evaluations of the activities adopted in Lessons 2–4. The scores, as noted previously, are transformed from the expressions that were used in our survey forms: "I like it very much" (four points), "I like it moderately" (three points), "I don't like it much" (two points), and "I don't like it at all" (one point).

The overall responses of the whole class of students showed widely differing evaluations of these twenty activities. Those that got an average score higher than three points were the warm-up activities in Lessons 2 and 4, the word-guessing game in Lesson 3, the practice of three set expressions in Lesson 2, the two times of role-play in Lessons 3 and 4, and the giving and reporting of utterances in a chain in Lesson 4. These seven highly valued activities had some common features. First, they were interesting. A student said in her response to our final investigation that they could play games in some of our activities. Second, they were suitable to the learning of particular language points. These activities were not chosen blindly, but in accordance with the needs of both the teaching materials and the students. For example, in one of these activities we asked the learners to give and report utterances in a chain in order to practice using indirect speech; the students both enjoyed the activity and learned the structure by practicing it. Third, these activities cherished students' cooperation with each other and sometimes moderate competition. For example, in the warm-up of Lesson 4, *yes* and *no* are the forbidden words in the responses to "yes/no" questions; lighthearted competition took place between the questioners and questioned as the former tried to trick the latter into using the forbidden words.

Although some activities with serious topics listed here were not the most popular ones, they still got moderately high scores. Scores of 3.0 were given to these three activities: conversations in two concentric circles (Lesson 3, Number 3); group discussion of the topic, "Environment and Me" (Lesson 3, Number 7); and group conversations about the telephone service in China (Lesson 4, Number 5). The latter two involved factual topics while the former one needed some imagination.

The least popular activities among the twenty fell into the two types of dialogue presentation: role-play by students and tape-playing. The mean

Table 7-4
Students' evaluation of activities in Lessons 2–4

Activities	# Giving 4 Points	# Giving 3 Points	# Giving 2 Points	# Giving 1 Point	Total Scores	Mean Scores
Lesson 2						
1. Warm-up	10	12	3	0	82	3.3
a. relay messages						
b. yes/no questions						
(students-teacher)						
2. Discussion (pair work)	0	14	11	0	64	2.6
3. Story-making (group work)	5	14	5	1	73	2.9
4. Tape-playing	2	9	14	0	63	2.5
5. Discussion (teacher-students)	3	11	11	0	67	2.7
6. Question-answer (teacher-students)	4	11	9	1	68	2.7
7. Practice of 3 set expressions (pair work)	8	14	3	0	80	3.2
Lesson 3						
1. Warm-up (group work)	6	11	8	0	73	2.9
2. Word guessing game (students-student)	20	3	2	0	93	3.7
3. Conversations (two circles)	6	13	6	0	75	3
4. Students' reports	4	9	11	1	66	2.6
5. Students' role-play demonstration	1	10	12	2	60	2.4
6. Students' role-play (pair work)	9	12	4	0	80	3.2
7. Discussion (group work)	4	17	4	0	75	3
Lesson 4						
1. Warm-up (students-student)	23	3	0	0	101	3.9
2. Reporting utterances (pair work)	5	10	9	2	70	2.7
3. Reporting utterances (chain)	9	12	5	0	82	3.2
4. Interpretation of dialogue (pair work)	5	11	6	4	69	2.7
5. Conversation (group work)	9	10	6	1	79	3
6. Role play (pair work)	10	9	7	0	81	3.1

scores they got were 2.4 and 2.5, respectively. It was not strange that students did not welcome such kinds of activities, since in them, either all the students had nothing to do but passive listening or no more than two of them had a chance to speak. In addition, most students did not like the activities that tightly limited the sentence structures they could use. Both the discussion on the differences of sentence structures in Lesson 2 (Number 2) and reporting on the conversations in two concentric circles got only 2.6 points, maybe because they put more focus on form than on meaning.

We must be cautious in interpreting these data, however, because each student's evaluations were very subjective, affected by a variety of personal factors: whether she liked the teacher or the teaching style, whether she herself was in good mood that day, whether she preferred being challenged or being secure, and so on. A response might be more negative simply because it was raining. Therefore, we can only regard these evaluations as a rough guide in our attempts to design or choose teaching techniques.

Two Case Studies   While we were observing Lesson 1, we discovered that the regular teacher was very willing to appoint Li to answer his questions or do his tasks. As a result, she talked as many as nine times in that lesson. Wu, by contrast, had few chances to speak. Apart from one time when the whole class took turns to talk, she was only called once to repeat a drill with her partner.

In Lessons 2–4, Li talked six, five, and six times, respectively. She was still one of the most active students. But Wu's talking also went up to four, four, and five times, respectively. There was no longer a great difference between them in respect to the numbers of times they talked. This was because many of our activities were designed to give every student a chance to talk, in turn or simultaneously. So, even the most silent student had no alternative but to open her mouth if she did not want to lose face.

Then let us turn to the duration of the two individuals' talk time in each lesson. In Lessons 2, 3, and 4, Li talked for eighteen, twenty-six, and twenty-one minutes, respectively, while Wu talked for seven, fifteen, and eleven minutes only (the figures are only approximate). Thus, Li's total time of talking was about twice as much as Wu's in each of the three lessons. That may suggest that Wu's talk in the same activity had a shorter duration than Li's. This was proved by our actual observation. In pair work, many times when Li was still actively conversing with her partner, Wu and her partner had already stopped talking and were doing something else. Similarly, in group work, Wu only made brief and fragmentary oral contributions.

During our observation, we never saw Wu volunteering to say anything when the teacher called for volunteers to present a certain performance. She always lowered her head and avoided the teacher's eyes. She stated in her response to our final survey: "I really want to speak, but I'm so shy and easily get nervous that I dare not to speak. But I'm managing to overcome it." We came to realize that Wu's problem existed mainly in her timid personality rather than her attitude. We were very sorry that we could not help her out of her trouble during the short period of the teaching practicum.

If we can assume that Wu's changes were chiefly in respect to quantity, to Li more changes happened in regard to quality. In the original lesson, except for one time of substitution drill performance with her partner, each of Li's oral contributions involved only one utterance, either giving an answer to the teacher's question or presenting a solution to the teacher's task. In contrast, Li's speech in Lessons 2–4 involved many interactions with the teacher, her partner, the other group members, or the whole class. Also, she used the target language to talk about her own experiences, feelings, and opinions and to solve practical problems.

Li was always ready to speak if she was offered a chance. She could fulfill most of the tasks well. In the activity "act out a court scene" (not included in the four lessons analyzed here), she volunteered to act as the defending counsel—the most challenging role—and she gave an excellent performance. She was also the natural director of the activity. Her direction and performance, as well as the good cooperation of her classmates, made the play a successful one.

In group development of a story using the basic structures, Li acted as both facilitator and reporter. She reported the following story:

> I was wandering in the street when I saw a million-pound note lying on the ground. I had been looking forward to such kind of lucky experiences for years. I picked it up as quickly as possible, making sure that no one noticed me. I walked into a luxurious restaurant. I ordered a lot of expensive food, which I had been dreaming of for a long time. While I was gulping, the waiter came and stared at me. I didn't stop eating until he interrupted me: "Do you have enough cash with you?" "Certainly!" I threw the million-pound note on the table with pride. When I was waiting for my change, two policemen came to me and asked: "Where did you get this forged bank note?"

From the quotations of Li's actual speech, we may claim that those activities that we tried did bring about large qualitative changes in her talk as well as in the speech of other similar students.

But how about the students whose personalities were originally quiet like Wu? Were these activities also effective for them? We must confess, although this group of students also talked considerably more during those activities employed in the classes during our teaching practicum period, there were no obvious qualitative changes in their talk. We are wondering if we should have made some of our tasks easier and our activities more attractive to this group of students.

Conclusion

From our personal experiences during these few weeks of teaching practice, we realize that, although currently Chinese college English-teaching is examination-oriented, communicative-language teaching is still very welcome and ready to be received by Chinese students. This alternative teaching approach greatly stimulated the interest and enthusiasm of our students at Jinling Women's College to participate in the classroom activities and made them actively think, talk, and cooperate with each other, rather than just passively listening and receiving what they were instructed or mechanically responding to the given tasks, as they did in the traditional class.

Our communicative activities were designed in accordance with the Chinese reality. We also dealt with grammar, which occupies an important place in various types of examinations, but we helped the students discover the grammatical rules for themselves. At the same time, these activities around grammar learning, together with those around vocabulary and content learning, provided many opportunities for the students to talk with each other. As one student wrote in her response paper: "Your activities . . . made us remember well the knowledge in the textbook and also let us learn many things that don't exist in it."

So maybe we should say there is no absolute division line between communicative-language teaching and the Band 4 and other similar examinations. At the same time as we work to serve the communicative purpose, we can also take care of language learning. The challenge before us, as well as our colleagues, is to design a variety of activities to bring benefit to both the good and poor students, and to bring changes not only to the quantity, but also to the quality of all students' talk.

Conclusions

The project reported in this book had three main purposes. First, it was an attempt to answer a question: What is the relationship between first-language literacy and second-language learning? My intention was to elicit specific information about the Chinese writing system and the social circumstances in which Chinese people learn how to use it, and I hoped to relate that information to accounts of Chinese students' strategies for reading English. Second, the project was an exercise in teaching reading and writing skills in English as a foreign language at an advanced level. Specifically, I hoped that the participants would acquire useful professional vocabulary, learn the forms and conventions of English academic prose, adopt appropriate strategies for reading articles in their field, and develop the ability and confidence to write professional papers themselves. Finally, the project was intended to help the participants grow as teachers. The readings would serve, I hoped, not only as models of academic discourse, but also as stimuli to thinking about the processes of language learning and the social circumstances by which such learning is conditioned. Through their writing, the participants would be encouraged to relate what they read to their own experience as teachers and learners. It was an ambitious project, but, as the participants' contributions to this book testify, it succeeded beyond my expectations.

I do not claim, of course, to have found a conclusive answer to the question of the relationship between first-language literacy and second-language reading. The cultural practices associated with literacy and the individual behavior associated with reading are too complex for any straightforward correlation to be possible. Consider, for one thing, the diversity of China. It is a huge country in which geographical variation—between north and south, between coastland and interior, and between urban and rural—interacts with social distinctions—between educated and uneducated, between modernizing and traditional, and, increasingly now, between rich and poor. All these factors contribute to how literacy is acquired and used, creating great variation in the experience of people of different regions and different social groups. The society is, moreover, in a constant state of change, and over the course of the last few decades, the changes have been particularly dramatic. They affect literacy practices as they do other aspects of social life: Today's children, in the cities at least, enjoy more parental teaching and more access to written materials than the children of the Cultural Revolution ever did; on the other hand, they suffer more from pressures to study and to do well in their schoolwork, and they have little time to enjoy the materials available to them. In addition, those who aspire to be well educated in today's China must not only be highly literate in Chinese; they must also, whatever their discipline, be able to pass a stiff exam in English, and for some, the pressure to learn English begins very early in life (see Qin Haihua's essay in Chapter One, p. 29).

If social practices vary, diachronically as well as synchronically, individual strategies do so even more. The contributions to this book give some indication of how much their writers vary in personality: some are introvert, some extrovert, some self-confident, some diffident, some phlegmatic, some anxious, some obedient, some rebellious. Such differences have important effects on how people approach learning tasks, including the task of reading in a foreign language. And, like societies, individuals change, so that what a particular person does at one stage of learning a language may be quite different from what he or she does later. Finally, there is the problem that bedevils all reading research: It is impossible to be aware of all the complex interactions that take place as one reads and still more difficult to articulate them, so the introspective accounts presented here necessarily give only a partial and undoubtedly simplified picture.

Given two such complex and dynamic phenomena, we cannot expect to identify a constant relationship between them. Yet the participants' writings do suggest strongly that their behavior as English-language learners has grown out of their experiences as literate Chinese people, and that there are common elements in those experiences that can help us understand, if not predict, the behavior of other Chinese students of English. More generally, too, an awareness of what literacy means in China and of how it relates to the learning of English may help us to ask questions about and so to interpret the behavior of students who come to English from other cultural backgrounds. To help in such a process, I will summarize here what the program participants have written about Chinese literacy and about its effects on their approach to English.

One of the most salient points to arise from our discussions was the enormously high value the participants place on literacy, not just as a useful practical skill, but also as an aesthetic experience and a moral discipline. The writing system itself is seen as a thing of beauty, with its enormous numbers of characters, each perceived as having its own meaning, and the ingenious ways in which the characters are related to each other so that they can be remembered (see Li Xiaozhong, Chapter One, p. 25). Furthermore, once the characters are known, a Chinese reader gains access to a rich literary heritage, including history, philosophy, fiction, and poetry, which expresses the whole range (as it seems) of human experience, wisdom, and emotion (for powerful responses to such material, see Zhu Xiaowen in Chapter One, p. 11, and Wang Kui in Chapter Three, p. 87).

The rewards of Chinese literacy are great, and perhaps they are all the more valued because of the hard work required to obtain them. It takes time and effort to learn the writing system, and the discipline involved is particularly emphasized in the teaching of calligraphy, as Ding Lu suggests in Chapter One (p. 17). Thus, literacy is associated not only with beauty, but also with desirable personal qualities, and this association is reinforced as children learn to read whole texts. Many of the materials used have obvious morals—consider, for example, the references made to the Lei Feng stories by Zhu Xiaowen in Chapter One (p. 9) and by Lu Wanying in Chapter Two (p. 52)—and when students begin to study classical Chinese, they are exposed to the ancient tradition of Confucian moral philosophy (see Wu Lili's essay in Chapter Three, pp. 89–97).[1]

According to the accounts given here, Chinese literacy is seen as not only encouraging good behavior at the individual level, but also as supporting the ideal of the state as the united Chinese "family" (see Liu Yuanyan, Chapter Four, pp. 106–107). One way in which it does this is, again, through the writing system itself. As Chang Qian suggests in Chapter Three (p. 67), the characters are perceived as representing not sounds so much as meaning, and the same text can, in fact, be read in any of the regional varieties of Chinese. (The participants demonstrated the point with much hilarity one evening, when several of them read one of my own Chinese compositions, each in her own dialect.) The writing system, therefore, is seen as having an important unifying function in that it transcends the variability of speech.[2] Now, moreover, the alphabetic writing system is used to further support national integration. In school textbooks, as shown by Wang Jian (Chapter Three, p. 73), the "correct" pronunciation of each character is shown in Pinyin, which is regarded strictly as a phonetic notation; thus, children from all over China learn to speak Putonghua, the dialect of educated people in and around Beijing.

The choice of texts used to teach literacy similarly promotes national unity. Despite the richness and variety of China's literary heritage, there seems to be widespread agreement as to which pieces should be selected from it for children to learn. Thus, in Chapter One, Xu Ju and Luo Ningxia both refer to the same poem and Ding Lu and Lu Wanying to the same stories (see pp. 23, 28, and 17). When children work on school textbooks, there is even greater

---

1. Confucianism, however, no longer enjoys the respect that it used to, for it was deeply undermined by the Cultural Revolution. Communism, in its turn, has lost much of its moral force, and many express concern about the resulting moral vacuum. It is in these circumstances that Christianity has attracted increasing interest among Chinese, and it is pertinent to note in a discussion of literacy that there is now an apparently insatiable demand for Chinese Bibles (information from the Amity Press, Nanjing, 1992).

2. In the present century, however, a distinctive way of writing Guangdonghua (Cantonese) has developed, especially in Hong Kong (Gargan 1996). The political significance of this fact is obvious.

uniformity, for the curriculum and choice of books is tightly controlled by the central government. It is not surprising, then, that the materials for literacy instruction reflect closely the current political ideology, as Lu Wanying demonstrates in Chapter Two (pp. 52–55).[3]

The association between literacy and socially acceptable behavior is further reinforced by the way in which it is taught. Qin Haihua describes eloquently in Chapter Two (pp. 56–57) the strict discipline of the classrooms in which she learned to read and write, and that impression is supported by the account of Wu Liangzhe in Chapter Two (pp. 40–41). Nor is it only in school that children are controlled by the requirement to do reading and writing tasks. Gu Tiexia in Chapter Two (pp. 58–60) emphasizes how parents cooperate with teachers to ensure that homework gets done; this, in turn, enables teachers to assign much more homework than they otherwise could.

Besides encouraging—indeed, requiring—diligence, the acquisition of Chinese literacy seems to encourage a particular kind of mental discipline. The essays by Wang Jian and Zhu Minghui in Chapter Three (pp. 73–84) describe a systematic presentation of material, starting with the smallest units and moving up to the largest. This analytical approach to written text is reinforced in many different ways, ranging from the stroke-by-stroke construction of characters at the elementary stage to the punctuation of ambiguous texts in the study of classical Chinese (see Wu Lili in Chapter Three, pp. 93–96); according to Wang Kui's informants (Chapter Six, pp. 189 and 191), college students still use it even when reading Chinese for pleasure.[4]

The participants, then, supported the suggestion made in the introduction that Chinese literacy is a distinctive kind of literacy, by virtue both of the writing system and of the social framework in which it is used and taught. How does this literacy affect their approach to English? How, in particular, does it affect the way in which they and their students read English text?

The essays in Chapter Four indicate clearly that there is considerable ambivalence towards English in China, even on the part of these writers, who have chosen it as their subject of specialization and who were undoubtedly enjoying their time studying it at Nanjing. The ambivalence springs partly from the unhappy history of China's relationship with Britain and the United States (see Chen Ting and Zhu Minghui, pp. 109–116), but it may also have roots in Chinese literacy and the evident pride that Chinese take in it. Liu

3. Literacy can of course be used in China, as it is elsewhere, to express dissent against the central government. A most distinguished example before the 1949 Revolution was Lu Xun, who, incidentally, was an ardent advocate of alphabetization precisely because it would allow regional differences in speech to be expressed in writing (DeFrancis 1984). For a full account of Lu Xun's career and for those of other prominent social critics, see Spence (1981).

4. Nobody claims, however, that Chinese-language reading strategies are exclusively bottom-up. The program participants were quite sure that they used top-down strategies for reading Chinese; and Zhu Minghui's and Wang Kui's descriptions of primary-school teaching in Chapter Three (pp. 79–88) show that in addition to analytical exercises, there is a good deal of oral presentation of text, which helps children develop and use appropriate text and content schemata.

Yuanyan (p. 106) argues that in the traditional Chinese view, individuals are necessarily either inferior or superior to the other individuals with whom they deal, and that this way of thinking is extended to relationships between nations and cultures. Perhaps it is extended to perceptions of different kinds of literacy, too, for this would explain the clear impression that written Chinese is regarded as better—more elegant, more subtle, more expressive—than English, even though learning English is universally recognized as necessary for professional and economic advancement in the modern world.

If this perception indeed exists (and I cannot be sure about it, for the program participants were too polite to tell me so directly), it is not altogether surprising when viewed from the perspective of Chinese literacy. Take the writing system, for a start: English has a mere twenty-six characters, none of which has meaning in itself. As a writing system, it may be relatively easy to learn, but it has none of the charm and fascination of Chinese. Then consider the literary tradition of English. It is as extensive as that of Chinese, if not as old, but little of that tradition is accessible to Chinese students, as is all too clear from Wang Kui's paper in Chapter Six (p. 193); only those who specialize in English at an advanced level have any opportunity to study it as literature. Finally, consider the circumstances in which English is taught. Du Qunhua (Chapter Four, pp. 117–118) shows quite plainly that for many Chinese the chief motivation for learning English is to pass an exam, and the accounts presented in Chapter Five (pp. 136–168) demonstrate how much that exam dominates the activities that take place in class. English, therefore, is presented at school (and school is the only place where most Chinese students come into contact with it) as a collection of "language points" to be committed to memory; the participants are quite exceptional in perceiving it as a real means of communication.

And what about English reading strategies? The participants were remarkably consistent in reporting the use of bottom-up strategies more than top-down ones, though there was some variation as to when they said they used them. According to the accounts in Chapter Six, some, like Bao Jingying (p. 176), used such strategies consistently right up to the time when they entered the program and embarked on my first reading assignment. Others, such as Du Qunhua and Zhu Xiaowen (pp. 178 and 182), reported that they would try to use top-down strategies when first approaching a text, but would resort to bottom-up ones when they encountered difficulties. Still others reported bottom-up strategies as an earlier stage of learning, which, in some cases at least, had been passed before they came to the program.[5] Amid all this variation, there seems to be one constant factor: an assumption that bottom-up reading is prior to top-down and that comprehension problems are dealt with by analyzing problematic items rather than by looking at the broader

---

5. There has not been space here to print the essays that illustrate this point, but they are quoted at length in Parry (1996a).

context. This view of reading seems to reflect clearly the way in which Chinese literacy is taught at an elementary level.

The participants' reading strategies could and did change, however—in some cases quite dramatically. This brings us to the second aspect of the project, as a course designed to develop skills in reading and writing academic English. Many of the participants chose for their essays on "Making Sense of English Text" to describe how their strategies had developed in the course of that term's work, and these accounts suggest strongly that, as a reading course, the project was remarkably successful (see Bao Jingying, Du Qunhua, and Zhu Xiaowen in Chapter Six, pp. 176–186, and other essays quoted in Parry 1995). It is worth pausing for a moment to consider why this was so.

The most important reason was the diligence and goodwill of the participants as students. Most of them worked tremendously hard on the readings, making sure that they understood before beginning to write their responses. The requirement to write responses helped too; as Du Qunhua points out (p. 180), it provided an important impetus to work on the readings to the point that they could be perceived as wholes, despite their length and the participants' tendency to read them word by word and sentence by sentence. The process of arriving at a holistic understanding, moreover, got easier as time went by; the vocabulary and rhetorical structures became increasingly familiar, and the ideas, so new to begin with, were reiterated from one reading to the next and were further reinforced in the courses on linguistics and methodology. Thus, while the participants were reading about and discussing the use of top-down strategies in interaction with bottom-up ones, they were steadily developing appropriate schemata for applying such strategies themselves. Finally, the essay-writing assignments served to reinforce the reading, for through them the participants could use the new vocabulary and relate the theories to their own experience, and thus they could assimilate both.

As a writing course, the project worked extraordinarily well too. A key factor in this was the fact that there was a real communication gap, because at the beginning I knew little about literacy in China and really wanted to learn about it. The questions that I wrote on the participants' first drafts were genuine questions, informed (it is true) by some understanding of the general issues involved in literacy, but arising chiefly out of my ignorance of the particular circumstances described. As the term progressed and I learned more, it was possible to elicit ever richer information, while the participants, for their part, were increasingly successful in anticipating my questions. As a result, many of them proved able by the end of the term to produce well-developed essays in two drafts instead of three. It should be said, too, that although I did not present grammatical complexity as a desideratum, the participants' style did, through that first term, become increasingly complex, and they took to using increasingly professional vocabulary. The outcome can be seen in the essays presented here and especially in the research papers. These papers were written through frequent consultation with me, but I did not mark them till the very end of the program. Thus, the articulation of the material in written form was largely the participants' own work; my only written contribution, in most cases, was final editing for publication here.[6]

This is not to say that the participants' work was entirely free of problems. Minor grammatical errors continued to crop up regularly and, in the research papers especially, there were often difficulties expressing accurately and clearly what was meant (first-language writers have such difficulties too). More seriously, the participants did not all successfully assimilate Western conventions of documentation and evidence: When citing secondary sources, they frequently gave incomplete bibliographic references and occasionally misquoted; when citing their own observations, they did not always transcribe accurately what was said—despite our discussions, in the course on discourse and style, of how to represent oral interactions in writing. Nevertheless, given the short time given to the work and the participants' previous lack of experience in both doing research and writing about it, their achievement must be recognized as a considerable one.

Finally, how successful was the project as part of a teacher-training program? When the participants first came to Nanjing, the greatest benefit that they expected to receive was an improvement in their own English proficiency, especially in listening and speaking.[7] As has been noted in similar programs in China (Sunderland 1990), they did not expect to learn much about how to teach. Yet, as Chapter Seven shows, they developed in the course of their teaching practice methods of teaching that were to them quite revolutionary, and several have claimed in letters written to Sarah Towle and me that they have continued to experiment since their return home.

The main factor in encouraging this innovative spirit was, I believe, the teaching practice itself; as described in Chapter Seven (see p. 208), it was set up so as to give the participants maximum support in any attempt to restructure their teaching along communicative lines. Another essential factor was the methodology course taught by Sarah Towle, in which, in the first term, the participants considered the principles underlying various methods of teaching (see Brown 1994; Nunan 1991) and, in the second, worked together on lesson plans to give practical expression to those principles. Equally important was an undergraduate course in intensive reading that Sarah Towle taught as a demonstration class in the first term. This course enabled the participants to see communicative-language teaching in action, and the discussions of

6. It gives me great pleasure to note, in this regard, that within a year of leaving the program, Zhu Xiaowen had presented a paper in English at a professional conference and Xu Ju had had a prize-winning article on teaching accepted for publication in one of China's major English newspapers. Then, in July 1997, several of the others presented papers at an English language teaching conference organized at Nanjing University.

7. This information is based on Zheng Guolong's research paper, which is not included in this collection. His purpose was to assess the value of foreign teachers to China, so he gathered information from his fellow participants about their experiences with such teachers both before and during the program.

particular lessons gave them an opportunity to articulate and explore the reservations that they felt about such teaching.

The reading and writing course, then, was far from being the only factor, nor was it even the major one, in the participants' development as teachers. It did, however, work well as a complement to the parts of the curriculum that dealt directly with pedagogy. First, it reinforced the methodology course and the demonstration class by modeling the kind of teaching advocated there, as Zheng Guolong reports in his research paper:

> The [present foreign teachers] make use of [the] Communicative Approach not only in listening and speaking, but also in reading and writing. Frequently, each class, one or two articles are distributed to be read and students are asked to write responses after class. During class, students are often organized into small groups to discuss, and then they are asked to present the interesting points and problems to the class. The whole class talk together.

Second, and perhaps still more important, the introspective emphasis of the course and its focus on processes of language learning caused the participants to be acutely aware of what was happening as their own proficiency developed. This made them both more interested in and more sensitive to what was happening to their students; the interest was shown in their choice of topics for research (see Appendix III) and the sensitivity in their descriptions of individual students' responses (e.g., Wang Jian's paper in Chapter Six, pp. 200–206; Lu Wanying also wrote for her research paper a deeply sympathetic account of students' writing processes).

Finally, it was not only the student participants in this project who benefited from such an increased awareness. While they were teaching me about Chinese literacy, I was myself learning to read and write Chinese,[8] and so had an opportunity to observe and think about my own language-learning strategies and to discuss them with the participants. I did not learn very much of the language (after a year of working an hour a day, I had a secure knowledge of less than two hundred characters), but I was able to see how my strategies were conditioned by my background of literacy in English and by my experience of learning other languages—and how, in consequence, I found myself sometimes resisting what my teacher wanted to do with me. Thus, my teacher and my students between them made me increasingly aware that I, too, was a product of my own culture even while I was, to some degree, moving away from it. Such self-knowledge is, I think, essential for teachers who wish to observe and interpret the culturally conditioned characteristics of their students, while at the same time doing justice to those students' individual personalities. A powerful way to develop it is for teachers to think about their own, as well as their students', second-language learning in relation to the literacy practices of the culture from which they themselves come.

8. I worked on this under the tutelage of Wu Zhanyun, to whom this book is dedicated.

Appendix I

Nanjing University/United Board
College English Teacher Training Program, 1994–5
Questionnaire for eliciting personal information

For preparing our book it would help me to have the following information. However, if you feel uncomfortable giving answers to any of the questions, please feel free to leave the space blank. If you don't have enough room for all the information under a particular heading, please write it on page 4, which is blank, giving the number of the question that it refers to.

1. Name (in English) _____ (in Chinese characters) _____

2. Address (in English) _____

_____

(in Chinese characters) _____

_____

3. Date of birth _____   4. Place of birth _____

5. Please list all the places you have lived for a year or more, giving for each the dates when you lived there, the name of the place, the province, and a brief description of it (i.e. village, town, small city, big city).

Dates   Name of place   Province   Description

_____

_____

_____

_____

_____

6. Please give the reason for each of the moves that you have listed above.

Date   From   To   Reason

_____

_____

_____

_____

_____

_____

7. Please indicate who were the adults you lived with when you were a child and what was their work and educational status.

Dates	Adults in the household	Work	Educational status

8. Please list all the institutions at which you have studied and indicate their status (e.g. key middle school, provincial university).

Dates	Name of institution	Status

9. Please list all the institutions where you have worked, indicate their status, and describe your own job there.

Dates	Name of institution	Status	Your job

10. Please list those who are in the household in which you live now, giving their age, occupation, and educational status.

Relationship to you	Age	Occupation	Educational Status

11. The above information is to enable me to give a broad sociological description of the class. If there is any further information about you that you think might be useful, please give it below.

_____

_____

_____

_____

_____

Thank you for your help!

Kate Parry

13 June 1995

Appendix II

Nanjing University/United Board
College English Teacher Training Program
Advanced Reading and Writing
Fall 1994
Assigned Readings

Theme 1: Literacy at Home

Hatano, G. 1986. "How Do Japanese Children Learn to Read?: Orthographic and Eco-cultural Variables." In *Acquisition of Reading Skills: Cultural Constraints and Cognitive Universals,* edited by B. R. Foorman and A. W. Siegel (pp. 81–114). Hillsdale, NJ: Lawrence Erlbaum Associates.

Heath, S. B. 1986. "What No Bedtime Story Means: Narrative Skills at Home and School." In *Language Socialization Across Cultures,* edited by B. B. Schieffelin and E. Ochs (pp. 97–124). Cambridge: Cambridge University Press.

Lee, S., J. W. Stigler, and H. W. Stevenson. 1986. "Beginning Reading in Chinese and English." In *Acquisition of Reading Skills: Cultural Constraints and Cognitive Universals,* edited by B. R. Foorman and A. W. Siegel (pp. 123–50). Hillsdale, NJ: Lawrence Erlbaum Associates.

Parry, K. 1993. "The Social Construction of Reading Strategies: New Directions for Research." *Journal of Research in Reading* 16 (2): 148–158.

Theme 2: Literacy in School

Collins, J. 1986. "Differential Instruction in Reading Groups." In *The Social Construction of Literacy,* edited by J. Cook-Gumperz (pp. 117–137). Cambridge: Cambridge University Press.

Gee, J. P. 1986. "Orality and Literacy: From *The Savage Mind* to *Ways with Words.*" *TESOL Quarterly* 20 (4): 719–46.

Goody, J., and I. Watt. 1968. "The Consequences of Literacy." In *Literacy in Traditional Societies,* edited by J. Goody (pp. 27–68). Cambridge: Cambridge University Press.

Hill, C. A., and K. J. Parry. (1992). "The Test at the Gate: Models of Literacy in Reading Assessment." *TESOL Quarterly* 26 (3): 433–61.

Philips, S. U. 1972. "Participant Structures and Communicative Competence: Warm Springs Children in Community and Classroom." In *Functions of Language in the Classroom,* edited by C. B. Cazden, V. P. John, and D. Hymes (pp. 370–94). New York: Teachers College Press.

Theme 3: Approaching English

Braine, G. 1994. "Comments on A. Suresh Canagarajah's 'Critical Ethnography of a Sri Lankan Classroom.'" *TESOL Quarterly* 28 (2): 609–13.

Campbell, K. P., and Y. Zhao. 1993. "The Dilemma of English Language Instruction in the People's Republic of China." *TESOL Journal* 2 (4): 4–6.

Canagarajah, A. S. 1993. "Critical Ethnography of a Sri Lankan Classroom: Ambiguities in Student Opposition to Reproduction Through ESOL." *TESOL Quarterly* 27 (4): 601–26.

Masani, Z. 1987. *Indian Tales of the Raj.* Berkeley, CA: University of California Press.

Widdowson, H. G. 1994. "The Ownership of English." *TESOL Quarterly* 28 (2): 377–89.

Theme 4: Making Sense of English Text

Block, E. L. 1992. "See How They Read: Comprehension Monitoring of L1 and L2 Readers." *TESOL Quarterly* 26 (2): 319–43.

Gu, Y. 1994, March. "Vocabulary Learning Strategies of Good and Poor Chinese EFL Learners." Paper presented at the International TESOL Convention; Baltimore, MD.

Kern, R. G. 1994. "The Role of Mental Translation in L2 Reading." *Studies in Second Language Acquisition* 16 (4): 441–61.

Parry, K. 1991. "Building a Vocabulary Through Academic Reading." *TESOL Quarterly* 25 (4): 629–53.

Pritchard, R. 1990. "The Effects of Cultural Schemata on Reading Processing Strategies." *Reading Research Quarterly* 25 (4): 273–95.

Appendix III

Nanjing University/United Board
College English Teacher Training Program
Advanced Reading and Writing
Spring 1995
Research Topics

Bao Jingying — Secondary-school English teaching

Chang Qian* — Students' reluctance to speak in class—means of overcoming

Chen Ting — Motivation for learning English and its effects on behavior in class

Ding Lu — How individuals remember Chinese characters

Du Qunhua — CEE and CET Band 4—effects on teaching

Gu Tiexia — Differences between secondary-school and college English teaching

He Yue — Communicative language teaching in college English classes

Li Xiaozhong — A student-centered approach to teaching vocabulary through intensive reading

Lu Wanying — Problems with Band 4 writing

Luo Ningxia — Motivation and opportunity as factors in students' learning of English

Qin Haihua** — Chinese behavioral patterns in English communication

Rao Zhiren — Computer literacy in Chinese

Sheng Ping* — Students' reluctance to speak in class—means of overcoming

Sun Wenjing — Problems of learning vocabulary in medical English

Wang Jian — How students read a difficult English text

Wu Liangzhe — Students' perceptions of what constitutes good and bad language teaching

Wu Lili** — Chinese behavioral patterns in English communication

Xu Ju* — Students' reluctance to speak in class—means of overcoming

* Joint project, three researchers
** Joint project, two researchers

Yang Hongqi	Students' ability to understand words in writing and in speech
Zhang Weinian	Using cohesion/coherence and background knowledge in teaching intensive reading
Zhao Guangzhu	Relationship between students' ability to interpret a word in writing, recognize it in speech, and produce it in writing
Zheng Guolong	Students' reactions to foreign teachers
Zhu Minghui	Teaching English with the new textbooks in junior-secondary school
Zhu Xiaowen	The relationship between English as taught in college and English as needed in the workplace

Contributors

鲍静英	Bao Jingying	Nanjing Higher College of Finance
常倩	Chang Qian	Jinling Women's College, Nanjing Normal University
陈婷	Chen Ting	Nanjing Educational College
丁路	Ding Lu	Nanjing Educational College
杜群华	Du Qunhua	Hubei Academy of Fine Arts
谷铁霞	Gu Tiexia	Anshan Normal College
何悦	He Yue	Nanjing Auditing Institute
李小重	Li Xiaozhong	Central China Normal University
刘远燕	Liu Yuanyan	Hwanan Women's College
吕万英	Lu Wanying	South-Central Nationality Institute
罗宁霞	Luo Ningxia	Ningxia University
秦海花	Qin Haihua	Jinling Women's College, Nanjing Normal University
饶志仁	Rao Zhiren	Nanjing University
盛萍	Sheng Ping	Central China Normal University
苏晓军	Su Xiaojun	Suzhou University
孙文静	Sun Wenjing	Qinghai Medical College
王健	Wang Jian	Nanjing University
王葵	Wang Kui	Xinjiang University
武亮哲	Wu Liangzhe	formerly of Suzhou Institute of Silk Textile Technology
吴莉莉	Wu Lili	formerly of East China University of Science and Technology
许菊	Xu Ju	South-Central Nationality Institute
杨红旗	Yang Hongqi	Nanjing University of Chemical Technology
张建颖	Zhang Jianying	Nanjing Auditing Institute
张伟年	Zhang Weinian	Nanjing International Studies University
赵广竹	Zhao Guangzhu	Anshan Normal College

郑国龙	Zheng Guolong	Shazhou Institute of Technologies
朱明慧	Zhu Minghui	Nanjing Educational College
朱筱雯	Zhu Xiaowen	Agricultural College of Yangzhou University

References

Allwright, R. 1977. "Language Learning Through Communicative Practice." *ELT Documents* 76 (3): 5.

Block, E. L. 1992. "See How They Read: Comprehension Monitoring of L1 and L2 Readers." *TESOL Quarterly* 26 (2): 319–43.

Bloom, A. 1987. *The Closing of the American Mind.* New York: Simon and Schuster.

Braine, G. 1994. Comments on A. Suresh Canagarajah's "Critical Ethnography of a Sri Lankan Classroom." *TESOL Quarterly* 28 (3): 609–13.

Brown, G., and G. Yule. 1983. *Discourse Analysis.* Cambridge University Press.

Brown, H. D. 1994. *Teaching by Principles.* Englewood Cliffs, NJ: Prentice Hall Regents.

Bruner, J. S. 1993. "Learning the Mother Tongue." In *Linguistics for Teachers,* edited by L. M. Cleary and M. D. Linn. New York: McGraw-Hill.

Burnaby, B., and Y. L. Sun. 1989. "Chinese Teachers' Views of Western Language Teaching: Context Informs Paradigms." *TESOL Quarterly* 23 (2): 219–38.

Campbell, K. P., and Y. Zhao. 1993. "The Dilemma of English Language Instruction in the People's Republic of China." *TESOL Journal* 2 (4): 4–6.

Canagarajah, A. S. 1993. "Critical Ethnography of a Sri Lankan Classroom: Ambiguities in Student Opposition to Reproduction through ESOL." *TESOL Quarterly* 27 (4): 601–26.

Carrell, P. L. 1987. "A View of Written Text as Communicative Interaction: Implications for Reading in a Second Language." In *Research in Reading in English as a Second Language,* edited by J. F. Devine, P. L. Carrell, and D. E. Eskey. Washington DC: TESOL.

Carrell, P. L., J. Devine, and D. Eskey. 1988. *Interactive Approaches to Second Language Reading.* Cambridge: Cambridge University Press.

Carrell, P. L., and J. C. Eisterhold. 1983. "Schema Theory: ESL Reading Pedagogy." *TESOL Quarterly* 17 (4): 553–73.

Carter, R. A. 1987. *Vocabulary: Applied Linguistic Perspectives.* London: Allen and Unwin.

Cathcart, R. L. 1989. "Authentic Discourse and the Survival English Classroom." *TESOL Quarterly* 23 (1): 105–26.

Cazden, C. B., V. P. John, and D. Hymes, eds. 1972. *Functions of Language in the Classroom.* New York: Teachers College Press.

Chaika, E. 1994. "Discourse Routines." In *Language: Introductory Readings,* 5th edition, edited by V. P. Clark, P. A. Eschholz, and A. F. Rosa. New York: St. Martin's Press.

Chang, J. 1991. *Wild Swans: Three Daughters of China.* London: HarperCollins.

Cheng, N. 1986. *Life and Death in Shanghai.* New York: Grove Press.

Chomsky, N. 1957. *Syntactic Structures.* The Hague: Mouton.

Chomsky, N. 1965. *Aspects of the Theory of Syntax.* Cambridge: MIT Press.

Clanchy, M. T. 1993. *From Memory to Written Record: England 1066–1307.* Oxford: Blackwell.

Clark, H. H., and E. V. Clark. 1977. *Psychology and Language: An Introduction to Psycholinguistics.* New York: Harcourt Brace Jovanovich.

Clarke, M. A. 1980. "The Short-Circuit Hypothesis of ESL Reading—or When Language Competence Interferes with Reading Performance." *Modern Language Journal* 64 (2): 203–9.

Coady, J. 1979. "A Psycholinguistic Model of the ESL Reader." In *Reading in a Second Language,* edited by R. Mackay, B. Barkman, and R. R. Jordan. Rowley, MA: Newbury House.

Cohen, A. 1994. "English for Academic Purposes in Brazil." In *From Testing to Assessment: English as an International Language,* edited by C. A. Hill and K. J. Parry. London: Longman.

Collins, J. 1986. "Differential Instruction in Reading Groups." In *The Social Construction of Literacy,* edited by J. Cook-Gumperz. Cambridge: Cambridge University Press.

Cook-Gumperz, J., ed. 1986. *The Social Construction of Literacy.* Cambridge: Cambridge University Press.

Cortazzi, M., and L. X. Jin. 1996. "English Teaching and Learning in China." *Language Teaching* 29: 61–80.

Cremin, L. A. 1980. *American Education: The National Experience.* New York: Harper and Row.

Davis, J. N., and L. Bistodeau. 1993. "How Do L1 and L2 Reading Differ? Evidence from Think-aloud Protocols." *Modern Language Journal* 77 (4): 459–72.

DeFrancis, J. 1984. *The Chinese Language: Fact and Fantasy.* Honolulu: University of Hawaii Press.

DeFrancis, J. 1989. *Visible Speech: The Diverse Oneness of Writing Systems.* Honolulu: University of Hawaii Press.

Dong, L. 1995. "English in China." *English Today 41* 11(1): 53–56.

Duckworth, E. 1987. *"The Having of Wonderful Ideas" and Other Essays on Teaching and Learning.* New York: Teachers College Press.

Dunn, R., and K. Dunn. 1972. *Practical Approaches to Individualizing Instruction.* Englewood Cliffs, NJ: Prentice-Hall.

Durrell, G. 1978. "The Talking Flowers." Adapted from *My Family and Other Animals,* in *Reader's Choice,* edited by E. M. Baudoin, E. S. Bober, M. A. Clarke, B. K. Dobson, and S. Silberstein. Ann Arbor: University of Michigan Press.

Dzau, Y. F. 1990a. "Historical Background." In *English in China,* edited by Y. F. Dzau. Hong Kong: API Press.

Dzau, Y. F. 1990b. "How English Is Taught in Tertiary Educational Institutions." In *English in China,* edited by Y. F. Dzau. Hong Kong: API Press.

Edge, J. 1996. "Cross-cultural Paradoxes in a Profession of Values." *TESOL Quarterly* 30 (1): 9–30.

Erbaugh, M. S. 1990. "Taking Advantage of China's Literary Tradition in Teaching Chinese Students." *Modern Language Journal* 74 (1): 15–27.

Eskey, D. E. 1970. "A New Technique for the Teaching of Reading to Advanced Students." *TESOL Quarterly* 4 (4): 215–21.

Faerch, C., K. Haastrup, and R. Phillipson. 1984. *Learner Language and Language Learning.* Clevedon, England: Multilingual Matters.

Faerch, C., and G. Kasper, eds. 1987. *Introspection in Second Language Research.* Clevedon, England: Multilingual Matters.

Fairbank, J. K. 1992. *China: A New History.* Cambridge: Harvard University Press.

Fairbank, J. K., and E. O. Reischauer. 1979. *Tradition and Transformation.* Boston, MA: Houghton Mifflin.

Foorman, B. R., and A. W. Siegel, eds. 1986. *Acquisition of Reading Skills: Cultural Constraints and Cognitive Universals.* Hillsdale, NJ: Lawrence Erlbaum Associates.

Freire, P. 1970. *The Pedagogy of the Oppressed.* New York: Herder and Herder.

Gairns, R., and S. Redman. 1986. *Working with Words: A Guide to Teaching and Learning Vocabulary.* Cambridge: Cambridge University Press.

Gargan, E. A. 1996. "The New Mandarins, and a New Language Muddle." *The New York Times.* 9 December, Sec. A, p. 4.

Gee, J. P. 1986. "Orality and Literacy: From *The Savage Mind* to *Ways with Words.*" *TESOL Quarterly* 20 (4): 719–46.

Goodman, K. S. 1967. "Reading: A Psycholinguistic Guessing Game." *Journal of the Reading Specialist* 4: 13–26.

Goodman, K. S. 1982. *Language and Literacy: The Selected Writings of Kenneth S. Goodman.* Two vols., edited by F. V. Gollasch. London: Routledge and Kegan Paul.

Goodman, Y. 1993. "I Never Read Such a Long Story Before." In *Linguistics for Teachers,* edited by L. M. Cleary and M. D. Linn. New York: McGraw-Hill.

Goody, J., and I. Watt. 1968. "The Consequences of Literacy." In *Literacy in Traditional Societies,* edited by J. Goody. Cambridge: Cambridge University Press.

Grabe, W. 1991. "Current Developments in Second Language Reading Research." *TESOL Quarterly* 25 (3): 375–406.

Graff, H. J. 1979. *The Literacy Myth: Literacy and Social Structure in the 19th Century City.* New York: Academic Press.

Graff, H. J. 1987. *The Legacies of Literacy: Continuities and Contradictions in Western Culture.* Bloomington: Indiana University Press.

Gu, Y. Q. 1994, March. "Vocabulary Learning Strategies of Good and Poor Chinese EFL Learners." Paper presented at the International TESOL Convention; Baltimore, MD.

Hansen-Strain, L. 1989. "Orality/Literacy and Group Differences in Second-language Acquisition." *Language Learning* 39 (4): 469–96.

Hasuike, R., O. Tzeng, and D. Hung. 1986. "Script Effects and Cerebral Lateralization: The Case of Chinese Characters." In *Language Processing in Bilinguals: Psycholinguistic and Neurological Perspectives,* edited by J. Vaid. Hillsdale, NJ: Lawrence Erlbaum Associates.

Hatano, G. 1986. "How Do Japanese Children Learn to Read? Orthographic and Ecocultural Variables." In *Acquisition of Reading Skills: Cultural Constraints and Cognitive Universals,* edited by B. R. Foorman and A. W. Siegel. Hillsdale, NJ: Lawrence Erlbaum Associates.

Hayhoe, R., ed. 1992. *Education and Modernization: The Chinese Experience.* Oxford: Pergamon Press.

Heath, S. B. 1983. *Ways with Words: Language, Life, and Work in Communities and Classrooms.* Cambridge: Cambridge University Press.

Heath, S. B. 1986. "What No Bedtime Story Means: Narrative Skills at Home and School." In *Language Socialization Across Cultures,* edited by B. B. Schieffelin and E. Ochs. Cambridge: Cambridge University Press.

Hedley, C. N., and A. N. Baratta, eds. 1985. *Contexts of Reading.* Norwood, NJ: Ablex.

Heny, J. 1994. "Learning and Using a Second Language." In *Language: Introductory Readings,* 5th ed., edited by V. P. Clark, P. A. Eschholz, and A. F. Rosa. New York: St. Martin's Press.

Henze, J. 1992. "The Formal Education System and Modernization: An Analysis of Developments Since 1978." In *Education and Modernization: The Chinese Experience,* edited by R. Hayhoe. Oxford: Pergamon Press.

Hill, B. 1994. "Self-managed Learning." *Language Teaching* 27 (4): 213–23.

Hill, C. A., and L. Anderson. 1994. "Adult Education in the United States: Adapting Material for Reading Tests." In *From Testing to Assessment: English as an International Language,* edited by C. A. Hill and K. J. Parry. London: Longman.

Hill, C. A., and K. J. Parry. 1989. "Autonomous and Pragmatic Models of Literacy: Reading Assessment in Adult Education." *Linguistics and Education* 1 (3): 233–83.

Hill, C. A., and K. J. Parry. 1992. "The Test at the Gate: Models of Literacy in Reading Assessment." *TESOL Quarterly* 26 (3): 433–61.

Hill, C. A., and K. J. Parry. 1994a. "Models of Literacy: The Nature of Reading Tests." In *From Testing to Assessment: English as an International Language,* edited by C. A. Hill and K. J. Parry. London: Longman.

Hill, C. A., and K. J. Parry. 1994b. "Assessing English Language and Literacy Around the World." In *From Testing to Assessment: English as an International Language,* edited by C. A. Hill and K. J. Parry. London: Longman.

Hino, N. 1992. "The Yakudoku Tradition in Foreign Language Literacy in Japan." In *Cross-cultural Literacy: Global Perspectives on Reading and Writing,* edited by F. Dubin and N. Kuhlman. Englewood Cliffs, NJ: Regents/Prentice Hall.

Hirsch, E. D. 1987. *Cultural Literacy: What Every American Needs to Know.* Boston, MA: Houghton Mifflin.

Hirsch, E. D. 1996. *The Schools We Need and Why We Don't Have Them.* New York: Doubleday.

Ho, P. T. 1982. *The Ladder of Success in Imperial China.* New York: Columbia University Press.

Hu, Y. N. 1990. "Teaching English in Chinese Secondary Schools." In *English in China,* edited by Y. F. Dzau. Hong Kong: API Press.

Huang, X. 1993. "Improper Method in Teaching a Foreign Language Affects Chinese Students' Psychology in Learning a Foreign Language." *Foreign Language World* 49 (2): 13–15.

Huckin, T., and J. Bloch. 1993. "Strategies for Inferring Word Meaning in Context: A Cognitive Model." In *Second Language Reading and Vocabulary Learning,* edited by T. Huckin, M. Haynes, and J. Coady. Norwood, NJ: Ablex.

Hudson-Ross, S., and Y. R. Dong. 1990. "Literacy Learning as a Reflection of Language and Culture: Chinese Elementary School Education." *The Reading Teacher* 44: 110–23.

Hymes, D. 1974. *Foundations in Sociolinguistics: An Ethnographic Approach.* Philadelphia: University of Pennsylvania Press.

Ingulsrud, J. E., and K. O. Allen. 1992, March. "Literacy and Learning a Standard Language." Paper presented at the International TESOL Convention; Vancouver, BC.

Johnson, D. W., R. Johnson, and E. Holubec, eds. 1986. *Circles of Learning: Cooperation in the Classroom.* Edina, MN: Interaction Book Company.

Johnson, R. K., C. K. W. Shek, and E. H. F. Law. 1989. "Text Processing: Investigating L2 in Strategies and Styles." In *Language Teaching and Learning Styles Within and Across Cultures,* edited by V. Bickley. Hong Kong: Institute of Language in Education.

Kachru, B. B. 1992. *The Other Tongue: English Across Cultures.* Champaign: University of Illinois Press.

Katz, S. R. 1993. "The King of France *Is* Bald: An Introduction to Cognitive Linguistics." In *Linguistics for Teachers,* edited by L. M. Cleary and M. D. Linn. New York: McGraw-Hill.

Koda, K. 1988. "Cognitive Process in Second Language Reading: Transfer of L1 Reading Skills and Strategies." *Second Language Research* 4 (2): 133–56.

Koda, K. 1990. "The Use of L1 Reading Strategies in L2 Reading: Effects of L1 Orthographic Structures on L2 Phonological Recoding Strategies." *Studies in Second Language Acquisition* 12 (4): 393–410.

Krashen, S. D. 1981. "The Case for Narrow Reading." *TESOL Newsletter* 15 (6): 23.

Kristof, N., and S. WuDunn. 1994. *China Wakes: The Struggle for the Soul of a Rising Power.* New York: Times Books.

Lee, S., J. W. Stigler, and H. W. Stevenson. 1986. "Beginning Reading in Chinese and English." In *Acquisition of Reading Skills: Cultural Constraints and Cognitive Universals,* edited by B. R. Foorman and A. W. Siegel. Hillsdale, NJ: Lawrence Erlbaum Associates.

Li, G. Y. 1986. *A New English Course.* Shanghai: Foreign Language Education Press.

Li, X. J. 1990. "In Defence of the Communicative Approach." In *English in China,* edited by Y. F. Dzau. Hong Kong: API Press.

Link, P. 1993. *Evening Chats in Beijing: Probing China's Predicament.* New York: W. W. Norton.

Lo, B. L. C. 1984. "Primary Education in China: A Two-track System for Dual Tasks." In *Contemporary Chinese Education,* edited by R. Hayhoe. Armonk, NY: M. E. Sharpe.

Logan, R. K. 1987. *The Alphabet Effect: The Impact of the Phonetic Alphabet on the Development of Western Civilization.* New York: St. Martin's Press.

Mann, V. A. 1984, July. *The Relation Between Temporary Phonetic Memory and the Acquisition of Japanese Kana and Kanji.* Paper presented at the Third International Symposium on Psychological Aspects of the Chinese Language. Hong Kong.

Masani, Z. 1987. *Indian Tales of the Raj.* Berkeley: University of California Press.

McCarthy, M. 1990. *Vocabulary.* Oxford: Oxford University Press.

Nunan, D. 1991. *Language Teaching Methodology.* New York: Prentice Hall.

Nunan, D. 1992. *Research Methods in Language Learning.* Cambridge: Cambridge University Press.

Nuttall, C. 1982. *Teaching Reading Skills in a Foreign Language.* London: Heinemann.

Olson, D. R. 1994. *The World on Paper: The Conceptual and Cognitive Implications of Writing and Reading.* Cambridge: Cambridge University Press.

Oxford, R. L. 1990. *Language Learning Strategies: What Every Teacher Should Know.* Boston, MA: Heinle and Heinle.

Oxford, R. L., and N. J. Anderson. 1995. "A Crosscultural View of Learning Styles." *Language Teaching* 28: 201–15.

Paine, L. 1992. "Teaching and Modernization in Contemporary China." In *Education and Modernization: The Chinese Experience,* edited by R. Hayhoe. Oxford: Pergamon Press.

Parry, K. J. 1987. "Reading in a Second Culture." In *Research in Reading in English as a Second Language,* edited by J. Devine, P. L. Carrell, and D. E. Eskey. Washington, DC: TESOL.

Parry, K. J. 1991. "Building a Vocabulary Through Academic Reading." *TESOL Quarterly* 25 (4): 629–53.

Parry, K. J. 1992. "English in Nigeria." *Geolinguistics* 18: 49–65.

Parry, K. J. 1993a. "The Social Construction of Reading Strategies: New Directions for Research." *Journal of Research in Reading* 16 (2): 148–58.

Parry, K. J. 1993b. "Too Many Words: Learning the Vocabulary of an Academic Subject." In *Second Language Reading and Vocabulary Learning,* edited by T. Huckin, M. Haynes, and J. Coady. Norwood, NJ: Ablex.

Parry, K. J. 1994. "The Test and the Text: Readers in a Nigerian Secondary School." In *From Testing to Assessment: English as an International Language,* edited by C. A. Hill and K. J. Parry. London: Longman.

Parry, K. J. 1995. "First Language Literacy and Second Language Reading: Perspectives from China." In *Language Awareness in Language Education: Proceedings of the International Language in Education Conference 1994,* edited by D. Nunan, R. Berry, and V. Berry. Hong Kong: University of Hong Kong.

Parry, K. J. 1996a. "Culture, Literacy, and L2 Reading." *TESOL Quarterly* 30 (4): 665–92.

Parry, K. J. 1996b. "Vocabulary and Comprehension: Two Portraits." In *Vocabulary Acquisition: A Rationale for Pedagogy,* edited by J. Coady and T. Huckin. Cambridge: Cambridge University Press.

Philips, S. U. 1972. "Participant Structures and Communicative Competence: Warm Springs Children in Community and Classroom." In *Functions of Language in the Classroom,* edited by C. B. Cazden, V. P. John, and D. Hymes. New York: Teachers College Press.

Phillipson, R. 1992. *Linguistic Imperialism.* Oxford: Oxford University Press.

Pritchard, R. 1990. "The Effects of Cultural Schemata on Reading Processing Strategies." *Reading Research Quarterly* 25 (4): 273–95.

Raimes, A. 1983. "Tradition and Revolution in ESL Teaching." *TESOL Quarterly* 17 (4): 535–52.

Ramsey, S. R. 1987. *The Languages of China.* Princeton: Princeton University Press.

Rawski, E. S. 1979. *Education and Popular Literacy in Ch'ing China.* Ann Arbor: University of Michigan Press.

Read, C., Y. Zhang, H. Nie, and B. Ding. 1987. "The Ability to Manipulate Speech Sounds Depends on Knowing Alphabetic Writing." In *The Onset of Literacy,* edited by P. Bertelson. Cambridge: MIT Press.

Reid, J. 1994. "Responding to ESL Students' Texts: The Myths of Appropriation." *TESOL Quarterly* 28 (2): 273–92.

Reynolds, R. E., M. Taylor, M. S. Steffensen, L. L. Shirey, and R. Anderson. 1982. "Cultural Schemata and Reading Comprehension." *Reading Research Quarterly* 17: 357–66.

Rosen, S. 1984. "New Directions in Secondary Education." In *Contemporary Chinese Education,* edited by R. Hayhoe. Armonk, NY: M. E. Sharpe.

Rosen, S. 1992. "Women, Education, and Modernization." In *Education and Modernization: The Chinese Experience,* edited by R. Hayhoe. Oxford: Pergamon Press.

Ross, H. 1992. "Foreign Language Education as a Barometer of Modernization." In *Education and Modernization: The Chinese Experience,* edited by R. Hayhoe. Oxford: Pergamon Press.

Rumelhart, D. 1977. "Toward an Interactive Model of Reading." In *Attention and Performance VI,* edited by S. Dornic. Hillsdale, NJ: Lawrence Erlbaum Associates.

Scarcella, R. C., and R. Oxford. 1992. *The Tapestry of Language Learning: The Individual in the Communicative Classroom.* Boston, MA: Heinle & Heinle.

Schieffelin, B. B., and P. Gilmore, eds. 1986. *The Acquisition of Literacy: Ethnographic Perspectives.* Norwood, NJ: Ablex.

Schmied, J. 1991. *English in Africa: An Introduction.* London: Longman.

Scollon, R., and S. B. K. Scollon. 1981. *Narrative, Literacy, and Face in Interethnic Communication.* Norwood, NJ: Ablex.

Scribner, S., and M. Cole. 1981. *The Psychology of Literacy.* Cambridge: Harvard University Press.

Selinker, L. 1972. "Interlanguage." *International Review of Applied Linguistics* 10: 201–31.

Slavin, R. 1983. *Cooperative Learning.* New York: Longman.

Smith, F. 1982. *Understanding Reading.* 3rd ed. New York: Holt, Rinehart, and Winston.

Spence, J. D. 1981. *The Gate of Heavenly Peace.* New York: Viking Press.

Spence, J. D. 1990. *The Search for Modern China.* New York: W. W. Norton.

Steffenson, M. S., C. Joag-dev, and R. C. Anderson. 1979. "A Cross-cultural Perspective on Reading Comprehension." *Reading Research Quarterly* 15: 10–29.

Stevick, E. W. 1976. *Memory, Meaning, and Method.* Rowley, MA: Newbury House.

Street, B. V. 1984. *Literacy in Theory and in Practice.* Cambridge: Cambridge University Press.

Street, B. V., ed. 1993. *Cross-cultural Approaches to Literacy.* Cambridge: Cambridge University Press.

Sunderland, J. 1990. "Doing What the Romans Don't Do: Advanced Teacher Training Courses in China." In *English in China,* edited by Y. F. Dzau. Hong Kong: API Press.

Tang, G. T. 1988. *The Sociology of English Teaching.* Harbin, P.R.C.: Heilongjiang Educational Press.

Thomas, L. 1993. "The Lives of a Cell." In *Modern American Prose,* 2nd ed., edited by J. Clifford and R. DiYanni. New York: McGraw Hill.

Wenden, A., and J. Rubin, eds. 1987. *Learner Strategies in Language Learning.* London: Prentice Hall.

Widdowson, H. G. 1978. *Teaching Language as Communication.* Oxford: Oxford University Press.

Widdowson, H. G. 1994. "The Ownership of English." *TESOL Quarterly* 28 (2): 377–89.

Zamel, V. 1992. "Writing One's Way into Reading." *TESOL Quarterly* 26 (3): 463–85.